William Chauncey Fowler

The sectional controversy; or,

Passages in the political history of the United States, including the causes of the

war between the sections

William Chauncey Fowler

The sectional controversy; or,
Passages in the political history of the United States, including the causes of the war between the sections

ISBN/EAN: 9783337810412

Printed in Europe, USA, Canada, Australia, Japan

Cover: Foto ©ninafisch / pixelio.de

More available books at **www.hansebooks.com**

THE

SECTIONAL CONTROVERSY;

OR,

PASSAGES

IN THE

POLITICAL HISTORY OF THE UNITED STATES,

INCLUDING THE

CAUSES OF THE WAR

BETWEEN THE SECTIONS.

BY

WILLIAM CHAUNCEY FOWLER, LL. D.

NEW YORK:

CHARLES SCRIBNER, 124 GRAND STREET.

1862.

JOHN F. TROW,
PRINTER, STEREOTYPER, AND ELECTROTYPER,
46, 48 & 50 Greene Street,
New York.

PREFACE.

In the year 1850, the week before Mr. WEBSTER delivered his memorable speech on the seventh of March, I had the pleasure, in Washington, of taking tea with my old friend and classmate, Governor McDowell, then a member of Congress. When I rose to take my leave of him, he said he was not willing to part without telling me of a burden which was resting on his mind. "I am convinced, my dear friend," said he, "that there will be a disunion of the States. There is a great change going on at the South. Two years ago, when I delivered my speech for the Union, all were melted down into a common feeling of love for the whole country. Men of all parties in the House gave me their hands and congratulated me on what they were pleased to call my patriotic speech.

"But now some of the same men are not willing to hear a word on the subject of the Union. I am not in the councils of these Southern men, though I suppose I might be, if I would think and act with them. Every thing is tending to disunion; and I wanted to tell you so before you return to the North."

As he said this to me in earnest, tender tones, and with eyes filled with tears, I felt that his sad forebodings ought to be heeded, and their grounds investigated.

Not very far from this time, I made the acquaintance of Judge Burnet, of Cincinnati, at Union Hall, Saratoga, and was greatly interested in his intelligence, wisdom, and patriotism. In repeated conversations, he said to me, in substance: "These

States cannot long hold together—they will separate." On my replying, I can hardly believe that the Southern States will be so unwise, he answered, " Ah, my dear sir, the difficulty is with Northern men. Great numbers of them do not value the Union so much as they do their doctrines on slavery, which, in their working, are hostile to the Union. A spirit of disunion exists at the North which will continue to increase in extent and intensity until it has produced a separation of the States."

After hearing the testimony of these two patriot statesmen, the one speaking of the South and the other of the North, I resolved to investigate the following questions, chiefly for my own satisfaction :

I. Is the traditionary sentiment in favor of the Union dying out in the hearts of the people of the States ?

II. Is the bond of Union, namely, the Constitution, growing weaker in the respect and confidence of politicians ?

III. As a consequence, are the States drifting along, to some extent, unconsciously, toward disunion ?

IV. What are the causes of this alarming condition of the country ?

V. Which section of the Union is responsible for the opera· tion of these causes ?

While investigating these questions, my historical collections, in their bearing on their solution, grew to such an amount, and assumed so much importance in my estimation, that I concluded to present them to the public in the following pages, as furnishing a satisfactory answer to these questions. In adopting a chronological arrangement of my materials, I have endeavored to bring distinctly into view *the prominent questions in dispute between the two sections in the successive eras, from the first settlement of the country down to the close of President Buchanan's administration.* The answer to the former set of questions depends on the answer to the latter. For the statement of

these latter questions, and for the arguments on each side, I
have quoted Northern utterances and Southern utterances.
These, with the "Remarks" inserted at the close of each chapter, will enable the careful reader, *at a small expense of time,*
to obtain a knowledge of the *principal sectional questions*
which have agitated the country from the first to the present
time.   He cannot fail to see that the same questions, under different forms, appear, disappear, and reappear, on the tide of
time, as if they had not already been discussed, and as if one
generation of politicians must again settle what had been regarded as settled by a former generation.   Every political as-
pirant in each section has been ready to show his prowess in
attacking some supposed political heresy in the other section,
even though it had been often confuted; just as formerly
" every young churchman militant would try his arms in thun-
dering on Hobbes's Steel Cap."

Disguise it as we will, bitter feuds have existed between the
North and the South, for a generation at least, reckoning a
generation at thirty years.   In that period men have come forward into life in each section who think of those born in the
other section, only to hate them or despise them, or, at least, to
misunderstand them.   Where does the blame rest?   Not solely
on the North, nor solely on the South.   *Iliacos intra muros*
peccatur, et extra.   The careful reader of this small volume
will be satisfied that all the political intelligence and virtue of
the country is not to be found north of Mason and Dixon's
line, nor south of it; and that political and sectional pride, and
intolerance, and hatred, and desire of office, confined to neither
section, have brought the Union of the States to the verge of ruin.

When the rapid current of events in 1861 outran the fears of
the ridiculed " Union-savers," and hurried on the dreaded catas-
trophe, the civil war, then begun, was but the logical sequence
of foregoing events.   Bitter feelings long cherished, bitter

words often uttered, injuries inflicted, insults offered, naturally
germinated and grew into deeds of violence and blood. Dra-
gons' teeth had been plentifully sown, and they started up armed
men. And yet multitudes, at the time, were so ignorant of the
prevalent sectional feelings and purposes, that, in surprise, they
asked, " What are they fighting for ? "

The people of the two sections of the country, are, to a large
extent, ignorant of each other, and hence, in their estimate of
each other's institutions, they are misled by illusions of the
imagination.

For the purpose of distributing information among the people, this volume, which might be entitled " HISTORICAL COLLEC-
TIONS," is offered to various classes of readers.

I. To all, whether North or South, who are ignorant of the
political history of the United States, and who have not an opportunity of referring to original sources.

II. To all, whether North or South, who have strong sectional prejudices.

III. To all, whether North or South, who wish for the restoration and the preservation of the Union.

IV. To all, whether North or South, who wish to understand the causes of the war between the sections.

V. To all, whether North or South, who value the prosperity of the country more than they do the success of their party.

VI. To all, whether North or South, who believe that merely defeating the armies of the Southern States will bring back
the Union.

VII. To all, whether North or South, who wish to understand the constitutional relations between the States and the
Federal Government.

VIII. To all, whether North or South, whose hearts, not
limited by party or section, are large enough to embrace the
interests of the whole country, and of all the States.

The final issue of the sectional controversy lies in the future, beyond the ken of mortal vision, wrapped up in the hollow of God's mysterious hand. He only, who presides over the destiny of nations, " sees the end from the beginning." But though thus limited in vision, man can gather from the past the lessons of wisdom for his guidance in the future. And may we not indulge the pleasing hope that the people of the States, gathering wisdom from the mistakes of the past, in the sectional controversy, may become qualified to enjoy, in the long future, the blessings of union under the FEDERAL CONSTITUTION ?

W. C. F.

New York, 1862.

CONTENTS.

CHAPTER I.

CHAPTER II.

CHAPTER III.

CHAPTER VIII.

CHAPTER IX.

CHAPTER X.

CHAPTER XI.

CHAPTER XII.

CHAPTER XIII.

THE SECTIONAL CONTROVERSY.

CHAPTER I.

ORIGINAL SECTIONAL DIVERSITIES.

BEFORE the American Revolution, there were on the great eastern slope of North America, along the shores of the Atlantic Ocean, thirteen separate colonies. These colonies were, indeed, connected with England, as their mother country; but in their relations to each other they were independent and sovereign nations.

Moreover, they were, to some extent, alien to one another in race, in religion, and in political affinities. The inhabitants of New Hampshire, Massachusetts, and Connecticut, were descended from that class of the English who were Puritan in their religion, and Roundhead in their politics. The inhabitants of New York and New Jersey were largely descendants of the Dutch. The English Quakers, the original settlers, gave a certain character to Pennsylvania, just as the Roman Catholics did to Maryland, just as the prelatical cavaliers did to Virginia, just as did the French Huguenots to South Carolina.

ADDITIONAL SECTIONAL DIVERSITIES.

But other diversities were, in process of time, created by climate, education, industrial pursuits, social institutions, and government. The people of New Hampshire, New Jersey, Virginia, the Carolinas, and Georgia, were under what was called a *Provincial Government*, in which the Governors were appointed by the Crown. The people of Maryland, Pennsylvania, and Delaware, were under what was called a *Proprietary Government*, in which the Governors were appointed by certain individuals called proprietaries. Massachusetts, Rhode Island, and Connecticut, were under what was called a *Charter Government*, in which the· Governor was appointed by the freemen of the colony. In Massachusetts, after 1692, the Governors were appointed by the Crown.

Nor were the existing diversities diminished by personal intercourse between the colonies, or by the press. In those times there were but few travelling, whether for the purposes of business or pleasure; and the press had but a limited circulation for the few newspapers which it sent forth. So great were these diversities, that in Rivington's Gazette, p. 32, they are thus noticed : " Nothing has surprised people more than the Virginians and Marylanders joining with so much warmth with the New England Republicans in their opposition to their ancient Constitution, which has been the glory of the English in every part of the world. As there are certainly no nations under heaven more opposite than these colonies, it would be very difficult to account for it on the principle of religion and sound policy, had not the Virginians discovered their indifference to both, so highly revered by their illustrious ancestors."

BOND OF SYMPATHY BETWEEN THE COLONIES.

But it was also true that the colonies, generally, were of common blood, and spoke a common language, and were familiar with the same traditions, and, in relation to Great Britain, had common rights and interests at stake, and common habits of reasoning about them. It is not surprising, therefore, that when the crown encroached on the rights of Massachusetts, that all the colonies should express the liveliest interest in her sufferings. Her fate might soon be theirs. It is not surprising that Virginia should take the lead in the declaration, that the interests of all the colonies were concerned in what was done by the British

BOND OF SYMPATHY BETWEEN THE COLONIES.

Government, in respect to Massachusetts. The Assembly of Virginia warned the king of the danger that would ensue, "if any person in any part of America should be seized and carried beyond sea for trial," May 16, 1769.

Of the resolves passed by Virginia at this time, Bancroft says : " Is it asked who was the adviser of the measure? None can tell. Great things were done, tranquilly and modestly, without a thought of the glory that was their due. Had the Ancient Dominion been silent, I will not say that Massachusetts might have faltered ; but mutual confidence would have been wanting. American freedom was more prepared by courageous counsel for successful war." *His. Am. Rev.*, vol. iii., p. 310.

In another place he says : " The Boston committee were already (1774) in close correspondence with the other New England colonies, with New York, and Pennsylvania. Old jealousies were removed, and perfect harmony subsisted between all. " UNION " was the cry, a union which should reach from Florida to the icy plains of Canada ; " p. 541. Under a common impulse, in view of common interests at stake, all the colonies, except Georgia, sent delegates to the first CONTINENTAL CONGRESS, which assembled at Philadelphia on the 5th of September, 1774. It is not surprising that PATRICK HENRY should, in that Congress, scout the idea of sectional distinctions and of individual interests. "All America," said he, " is thrown into one mass. Where are your landmarks, your boundaries of colonies? They are all thrown down. The distinction between Virginians, Pennsylvanians, New Yorkers, and New Englanders are no more. *I am not a Virginian, but an American.*" Under a common impulse all the States sent delegates to the second Continental Congress, which assembled at Philadelphia on the 10th of May, 1775, which unanimously appointed George Washington commander-in-chief of the continental forces in the united colonies. Under a common impulse, all the colonies, on the 4th of July, 1776, voted, through their delegates, " that the united colonies ought to be Free and Independent States." Under the same common impulse, the States, eleven of them, adopted the articles of confederation in 1778, one in 1779, and the remaining one in 1781, by which the union of the States was consummated.

SECTIONAL FEELING YIELDING TO LOVE OF COUNTRY.

It is not to be supposed that the appointment of George Washington to the supreme command, or that the draft of the Declaration of Independence by another Virginian, or that the action of the Continental Congress would entirely avoid the manifestation of sectional feelings. Such feelings were, indeed, called forth, but they were expelled from the heart of the people of the colonies by the new and stronger affection, namely, love of country. The sectional feeling, which led some of the Northern delegates, in the Continental Congress in 1775, to prefer Artemas Ward or some New England man to be commander-in-chief, they nobly sacrificed on the altar of patriotism, and gave their voices and their votes for a Virginian, who was selected partly on sectional grounds. The sectional feelings naturally aroused by the first draft of the Declaration of Independence, prepared by Mr. Jefferson, was allayed by striking from it the objectional clauses. These are his words: "The clause, too, reprobating the enslaving of the inhabitants of Africa, was struck out in complaisance to South Carolina and Georgia, who had never attempted to restrain the importation of slaves, and who, on the contrary, wished to continue it. Our Northern brethren, also, I believe, felt a little tender under those censures; for, though their people had very few slaves themselves, yet they had been pretty considerable carriers of them to others."—*Jefferson's Works.*

SECTIONAL OPINIONS IN THE CONTINENTAL CONGRESS.

In the Continental Congress, it was proposed, July 12, 1776, "that the expenses of the Confederation should be borne by each colony, in proportion to the number of inhabitants of every age and quality, except Indians, not paying taxes in each colony; a true account of which, distinguishing the white inhabitants, shall be triennially taken and transmitted to the Assembly of the United States."

Mr. CHASE, of Maryland, moved "that the quota should be paid, not by the number of inhabitants, but by the *white* inhabitants."

JOHN ADAMS, of Massachusetts, and Mr. WILSON, of Pennsylvania, spoke in opposition to this amendment. The amendment was rejected by the votes of New Hampshire, Massachusetts, Rhode Island, Connecticut, New York, New Jersey, Pennsylvania, against those of Maryland, Virginia, North Carolina, South Carolina, Delaware; Georgia being divided.

March 28, 1783, on the same subject, it was voted that slaves be taxed 3 to 5. New Hampshire, *aye;* Massachusetts, *no;* Rhode Island, *no;* New Jersey, *aye;* Pennsylvania, *aye;* Delaware, *no;* Maryland, *aye;* Virginia, *aye;* North Carolina, *aye;* South Carolina, *no;* Connecticut, *no;* New York, *aye.*

PROPOSED SECTIONAL CONVENTION.

April 1, 1783. Mr. GORHAM, of Massachusetts, in the Congress of the Confederation, observed, as a cogent reason for hastening the business, "that the Eastern States, at the invitation of the Legislature of Massachusetts, were, with New York, about to form a convention for regulating matters of common concern, and that, if any plan should be sent out by Congress, they would probably coöperate with Congress in giving efficacy to it."

Mr. MERCER, of Virginia, expressed great disquietude at this information; considered it as a dangerous precedent; and "that it behooved the gentleman to explain fully the object of the Convention, as it would be necessary for the Southern States to be otherwise very circumspect in agreeing to any plans on the supposition that the general Confederacy was to continue."

Mr. OSGOOD, of Massachusetts, and Mr. GORHAM, explained "that the object of the proposed Convention was to guard against an interference of taxes among States whose local situation required such precautions."

Mr. BLAND, of Virginia, said "he always considered these conventions as improper, and contravening the spirit of the general government. He said they had the appearance of YOUNG CONGRESSES."

Mr. MADISON and Mr. HAMILTON disapproved of those partial conventions, not as absolute violations of the Confederacy, but, as ultimately tending to them, and as, in the mean time, excit-

2

ing pernicious jealousies; the latter observing, " he wished, instead of them, to see a GENERAL CONVENTION take place."

SECTIONAL FEELING IN THE ARMY OF THE REVOLUTION.

Nowhere were these sectional jealousies more prevalent than in the motley army assembled, from distant quarters, under Washington's own command. REED, the adjutant-general, speaking on this subject, observes: " The Southern troops, comprising the regiments south of the Delaware, looked with very unkind feelings on those of New England." " It is with great concern," says Washington, in one of his general orders, " that the general understands that jealousies have arisen among the troops from the different provinces, and reflections are thrown out which can only tend to irritate each other, and injure the noble cause in which we are engaged, and which we ought to support with one hand and one heart."

In a letter to Gen. Schuyler, 1776, he says : " I must entreat your attention to do away the unhappy and pernicious distinctions and jealousies between troops of different governments. Enjoin this upon the officers, and let them inculcate and press home to the soldiery the necessity of order and harmony among those who are engaged in one common cause, and mutually contending for all that freemen hold most dear."

JOHN ADAMS, speaking of the violent passions and discordant interests at work throughout the country, from Florida to Canada, observes : " It requires more serenity of temper, a deeper understanding, and more courage, than fell to the lot of Marlborough, to ride in this whirlwind." IRVING's *Life of Washington*, vol. ii., p. 287.

REMARKS.

It is then manifest :

1. That there were original and acquired diversities of character in the early settlers of the States, which were the foundation of sectional feelings at the commencement of the American Revolution.

2. That these feelings, for the time, were overborne by the

common dangers and the common interests in respect to Great Britain, which established a strong bond of sympathy between them.

3. That, nevertheless, sectional interests were recognized and sectional feelings manifested in the Congress of the Confederation, and in the army, that were a great embarrassment to the Government and to the commander-in-chief.

4. That, notwithstanding these sectional feelings in the minds of those who indulged them, and in the hearts of the people generally, national feelings so far prevailed through the several States, that they contended successfully through a seven years' war with the mother country, and won the independence which they had declared, and took their place by common consent among the civilized nations of the earth, as a Confederacy, styled, THE UNITED STATES OF AMERICA.

CHAPTER II.

THE common fear of Great Britain had caused the States to adopt the "Articles of Confederation." When that fear was removed by the treaty of peace, January, 1783, those articles had lost their power as a bond of union. The common fear of imbecility and anarchy, into which they were in danger of sinking down, after the excitements of the war had passed off, caused them to adopt the Constitution.

The Convention was composed of gentlemen of high moral principle, of undoubted patriotism, and of courteous manners, of broad views, some of them accustomed to act together in the Continental Congress or in the army, and all of them entertaining a great respect for Washington, the President. The Convention assembled in May, 1787.

Still sectional difficulties arose in that body, which, with others inherent in the subjects under discussion, threatened its dissolution, before they had accomplished the object for which they came together. These subjects were : 1. Navigation. 2. Slavery. The North insisted on having protection for their property in commerce ; the South insisted on having protection for their property in slaves.

NAVIGATION.

The Committee of Detail had reported the following proposal : " No navigation act shall be passed (by Congress) without the assent of two-thirds of the members present in each House." This clause the Southern States were anxious to retain, lest their commerce should be placed too much in the power of the Eastern States; but which the latter were anxious to reject, that thus a bare majority of Congress might pass navigation laws to their advantage, even though injurious to the Southern States.

THE SLAVE TRADE.

By the same committee, the slave trade was left just where the old Confederation had left it, without giving Congress the power to abolish it, or to lay any duty on imported slaves. This proposal was acceptable to the Southern States, but not to the Northern; for the delegates from the latter thought that slaves imported ought to be placed under the general provision for taxing imports, and some few of them also thought that they ought to favor morals by the abolition of the slave trade.

Mr. KING, of Massachusetts, "thought the subject ought to be viewed in *a political light only*. If two States (South Carolina and Georgia) will not agree to the Constitution as stated on one side, he could affirm with equal belief on the other, that great and equal opposition would be experienced from other States." He remarked that "the exemption of slaves from duty, while every other import was subject to it, is an inequality that could not fail to strike the *commercial* sagacity of the Northern and Middle States."

Gen. COTESWORTH PINCKNEY, of South Carolina, in his reply, said "that he thought himself bound to declare candidly, that he did not think that South Carolina would stop the importation of slaves in any short time, but only stop it occasionally, as she now does. He moved to commit the clause, that slaves might be made liable to an equal duty with other imports, which he thought right, and which would remove one difficulty which had been stated."

Tuesday, August 21 *and* 22, 1787.—Mr. ELLSWORTH, of Connecticut, was for leaving the clause (which did not prohibit the importation of slaves) as it now stands. "Let every State import what it pleases. *The wisdom or morality of slavery are considerations that belong to the States themselves.* What enriches a part enriches the whole; and the States are the best judges of their particular interests. The old Confederation had not meddled with this point, and he did not see any greater necessity for bringing it within the policy of the new one."

Mr. SHERMAN, of Connecticut, " was for leaving the clause as it now stands. He disapproved of the slave trade; yet, as the *States were now possessed of the right to import slaves,* and as the public good did not require it to be taken from them, and as it was expedient to have as few objections as possible to the proposed scheme of government, he thought it best to leave the matter as we find it; that is, not prohibit the importation of slaves."

Mr. GOUVERNEUR MORRIS, of Pennsylvania, wished to have the whole subject to be committed, including the clause relating to navigation acts. "These things, namely, the slave trade, to which some of the North was opposed, and the navigation act without a restriction, to which the South was opposed, may form a *bargain* between the Northern and the Southern States."

COMMITTEE OF ONE FROM EACH STATE.

The Committee of Eleven, to whom was referred the subject of the " bargain," reported, August 24, 1787, "in favor of not allowing the Legislature to prohibit the importation of slaves before 1800, but giving them power to impose a duty at a rate not exceeding the *average of other imports.*"

DEBATE IN THE CONVENTION.

General PINCKNEY, August 25, moved to strike out the year 1800, and insert 1808.

Mr. GORHAM, of Massachusetts, seconded the motion.

It was then passed in the affirmative; New Hampshire, Massachusetts, Connecticut, Maryland, North Carolina, and South Carolina, voting in the affirmative (6); New Jersey, Pennsylvania, Delaware, and Virginia, in the negative (4).

It was finally agreed, *nem. con.,* to make the clause read, " but a tax or duty may be imposed on such importation, not exceeding ten dollars for each person." Ten dollars was considered by some of the members a *"fair average of other imports,"*

comparing the price of a slave, at that time, with the price of
" other articles" of importation, or five per cent. *ad valorem*,
the money value of a slave. This sum, as a specific duty, therefore, was inserted instead of " a fair average of other imports,"
the phrase used in the report of the committee. Thus the price
of a slave was reckoned at two hundred dollars by the Convention.

Mr. CHARLES PINCKNEY, of South Carolina, August 29,
moved in Convention to postpone the report of the Committee
of Eleven in favor of the following proposal: " That no act of
the Legislature for the purpose of regulating the *commerce* of
the United States with foreign powers, *among* the United
States, (the several States,) shall be passed without the assent
of two-thirds of the members of each House." Mr. MARTIN
seconded the motion. Mr. PINCKNEY remarked, that there were
five different commercial interests: 1. The fisheries and West
India trade, which belonged to the New England States. 2.
The interests of New York lay in free trade. 3. Wheat and
flour are the staples of the two Middle States, New Jersey and
Pennsylvania. 4. Tobacco, the staple of Virginia and Maryland, and a part of North Carolina. 5. Rice and indigo, the
staples of South Carolina and Georgia. These different interests would be the source of oppressive regulations, if no check
to a bare majority should be provided. States pursue their
interests with less scruple than individuals. The power of regulating commerce was a pure concession on the part of the
Southern States. They did not need the protection of the
maritime States for the present."

General C. C. PINCKNEY, of South Carolina, said " that it was
the true interest of the Southern States to pass no regulation of
commerce; but, considering the *loss* brought on the *commerce*
of the Eastern States by the Revolution, their *liberal conduct*
towards the views of South Carolina, (permission to import
slaves,) and the interests the weak Southern States had in being
united to the strong Eastern States, he thought it proper that
no fetters should be imposed on the power of making commercial regulations, and that his constituents, though prejudiced
against the Eastern States, would be reconciled by this liberality,
(as to the slave trade.) He had himself, he said, prejudices,

against the Eastern States before he came here, but would acknowledge that he had found them as liberal and candid as any men whatever."

Mr. CLYMER, of Pennsylvania : "The diversity of commercial interests of necessity creates difficulties which ought not to be increased by unnecessary regulations. The Northern and Middle States *will be ruined*, if not allowed to defend themselves against foreign regulations."

Mr. SHERMAN, of Connecticut, and Mr. MORRIS, of Pennsylvania, in behalf of the Eastern States, spoke against Mr. CHARLES PINCKNEY's motion.

Mr. BUTLER, of South Carolina, "differed from those who considered the rejection of the motion as no concession on the part of the Southern States. He considered the interests of these and the Eastern States as different as the interests of Russia and Turkey. Being, notwithstanding, desirous of *conciliating the affections* of the Eastern States, he should vote against requiring two-thirds instead of a majority."

Colonel GEORGE MASON, of Virginia : "If the Government is to be lasting, it must be founded in the *confidence* and *affection* of the people, and must be so construed as to obtain these. The *majority* will be governed by their interests. The Southern States are in the minority in both Houses. Is it to be expected that they will deliver themselves, bound hand and foot, to the Eastern States, and enable these to exclaim, in the words of Cromwell on a certain occasion, 'The Lord hath delivered them into our hands'?"

Mr. PINCKNEY's motion having failed to pass, the report of the committee, striking out the clause requiring a two-thirds vote to pass a navigation act, was then agreed to *nem. con.*

THE SPIRIT OF THE COMMITTEE OF ELEVEN.

The spirit of the committee that reported the terms of the foregoing "bargain," may be understood from the following statement of LUTHER MARTIN, one of their number : "They met and took under their consideration the subjects committed to them. I found the Eastern States, notwithstanding *their aversion to slavery*, were very willing to *indulge the Southern States* with at least a temporary liberty to prosecute the slave trade, provided the Southern States would, in their turn, gratify them by laying no restriction on navigation acts; and, after a very little time, the committee, by a large majority, agreed on a report."

GAIN AND LOSS TO EACH SECTION BY THE BARGAIN.

In this *bargain*, the Northern States gained : first, the right to pass navigation acts by a bare majority ; to tax the tonnage of foreign nations for their own advantage as carriers ; to lay a duty on foreign imports for their own advantage as manufacturers ; secondly, to put an end to the slave trade in twenty years, and thereby to prevent, in some degree, the increase of slave representation, for their own political advantage. What did they lose? Nothing, except their share of the profits in importing slaves, after enjoying it for that period.

What did the Southern States gain by this bargain? They gained only the additional recognition of property in slaves by the Constitution ; while they lost much of what the Northern States gained. They did not gain the right to import slaves for twenty years which they enjoyed before ; while they lost the right to import them afterwards. They found themselves " bound hand and foot " by the tariff laws of 1828, and other tariffs.

VIRGINIA NOT A PARTY TO THE BARGAIN.

One reason why Virginia did not unite with the Southern and Eastern States in making that bargain probably was, that she neither derived the profits received by the one class, from transporting slaves to the country, nor the profits received from purchasing and working them after their importation, enjoyed by the other class. She already had slaves enough of her own, so that she had no occasion to purchase, and she had comparatively few ships for transporting them to others. She could raise slaves cheaper than she could import them, and if she had any slaves for sale, the price of them would be lessened by the importation of negroes.

Besides this, Virginia had a long standing quarrel with the

British king on account of his vetoing a bill for the suppression of the slave trade, drawn up by the youthful Jefferson, and introduced by him into the State Legislature, and then passed. The indignation caused by that regal act continued to burn in the heart of the mover, and in many a generous bosom throughout Virginia for a long time afterwards, and may have contributed to prevent her from voting to permit the continuance of the slave trade until 1808.

The course of Virginia in the Convention was somewhat equivocal, acting sometimes with the slave States, and sometimes with the non-slaveholding States. As she had taken the lead in forming a Constitution, she must have been anxious to carry it out to a successful issue. She felt the dignity of her position as the Ancient Dominion, as the mother of statesmen, and as having her favorite son acting as President of the Convention. Mr. Madison, especially, was anxious to prevent a failure, and was disposed to conciliate both sections. He and others, probably, desired to believe that the abolition of slavery would take place in all the States, and he was willing to encourage the hope of it in others. But after the completion of the " bargain " by which the slave trade was to be continued twenty years, he must have given up that belief. Indeed, he declared that, by that continuance, all the evils of allowing the permanent continuance of the slave trade would be accomplished. The Pinckneys and others, who were better circumstanced to judge correctly, never encouraged that belief, but the contrary. They made arrangements in the Constitution for the permanence of slavery in the United States, and for its increase : just what has happened.

SLAVES RECOGNIZED AS PROPERTY BY THE CONSTITUTION.

But while the " bargain " was in the course of negotiation, it was particularly objected to by ROGER SHERMAN, on the ground that, by laying a duty on slaves as on other imports, it recognizes them as "*property*."

There were men in the Convention who had no objections to slaves being property, and to owning them as property, who thought that it was not judicious to name them as such, or to recognize them as such in the Constitution. That instrument must go before the people of the several States, and was likely to encounter great opposition. They thought, therefore, that it was desirable that as few features as possible should belong to it, with which even the most scrupulous and fastidious could find fault.

But it became necessary to recognize them as property in the Constitution ; just as they were often spoken of as property in the debates, and classed as property by Northern and Southern delegates. Thus, Mr. WILSON, of Pennsylvania, in the debate on this very subject, remarked : "As the section now stands, all *articles* (imported) are to be taxed, slaves only exempt ;" he thought it "unreasonable that slaves alone should be exempt, when all *other articles* are taxed or *dutied*. They were, therefore, classed in the same category with other articles of property.

THE WORD SLAVE NOT USED IN THE CONSTITUTION.

In regard to using the word "persons" in this section, and elsewhere, when *slaves* were meant and spoken of, LUTHER MARTON has the following remark in his letter to the Legislature of Maryland : "The design of this clause is to prevent the general Government from prohibiting the importation of *slaves ;* but the same general reason which caused them to strike out the word "national," and not admit the word "stamp," influenced them to guard against the introduction of the word *slaves*. They anxiously sought to avoid any expression which might be *odious* in the ears of Americans ; although they were willing to admit into their system the *things* which the expression signified." It fully recognized slaves to be property, though it does not contain the word. Mr. Sherman liked "a description" better than the term, which was not pleasing to some people. Mr. Madison was unwilling to use the term *slaves* in the Constitution, or even to suggest the idea that they were property ; though he spoke of them as property in debate and elsewhere, and owned them as property. He would have the idea, but would not suggest the idea. The word *slaves*, would be disagreeable to men like the Quakers ; the word "national," would be offensive to the staunch supporters of State rights ; and the word "stamp," would be disagreeable, because it called up the remembrance of the "stamp act." The phraseology used in describing the slave trade was employed for the same purpose. Mr. Madison, in his letter to Robert Walsh, Nov. 1819, declares, in respect to the phrase the "migration and importation of such persons," that it means *the importation of slaves.* The word "migration" was added as an expletive, that would weaken the impression produced by the word *importation* when used alone. The one word would modify or explain the other.

Gouverneur Morris, of Pennsylvania, one of the leading Northern men in the Convention, was anxious that the protection of slavery should not be made *prominent* in the Constitution. His constituents were some of them Quakers, some of them members of abolition societies, who might oppose the adoption of the Constitution, if they saw, distinctly, the whole amount of protection afforded to slave property, as they would, if slaves were distinctly named. And yet he declared that, as a matter of fact, domestic slavery was the most *prominent feature in the aristocratic countenance of the proposed Constitution.*" His perceptive mind saw clearly the exact meaning of the descriptive terms employed instead of the terms themselves. "A person held to service or labor in one State under the laws thereof," was a description conveying as clear a meaning to his mind, as if the word *slave* had been used instead of the "description." A description of the meaning of a word in a dictionary is a definition of the word, and shows its meaning. These statesmen did the same that theologians sometimes do. Instead of using odious words, they used equivalent terms.

FUGITIVE SLAVES.

General C. C. Pinckney, of South Carolina, at an early stage of the proceedings, declared that, unless provision should be made to secure the Southern States in the possession of their property in slaves, by preventing their emancipation by escaping into other States, the Constitution would not be accepted by the State which he represented. After the committee of detail had made their report, without making this provision, he renewed his demand for a provision "in favor of property in slaves;" and in the course of the debate he and Mr. C. PINCK-NEY moved to require fugitive slaves to be delivered up like criminals."

Mr. WILSON, of Pennsylvania, said: "This would require the executive of a State to do it at public expense."

Mr. SHERMAN, of Connecticut: "I see no more propriety in the public seizing and surrendering a slave, or servant, than a horse." It appears that both of these gentlemen voted for this provision, notwithstanding these objections.

Mr. BUTLER, of South Carolina, moved to insert, after article 15, "if any person, bound to service or labor in any of the United States, shall escape into another State, he or she shall not be discharged from such service or labor in consequence of any regulation subsisting in the State to which they may escape, but shall be delivered up to the person justly claiming their service or labor." This was agreed to in Convention *nem. con.*

In the first revision of this clause, there were some changes in style not affecting the meaning of the terms. Thus, instead of "justly" the word "due" was substituted; and instead of "any of the United States," "any State" was substituted.

Thus the Convention, without a dissenting voice, secured to slaveholders their right of property in slaves, according to the demand of Gen. Pinckney, in every part of the country, and in every State where the slave could be found. The States were expected to aid in the rendition of slaves.

REPRESENTATION AND TAXATION.

In respect to the subject of taxation, it seemed to be the wish of delegates from the Southern States that slaves should be reckoned as property, and not as persons; while, with respect to representation, it was their wish, at least a portion of them, that the slaves should be reckoned as persons, and the full number of slaves should be counted as so many white men.

On the other hand, the delegates from the Northern States seemed disposed to consider the slaves as persons with respect to the subject of taxation, but to consider them as property in respect to the subject of representation.

It having just been established in the Convention, by the

votes of the States, that there should be a common measure for representation and taxation, it was afterwards decided, that, as slaves were viewed both as property and as persons, they should be taken into both representation and taxation in the proportion of three to five, that is, that five slaves should count as much as three whites. Thus slaves are recognized as "persons" in the words of the Constitution, but as persons under the disability of being regarded as property by the laws of the State in which they reside. Had they been reckoned in their whole number, it would have been because they were regarded, in this matter, only as persons ; had they been excluded from the reckoning, it would be because they were, in this matter, reckoned only as property, just as they were originally by the Continental Congress.

The constitutional Convention was dissolved September 14, 1787.

REMARKS.

1. When the Constitution came from the Convention before the several States for adoption, so strong was the opposition to it in some of them, that it became evident that it could not be ratified by all of them, unless it should be amended either before or after its adoption. It was finally concluded to adopt it on assurances that it would be amended afterwards. One of the proposed amendments respected State rights, which have since been the subject of sectional discussion.

One of the articles of the old Confederation was this : " Each State retains its sovereignty, freedom, and independence, and every power, jurisdiction, and right, which is not by this Confederation expressly delegated to the United States in Congress assembled." This was omitted in the new Constitution, not from any objection to it, so far as is known to the present writer. Delegated powers are, of course, limited to the subjects delegated.

Accordingly, after its adoption, the following article, among others, was added to it, as an equivalent to the above article of the old Confederation : " The powers not delegated to the United States, are reserved to all the States respectively, or the people," (that is, to the people of the States respectively.)

At the time the Constitution was adopted, the citizens of

the different States were familiar with the doctrine of the Declaration of Independence, that Governments derive their just "powers from the consent of the governed," and that " it is the right of the people to alter and abolish their Government, and to form a new one, laying its foundation on such principles, and organizing its powers in such a form, as to them shall seem most likely to effect their safety and happiness."

The "right of the people" here spoken of generally, is applied, in that instrument, to the right of the people of the colonies respectively, who were about to " alter their former systems of government." The very clause containing the Declaration recognizes the same fact : " We, therefore, the representatives of the United States of America, in Congress assembled, appealing to the Supreme Judge of the world for the rectitude of our intentions, do, in the name and by the authority of the good people of these colonies, solemnly declare that these United Colonies are, and of right ought to be, free and independent States." Each colony thus became an independent State. Thus each colony, acting for itself, but in concert with others, " altered its former system of government."

And in the very act of changing the Government from that of the old Confederation, which was established by " articles of perpetual union," the several States recognized the right of " the people of the several States" to change the form of their government ; inasmuch as by their delegates, and then by their people, they changed the government, making it binding if nine States consent to the union, leaving out the remaining four. If the people of the several nine States had the right to change the government, notwithstanding they had adopted the " articles of perpetual union," then the four residuary States, namely, Virginia, New York, Rhode Island, and North Carolina, would be left in an awkward position, and might have some reason to complain ; but they could not deny the right. And it is not known to the present writer that they did deny the right. The two former soon acceded to the Union, but Rhode Island delayed until May, 1790, nearly three years, and North Carolina until November, more than three years. It should be added that these two States were not brought into the Union by coercion of any kind, but by conciliation.

2. After encountering a powerful opposition in the Convention in Virginia, the Constitution was ratified with the implied recognition of the right of the people of that State to resume the powers granted under it. "We, the delegates of the people of Virginia, do, in the name and behalf of the people of Virginia, declare and make known, that powers granted under the Constitution, being derived from the people of the United States, *may be resumed by them* whensoever the same shall be perverted to their injury or oppression, and that every power not granted thereby remains with them and at their will," &c.

In like manner the Convention of the State of New York assert the right of the people of New York to resume the powers granted under the Constitution. They "declare and make known, that the powers of government may be resumed by the people, whensoever it shall become necessary to their happiness; that every power, jurisdiction, and right, which is not by said Constitution clearly delegated to the Congress of the United States, or the Departments of the Government thereof, remains to the people of the several States, or to their respective State Governments to whom they have granted the same," &c. The State of New York, or the people of the State, as a party to the compact, must judge when it shall be necessary to resume the powers granted. Without this recognition of the right of a State to resume the powers granted, there is no reason to believe that the Constitution would have been ratified by New York; as there was a very powerful opposition to the measure. This recognition seems to have been substituted for another proposition, namely, to expressly reserve the right to recede after five or six years. The Constitution, with this and other explanations, was ratified by a majority of only three.

Rhode Island, also, expressly reserved the right to resume the powers granted. Thus three States, at least, not satisfied with the right which all the colonies were acknowledged to have, to alter their form of government, made a distinct declaration of that right, when they ratified the Constitution. In those times, when the word "people" was used in reference to the civil Government, it was understood to mean the people who acted by a Legislature, and Judges, and Governors of their own—the *people of a State*. In this sense it is used in the articles of Confederation, and in the Constitution, though in the latter it is also used for smaller bodies; but in no instance is it used for all the citizens of the United States taken collectively. Who were the people that ordained and established the Constitution of the United States? Evidently, the people of the several States, each State acting separately and for itself. The people of Massachusetts could not act for Virginia, but only for Massachusetts. The people of Virginia, when they claimed the right to resume the powers delegated, claimed that right for each of the States.

3. In the Convention which assembled in Philadelphia, May, 1787, the greatest difficulty arose from diversity of views in respect to State rights, though it did not, as afterwards, assume a sectional form. This will be noticed hereafter.

4. In respect to the "bargain" concerning navigation and the slave trade, it appears from the speech of General PINCKNEY. that the delegates of the Southern States were influenced by generous and patriotic considerations.

5. The Northern States declared in the Convention that they had but one motive to form a Constitution, and that was "commerce." By the bargain they gained *what they wanted*. In accordance with this, FISHER AMES, in the Massachusetts Convention, assembled to ratify the Constitution, said : "But we shall put every thing to hazard by rejecting the Constitution. We have great advantages with respect of navigation ; and it is the general interest of the States that we should have them. But if we reject it, what security have we that we shall obtain them a second time against the local interests and prejudices of the other States?"

6. The Northern States have since gained more than all the advantages which they expected by the encouragement provided for their commerce and manufactures ; especially since high tariffs have been established by Congress.

7. The Southern States lost whatever of advantages there was in the slave trade, after twenty years ; but they gained the acknowledgment that slaves under the Constitution are property, being taxable or dutiable like other articles of property ; that they shall be deliv- ... ... slaveholding States ; and that, in case of the insurrection-or-

3

slaves, they shall be protected in their rights of property by aid, when necessary, from the non-slaveholding States.

8. In submitting to the rule of reckoning five slaves as equivalent to three whites in taxation and representation, the Southern States did not gain what it was expected they would gain in taxation, inasmuch as, with very few exceptions, Federal taxes have not been assessed in the States, as the expenses of the Federal Government have been supported chiefly by revenue from imports; while they have lost what they expected to lose in respect to representation, namely, two-fifths of the slaves, which are not reckoned as the basis of representation.

9. It should be added that in 1807, when the vote was taken in Congress to abolish the slave trade, the Southern States united with the Northern in passing that vote, which was nearly unanimous, showing that the power over the trade, which they gave up in the Constitution, they did not attempt to retain by Congressional action.

Whether the Northern States have been careful not to abuse the power acquired by the "bargain," respecting navigation laws and tariff laws, is a question not yet settled between the Northern and the Southern States. Whether Northern States have faithfully performed their obligations to "deliver up" fugitive slaves to their owners, is likewise a question between the two parties. An unprejudiced mind, acquainted with Congressional action for the last forty years, and with State legislation in passing personal liberty bills for the last ten years, can hardly fail to decide that the Northern States have abused their power in the one case, and have not been faithful in the other.

10. The Constitution was intended to secure to the Southern States the *peaceable possession of their slaves;* and had it not been supposed that it did so, it would never have been adopted by them. It made slavery a part of our national institutions, so far as we have any national institutions; and the Federal laws, and the decisions of the Federal judiciary, and the action of the Federal executive in treaties with Great Britain and otherwise, have recognized it as a national institution. That they have not enjoyed the peaceable possession of their slaves, events for the last forty years ... editors have, for political purposes,

extensively insinuated into Northern minds hatred of slavery and slaveholders.

11. Covert or open attacks have been made upon slavery, from political considerations. Some fifteen or twenty years ago, when Northern petitions, signed by men, women, and children, and negroes, were flooding the floor of the lower House, as a leading Northern member of Congress, who afterwards was a member of a Presidential Cabinet, was coming out from a heated debate, he was asked by the present writer, an old college friend, "Will you inform me what is the *real reason* why Northern members encourage these petitions?" After considering for a moment, he said to me, "The real reason is, that the South will not let us have a tariff, and we touch them where they will *feel* it."

12. The Constitution gives no authority to Congress to legislate in favor of morals and religion; these subjects are reserved for the action of the States. The Constitution treats slavery as a political matter only, and gives no authority to Congress to treat it in any other way.

CHAPTER III.

THE Constitution just adopted embodied the principles of our Government; the laws to be passed under it would furnish the rules for its administration. It was fortunate for the country that the friends of the Federal Constitution had a paramount influence in the practical application of its principles in the legislative, judicial, and executive departments. Especially was it fortunate that WASHINGTON, the President of the Convention, was President of the United States, and HAMILTON, a leading member, was Secretary of the Treasury, and RANDOLPH, who, in the Convention, brought forward the plan that was adopted, was Attorney-General, and JEFFERSON, the author of the Declaration of Independence, was Secretary of State.

But as in the Convention, so in the first Congress and afterwards, sectional disputes arose, which, though conducted for the most part with decorum, shadowed dimly forth those future heated discussions in that Department, that have, from time to time, shaken like an earthquake the country to its centre. The interests of the Northern States were different from those of the Southern States, and when Congress was called to legislate on subjects connected with those interests, it is not strange that the members from the South, at their stand-point, should take a view of those subjects differing from that taken by Northern members.

DUTIES ON TONNAGE AND IMPORTS.

The duties on foreign tonnage and imports, pressed more heavily on the South than on the North, inasmuch as the former had fewer ships and fewer manufactures to be benefited. Mr. SMITH, of South Carolina, said: "Gentlemen have endeavored to persuade us that a high tonnage duty will be beneficial to the Union; but I would as soon be persuaded to throw myself out of a two-story window, as to believe that a high tonnage will be favorable to South Carolina." And in respect to duties on imports, Mr. MADISON remarked, " If there is a disposition represented to complain of the oppression of government, have not the citizens of the Southern States more just ground of complaint than others? " "The system can only be acceptable to them, because it is, essentially, necessary to be adopted for the public good."

And yet, on another occasion Mr. MADISON said, in reference to the same subject, " I believe every gentleman who hears the observations from the different quarters of this House, discovers great reason for every friend of the United States to congratulate himself upon the evident disposition which has been displayed to conduct business with harmony and concert." And Mr. AMES said, " The gentlemen from the southward who suppose their States most likely to be affected by a discrimination in the tonnage duty, have concluded their arguments with a candor which does honor to their patriotism."

It is very evident that on this subject there was a spirit of conciliation on the part of leading men, and especially on the part of Southern gentlemen, who consented to sacrifice the interests of their States for the public good. The Northern States had wished for the establishment of the Constitution, chiefly, for the protection of their *commercial* interests. This legislation of the first Congress under the Constitution secured to them this protection. The South patiently, or rather cheerfully, acquiesced in bearing the burdens imposed by this legislation. "If," said Mr. AMES, "I may judge of the feelings of the people by those of their representatives on this floor, I may venture to say that there never was less reason to apprehend envy and discord than at this time. I believe the fact is so, because I feel it." He was conscious of a patriotic regard for the whole country. " I look," said he, " with an equal eye upon the success of every State through the whole extent of United America. I wish their interests to be equally consulted." Thus were the commercial sacrifices of the South appreciated, and their patriotism, which made them submit to the sacrifices, reciprocated by a representative man of the North.   In this contest the South yielded to the North for the general good of the country.

SECTIONAL DISCUSSION OF SLAVERY.

In the Constitutional Convention, the Southern States had obtained provisions which secured to them their property in slaves, and the right to import slaves for twenty years.   But in Congress, Feb. 11, 1790, "The Address of the Quaker Meeting," from certain Northern States, was presented against the continuance of the African slave trade, which was permitted by the Constitution, until 1808.   And Feb. 11, 1790, "The Memorial of the Pennsylvania Abolition Society" was presented, praying for the abolition of slavery in the United States, which, by the Constitution, was left under the States.

These two memorials were received in one spirit by Southern members, and in another and different spirit by Northern members.   The former saw clearly that the petitioners were aiming a blow at their pecuniary and their social interests, by urging Congress to pass unconstitutional laws on the subject of slavery, and by holding slaveholders up to the moral abhorrence of the world; as if Congress had the power to legislate for the promotion of morals and religion.

The Northern members, some of them, seemed to give a warm welcome to the petitions, as if they were glad to ventilate their abhorrence of slave-trading and slaveholding.

In this contest the Southern States retained, indeed, their constitutional rights, but they had to struggle earnestly for them. The temper of Northern members shown on this occasion was manifested at times afterwards.   Thus, Jan. 1795, Mr. DEXTER, of Massachusetts, moved, as an amendment to a motion for naturalizing foreigners, "that each man naturalized should renounce the possession of slaves," and, as an amendment to this amendment, Mr. THATCHER, of Massachusetts, moved, "and he never would possess slaves."

Mr. MADISON, in reply to Messrs. DEXTER and THATCHER,

said " that the mention of such a thing would have a very bad effect on that species of property."

Mr. W. SMITH, of South Carolina, a distinguished member, in the course of the discussion on slavery, said "that the Southern States never would have entered into the Confederation unless their property (in slaves) had been guarantied to them."

Mr. BOUDINOT, of New Jersey, said : " There is a wide difference between justifying the ungenerous traffic, and supporting a claim to property vested at the time of the formation of the Constitution, and guarantied thereby."

The effect of the motions of Messrs. DEXTER and THATCHER, if they had prevailed, would have been to lessen emigration to the slave States, and thus to lessen their political power.

BANK OF THE UNITED STATES.

The Secretary of the Treasury, Mr. HAMILTON, had advocated the establishment of a National Bank, on the ground that it would promote the prosperous administration of the finances, and help to support the public credit. When a bill in conformity to his plan was, in 1791, sent down from the Senate, it was suffered to pass to its third reading without opposition. On the final question a powerful opposition was made to its passage by Mr. MADISON and others.

It was asserted by them that the powers of the Government of the United States which it might legitimately exercise, were *enumerated* in the Constitution. In this enumeration, the power to charter a bank was not to be found. They, moreover, insisted that it could not be implied from the powers that were given to the Government, and that, by any fair construction, no clause in the Constitution could be understood to imply so important a power as that of creating a corporation.

On the other side, in favor of the establishment of a bank, it was asserted, that incidental as well as express powers must, necessarily, belong to every government, and that when a power is delegated to effect particular objects, all the known and usual means of effecting them must pass also, and after taking a comprehensive view of the powers given to the General Government.

it was contended that a bank was a known and usual instrument, by which several of them were exercised. Taking into consideration the utility of a bank in managing the finances, and supporting public credit, the bill was passed in the House by a majority of nineteen voices. In the cabinet, the Attorney-General, Mr. RANDOLPH, and the Secretary of State, Mr. JEFFERSON, were opposed to it on constitutional grounds, while the Secretary of the Treasury was in favor of it, and the President added his signature to the bill.

While the bill was under debate, Mr. TUCKER, of Georgia, remarked, " That a gentleman from Virginia has well observed that we appear to be divided by a geographical line ; not a gentleman North of that line is opposed to the bill ; and where is the gentleman to the Southward that is in favor of it ? " The Northern States won the victory over the Southern, if not over the Constitution.

THE EXCISE LAW.

The Excise law, by which a duty was laid on *spirits distilled within the United States,* was opposed, very strongly, by a majority of the members of Southern and Southwestern States, on the ground that it would operate very unequally and against the interests of their constituents, who used foreign distilled liquor to a very inconsiderable amount. The bill was passed by Northern members, influenced, it was said, by the fact that the commercial States depended chiefly on foreign spirits. The whiskey insurrection grew chiefly out of the opposition to this law. The law, thus operating unequally, was wisely repealed.

THE ASSUMPTION OF STATE DEBTS.

On the 9th of January, 1790, Mr. HAMILTON, Secretary of the Treasury, gave notice to the House of Representatives that he was ready to make his report on public credit, which he had prepared in obedience to the resolution of the 21st of Sept., 1789. In that celebrated report he proposed the Assumption of State debts, and to fund them in common with that which constituted the proper debt of the Union.

This proposal was opposed by Southern members, on the ground that it would give undue influence to the General Government, and would thus weaken the State Governments; that it would not be justified by the Constitution, the powers of that instrument being specified, and this was not among them; that it was unjust, because it would make no discrimination between those States which had taxed themselves to discharge the claims against them, and those which had not made the same exertions.

In favor of the measure it was asserted by Northern members, that the debts contracted by the States were not contracted for the benefit of the individual States, but for the common good of the Union, in the war against the common enemy; that the measure would put an end to speculation, by fixing the value of the securities; that it would restore public confidence.

A large amount of these securities were owned at the North, where they were obtained in the course of trade. Many of them had been purchased at very low rates, as was said, for a song.

After a very heated debate, highly irritating to the parties, the resolution failed to pass, by a majority of two against it.

LOCATION OF THE SEAT OF GOVERNMENT.

July 9, 1790. Mr. GOODHUE, of Massachusetts, moved in the House: "That the permanent seat of the General Government ought to be at some convenient place, on the east bank of the river Susquehanna, in the State of Pennsylvania." In support of his motion, he prefaced it with the following remark: "The Eastern members, with the members from New York, have agreed to fix on a place upon national principles, without regard to their own convenience, and have turned their minds to the Susquehanna." The place contemplated was Wright's Ferry, about 35 miles from navigable water.

This sectional movement on the part of Eastern and Northern members, in favor of a place which had not a great deal to recommend it, awakened very strong sectional feelings on the part of the Southern members, who were in favor of the bank of the Potomac, as an appropriate place. To this place the Northern members were strongly opposed, proposing, instead of it, if not Wright's Ferry, Germantown and Baltimore.

In view of the above-mentioned combination of Northern members, RICHARD H. LEE, in the course of his speech, said : "It is well known with what difficulty the Constitution was adopted in Virginia. It was then said that there would be Confederacies of the States east of Pennsylvania, which would destroy the Southern States; that they would unite their councils in discussing questions relative to their particular interests, and the Southern States would be disregarded. To these suspicions it was answered: "No! It was contended that the magnanimous policy, arising from mutual interests and common dangers, would unite all the States, and make them pursue objects of general good. But if it should be found that there were such Confederacies as were predicted, that the Northern States did consult their partial interests, and form combinations to support them without regard to their Southern brethren, they would be alarmed, and the faith of all south of the Potomac would be shaken."

Mr. MADISON said, in the course of his remarks : "But give me leave now to say that, if prophets had arisen in that body, (the Convention of Virginia,) and brought the declarations and proceedings of this day to view, I as firmly believe Virginia might not have been a part of the Union at this moment."

BARGAIN IN CONGRESS.

This measure became combined with the Assumption Bill. Each had failed by small majorities; both were afterwards passed. The Eastern and Middle States were for the assumption; the Southern States were against it; the latter were for the Potomac for the seat of Government; the former were for the Susquehanna. The discontent was extreme on each side, at losing its favorite measure. At last the two measures were combined. Two members from the Potomac, who had voted against the assumption, agreed to change their votes : a few from the Eastern and Middle States, who had voted against the Potomac agreed to change in its favor; and so the two measures were passed.

Mr. JEFFERSON gave this account of it, omitting his strictures : "This measure (the Assumption of State debts) produced

the most bitter and angry contest ever known in Congress before
or since the Union of the States. I arrived in the midst of it ;
but a stranger to the ground, a stranger to the actors in it, so
long absent as to have lost all familiarity with the subject, and
as yet unaware of its object. I took no concern in it. The
great and trying question, however, was lost in the House of
Representatives. . So high were the feuds excited on this subject, that, on its rejection, *business was suspended, Congress met
and adjourned from day to day without doing any thing,* the
parties being too much out of temper to do business together.
(The Eastern members *threatened secession and dissolution.*)
HAMILTON was in despair. As I was going to the President's
one day, I met him in the street. He walked with me back-
wards and forwards before the President's door for half an hour.
He painted pathetically the temper into which the Legislature
had been wrought ; the disgust of those who were called the
creditor States, (the Northern,) the danger of the secession of
their members, and of the separation of the States. He observed that the members of the Administration ought to act in
concert ; that though this question was not of my department,
yet a common duty should make it a common concern ; that the
President was the centre, in which all administrative questions
ultimately rested, and that all of us should rally round him, and
support, with joint efforts, measures approved by him, and that
the question having been lost by a small majority only, that an
appeal from me to the judgment and discretion of some of my
friends might effect a change in the vote, and the machine of
government, now suspended, might be again set in motion.}/ I
told him I was really a stranger to the whole subject ; that, not
having yet informed myself of the system of finances adopted, I
knew not how far this was a necessary sequence ; that undoubtedly, if its rejection endangered the dissolution of the Union at
this incipient stage, I should deem that the most unfortunate of
all consequences, to avert which all partial and temporary evils
should be yielded. I proposed, however, to him, to dine with
me, next day, and I would invite another friend or two, bring
them into conference together, and I thought it impossible that
reasonable men, consulting together coolly, could fail, by some
mutual sacrifice of opinion, to form a compromise which would

save the Union. The discussion took place. I could take no part in it but an exhortatory one, because I was a stranger to the circumstances which should govern it. But it was finally agreed that whatever importance was attached to the rejection of this proposition, the preservation of the Union and concord among the States was more important, and therefore it would be better that the vote of rejection should be rescinded—to effect which, some members should change their votes. But it was observed that this pill would be peculiarly bitter to the Southern States, and that some concomitant measure should be adopted to sweeten it to them. There had before been propositions to fix the seat of Government either at Philadelphia or at George-town, on the Potomac ; and it was thought that by giving it to Philadelphia for ten years, and to Georgetown permanently' af-terwards, this might, as an anodyne, calm the ferment which might be excited by the other measure alone : so two of the Potomac members (WHITE and LEE, but the former with a re-vulsion of stomach almost convulsive) agreed to change their votes, and HAMILTON undertook to carry the other point." *Abridgment of Debates,* vol. i., p. 250.

The Northern members contended with great earnestness against the Potomac for the seat of Government; Mr. BOUDINOT, Mr. AMES, Mr. LAWRENCE, severally, proposing the Delaware, Germantown, Baltimore, instead of the Potomac, which latter finally received a majority of the votes, probably through the influence of HAMILTON. The Northern States, by the assumption of State debts by Congress, obtained millions, which en-riched many of their inhabitants, indeed, some of the members who helped to pass the bill. The Southern States obtained for the seat of Government their favorite location, and a much bet-ter location than Wright's Ferry, which had been selected by the combination of Eastern members.

This is the first *sectional combination* in Congress for carry-ing a measure that I have seen noticed. The assumption of State debts furnished the occasion of the first threat of secession, and breaking up the Government. It was made by the North-ern members.

FUGITIVES FROM JUSTICE AND FROM LABOR.

July 5, 1793. The House proceeded to consider the bill sent from the Senate, entitled " An act respecting fugitives from justice and persons escaping from the service of their masters," which lay on the table; whereupon the said bill, with the amendments agreed to yesterday, was read the third time ; and on the question that the same do pass, it was resolved in the affirmative ; yeas, 48, nays, 7.

The bill came down from the Senate, whose debates were not published, and seems to have passed the House without debate, and almost without discussion, there being but seven votes against, and two of these, Messrs. MERCER and PARKER, from slave States. Nor does it appear to what part of the bill they objected, whether to the part in relation to fugitives from justice, or to those who fled from service, for both classes of fugitives were comprehended in the same bill. It was passed on a message from President Washington, founded on a communication from the Governor of Pennsylvania in relation to a fugitive from justice who had taken refuge in Virginia, and because it was necessary to have an act of Congress to give effect to the rendition clause in the Constitution. There was but little necessity, in those times, and long after, for an act of Congress to authorize the recovery of fugitive slaves. The laws of the States and still more, the force of public opinion, were the owners' best safeguards. Public opinion was against the abduction of slaves ; and, if any one was seduced from his owner, it was done furtively and secretly, without show or force, and as any other moral offence would be committed. State laws favored the owner to a greater extent than the acts of Congress did or could. In Pennsylvania an act was passed in 1780, and repealed only in 1847, discriminating between the traveller and sojourner and the permanent resident, allowing the former to remain six months in the State before his slaves could become subject to emancipation laws ; and, in the case of a Federal Government officer, allowing as much more time as his duties required him to remain. New York had the same act, only varying in time, which was nine months. While these two acts were in force, and supported by public opinion, the traveller and sojourner was safe with his slaves in these States, and the same in the other States. There was no trouble about fugitive slaves in those times. This act of 1793 did not grow out of any such troubles, but out of the case of a fugitive from justice. It was that case which brought the subject before Congress, and in the act that was passed, the case of fugitives from justice was first provided for, the first and second sections of the act being given to that branch of the subject, and the third and fourth to the other—all brief and plain, and executable without expense or fuss. In the case of a slave, the owner was allowed to seize him wherever he saw him, by day or by night, and Sundays or week days, just as if he were in his own State, and a penalty of $500 attached to any person who obstructed him in this seizure. The only authority he wanted was after the seizure, and to justify the carrying back, and for that purpose the affidavit of the owner or his agent was sufficient. This act was perfect except in relying upon State officers not being subject to the Federal law, and being forbid to act after slavery became a subject of political agitation.—*Benton's Debates*, vol. i., p. 412.

The law was judiciously drawn, and entirely satisfactory to both sections of the country; but the Northern States, in the progress of years, refused to carry it out, and placed obstacles in the way.

MR. JEFFERSON'S LETTER TO GENERAL WASHINGTON.

"PHILADELPHIA, *May* 23, 1792.

❋ ❋ ❋ "True wisdom would direct, that they (means) should be temperate and peaceable; but the division of sentiment and interest happens, unfortunately, to be so *geographical*, that no mortal can say that what is most wise and temperate would prevail against what is most easy and obvious. I can scarcely contemplate a more incalculable evil than the breaking up of the Union into two or more parts. Yet, when we consider the mass which opposed the original coalescence; when we consider that it lay chiefly in the Southern quarter; that the Legislature have availed themselves of no occasion of allaying it, but on the contrary, when Northern and Southern prejudices have come into conflict, the latter have been sacrificed and the former soothed, that the owners of the debt are in the Southern, and the holders in the Northern division; that the anti-federal champions are now strengthened in their arguments by the fulfilment of their predictions; that this has been brought about by the monarchical federalists themselves, who have been for the new Government merely as a stepping-stone to monarchy, and who have adopted the very construction of the Constitution of which, when advocating its acceptance before the tribunal of the people, they had declared it unsusceptible; that the republican federalists who espoused the same Government for its intrinsic merits, are disarmed of their weapons; that which they deemed as prophecy having become true as history; who can be sure that these things may not proselyte the small number which was wanting to place the majority on the other side? And this is the event at which I tremble, and to prevent which I consider your continuing at the head of affairs as of the last importance. The confidence of the whole Union is centred in you. Your being at the helm will be more than an answer to every argument which can be used to alarm and lead the people in any quarter into violence and secession. North and South will hang together, if they have you to hang upon."

We have here the fact that sectional differences of opinion and sectional feelings existed of a dangerous character, and that Washington was urged to accept of the Presidency a second time, in order to prevent " violence and secession." Allusion is also made to the large construction given to the text of the Constitution by those who controlled some of the departments of the Government. A dominant party are always under a temptation to enlarge the powers of the General Government at the expense of the powers reserved to the people of the several States. They are apt to think that their favorite measure had better be passed in Congress, or sanctioned by the Executive, even at the expense of the Constitution. Party leaders, even during the administration of Washington, form no exception to this love of power.

REMARKS.

1. The administration of General Washington was distinguished for the wisdom of its measures, for the energy with

which they were carried out, and for the great success which attended them. The several departments, the legislative, the judicial, and executive taking form, now for the first time, and filled with men of experience, of undoubted patriotism, and of high talent, were in harmony with one another.

2. And yet, there was a difference of opinion in Congress, and in the cabinet, as to the construction to be given to the Constitution, in its application to the purposes for which it was framed. Alexander Hamilton, Secretary of the Treasury, the leading spirit in the Executive Department, was, in the Convention, in favor of forming a strong government, and what he failed to accomplish in that body in the framework of the Constitution, he endeavored to work out in practice by a broad construction of that instrument, by magnifying its "implied powers," and the "necessary powers." "Necessary powers" were understood to mean those powers that were deemed necessary to put the government in operation under the Constitution.

The terms "necessary powers" and "implied powers" were vague, and would vary according to the character of the mind that should exercise a judgment concerning them. What would seem to be "necessary" and "implied" to one mind, would not seem "necessary" or "implied" to another mind. With Hamilton, his old companion in arms, Knox, the Secretary of War, acted in promoting his views.

Jefferson, Secretary of State, and Edmund Randolph, Attorney-General, differed from Hamilton in their views of the power granted to the General Government in the Constitution, and looked at the powers reserved to the States as well as at those delegated to the General Government.

Hamilton, with his penetrating and logical mind, with his extraordinary energy, with his constructive and productive genius, had the ear of Washington as well as of Knox, all of them military men, and all of them disgusted with the weakness of the old Confederation.

Jefferson, with his gift of language, with his insight and foresight, with his constructive mind, accustomed to deal with principles, was aided, in his view, by Randolph, whose plan of a Constitution had been adopted in the Convention, and who understood accurately what was its meaning, and who was not disposed to magnify its implied powers.

In both Houses of Congress were leading men, who were also divided in their views as to the "implied powers" of the Constitution, a portion of them being in favor of a "broad construction" of its powers, and another portion being in favor of a "strict construction." The practical men of the Northern States, who valued the Constitution chiefly for "commercial purposes," and who felt the value of public credit, generally adopted the views of Mr. Hamilton. The statesmen of the South, who looked at political principles and relations, generally adopted the views of Mr. Jefferson.

3. Mr. Hamilton was an admirer of the British government, in which parliament has almost unlimited powers; and it was supposed that he endeavored to assimilate the General Government to that, notwithstanding the rights reserved to the States. In his celebrated report of 1791 he claimed power for the Federal Government to encourage learning, agriculture, and manufactures, all under the authority to levy imports for the "general welfare." Mr. Jefferson was an admirer of the early principles of the French Revolution, and was a hater of Great Britain, and in these respects he had the sympathy of the people of the United States, who remembered the wrongs they had received from the one nation, and the favors they had received from the other. The policy of the Administration in respect to the two nations was, to some extent, the ground of sectional difference of opinion, the leaders of the opposition being principally in the Southern States.

CHAPTER IV.

To the election of Mr. ADAMS there was an opposition in the Southern States, but not violent. It was generally conceded that his patriotism, his talents, his experience, and services, entitled him to the Presidency.

But in the course of his administration, this sectional opposition gained strength, chiefly on account of his war measures, by which eighty thousand men were subjected to his order, which was supposed to be contrary to the theory of our Government; the acts for increasing the navy; and especially on account of the passage of the alien and sedition laws, and prosecutions under them. This opposition was largely sectional, and was based chiefly on the exorbitant powers supposed to be claimed by the General Government. The leading men in the opposition, for their defence, fell back on the *residuary power* of the States secured by the Constitution, as the means of preventing the establishment of a consolidated government instead of a Federal one.

THE ASSERTION OF STATE RIGHTS.

Virginia, at a meeting of her Legislature, early in the session of 1798, passed a series of resolutions declaratory of State rights, and condemnatory of the alien and sedition laws, and other measures of the Government, as having a tendency to change its character from a Federal to a national Government. Among other things, these resolutions affirm, that "it (the Legislature) views the powers of the General Government as resulting from the compact to which the States are parties, as limited by the plain sense and intention of the instrument constituting that compact, as no further valid than they are authorized by the grants enumerated in that compact; and that in case of a deliberate, palpable, and dangerous exercise of powers not granted in said compact, the States who are parties thereto have the right, and are in duty bound to interpose for arresting the progress of the evil, and for maintaining within their respective limits the authorities, rights, and liberties appertaining to them."

In the resolutions passed by the Legislature of Kentucky in 1798, it is declared " that whensoever the General Government assumes and delegates powers, its acts are unauthoritative, void, and of no force; that each State acceded as a State, and is an integral party, its co-States forming as to itself the other party; that the Government created by this compact was not made the exclusive or final judge of the extent of the powers delegated to it, since that would have made its discretion and not the Constitution the measure of its powers; that, as in all other cases of a compact among parties having no common judge, each party has an equal right to judge for itself, as well of the infractions as the mode and measure of redress."

The resolutions of Virginia were drawn up by Mr. MADISON; those of Kentucky were said to be sketched, but not fully prepared, by Mr. JEFFERSON.

It was believed that the Administration, under the guidance of Northern men, had assumed powers not enumerated in the Constitution, and, in this way, had usurped powers belonging to the States.

THE DOCTRINE OF STATE RIGHTS.

As the doctrine of State rights has been adopted at different times, by both the South and the North, in their relations to the General Government, it seems proper to give some account of its origin and its sectional influences.

LUTHER MARTIN'S LETTER.

LUTHER MARTIN wrote a letter to the Legislature of Maryland on the formation of the Federal Constitution in 1787, and the composition of the Convention, of which the following is an extract:

_//_ " There was one party, whose object and wish is to abolish and annihilate all State Governments, and bring forward one General · Government over this extensive continent, of a monarchical nature, under certain restrictions and limitations. Those who openly avowed this sentiment were, it is true, but few; yet it is equally true that there was a considerable number who did not openly avow it—who were, by myself and many others of the Convention, considered as being in reality favorers of that sentiment, and, acting upon those principles, covertly endeavoring to carry into effect what they well knew openly and avowedly could not be accomplished.

" The second party was not for the abolition of State Governments, nor for the introduction of a monarchical Government in any form; but they wished to establish such a system as could give their own States undue power and influence in the Government over the other States.

" A third party was what I considered truly Federal and Republican. This party was nearly equal in number with the other two, and was composed of the delegations from Connecticut, New York, New Jersey, and in part Maryland; also of some individuals from other representations." _//_

The first party here mentioned by Mr. MARTIN was supposed to include Mr. HAMILTON, GOUVERNEUR MORRIS, and some others. The second party was supposed to include the delegates from Virginia, Pennsylvania, Massachusetts, and some other of the larger States.

Colonel HUMPHREYS, in his letter to General WASHINGTON, of the 20th of January, 1787, describes the temper of a number of the States in the following language: " They have a mortal reluctance to divest themselves of the smallest attribute of independent, separate sovereignties." This temper showed itself in the convention in the speeches of the delegates.

Friday, June 29, 1787.—Doctor JOHNSON, of Connecticut,

said, in the Federal Convention: "The controversy must be endless, whilst gentlemen differ in the grounds of their arguments; those on one side considering the States as districts of people composing one political society; and those on the other considering them as so many political societies. The fact is, the States *do exist as so many political societies;* and a government is *to be formed for them in their political capacity,* as well as for the individuals composing them. Does it not seem to follow, that, if the States as such are to exist, they *must be armed with some power of self-defence?*"

Mr. ELLSWORTH, in the same debate, said: "Under a national Government he should participate in the national security, as remarked by Mr. KING; but that was all. What he wanted was domestic happiness. The national Government could not descend to the local objects on which this depended. It could only embrace objects of a general nature. He turned his eyes, therefore, for the *preservation of his rights, to the State Governments.* From these alone he could derive the greatest happiness he expected in this life. His happiness depends on their existence as much as a new-born infant on its mother for nourishment."

So anxious was that distinguished statesman to preserve the *rights of the States,* that he moved in the Federal Convention that the term "*national*" should be stricken out of the Constitution; and his motion was passed without opposition, and the objectionable term was stricken out.

He and others preferred the term "Federal," because it described more accurately the nature of the Government which they were forming. The term "*Federal* pertains to a league or compact, and is derived from an agreement or covenant between parties, particularly between nations." Hence the friends of the Constitution, which was a compact or league between the States, were called *Federalists.*

In a letter to Governor HUNTINGTON, dated New London, September 26, 1787, Mr. ELLSWORTH and Mr. SHERMAN unite in saying:

"Some additional powers are vested in Congress, which was the principal object the States had in view in appointing the Convention; those powers extend only to matters respecting the common interests of the Union, and are *specially defined*, so that *the particular States retain their sovereignty in other matters.*"

Dr. Johnson, in the State Convention in Hartford, convened January 14, 1788, to ratify the Federal Constitution, said: "The Constitution vests in the general Legislature a power to make laws in matters of national concern; to appoint judges to decide upon those laws; and to appoint officers to carry them into execution. *This excludes the idea of an armed force.* The power which is to enforce these laws is to be a legal power, vested in the magistrates. [Not military.] The force which is to be employed, is the energy of law; and this force is to be employed *only upon individuals* who fail in their duty to their country. This is the glory of the Constitution, that it depends upon the mild and equal energy of the magistracy for the execution of the laws." [Not upon military coercion.]

Oliver Ellsworth, Jan. 7, 1788, in the State Convention, Hartford, 1788, said : "We see how necessary for the Union is a coercive principle. No man pretends to the contrary. We all see and feel this necessity. The only question is, Shall it be a coercion of law, or a coercion of arms? There is no other possible alternative. Where would those, who oppose a coercion of law, come out? Where will they end? A necessary consequence of their principles is a war of the States, one against the other. I am for coercion by law; that coercion which acts only upon delinquent individuals. *The Constitution does not attempt to coerce sovereign bodies*—States in their political capacity. No coercion is applicable to such bodies but that of armed force. If we should attempt to execute the laws of the Union *by sending an armed force* against a delinquent State, it would involve the good and bad, the innocent and guilty, in the same calamity. But this legal coercion singles out the guilty individual, and punishes him for breaking the laws."

Mr. Law, in the same Convention, said : "Some suppose that the General Government, which extends over the whole, will annihilate the State Governments. But we ought to consider that this General Government rests on the State Governments for its support. It is like a vast and beautiful bridge built upon thirteen strong and stately pillars. Now the rulers, those who occupy the bridge, cannot be so beside themselves as to knock away the pillars that support the whole fabric."

The Constitution was formed on the idea that all powers granted to the General Government were " *specially defined*" or "*enumerated*," and that all powers, not " specially defined " or " not enumerated," are retained by each of the States.

In the formation and adoption of the Constitution, the States were the only agents. The State Legislatures appointed the delegates to the Convention. While there, they voted by States. Each delegation made its report to the Legislature or Governor of the States. The Convention which assembled in the several States to ratify or reject the Constitution, was appointed by the people of the several States. The parties to the " Constitutional Compact " were the States. ROGER SHERMAN says : " And the Government of the United States being Federal, and instituted by a number of sovereign States for the better security of their rights, and the advancement of their interests," &c.—*Letter to John Adams.*

The motion was made in the Convention to give Congress power to negative all State laws contravening the articles of Union, and thus to abridge the rights of the several States. This motion was rejected by a vote of seven States against three.

. *Thursday, May* 31, 1787.—In the plan of a Constitution proposed by Governor RANDOLPH, and generally adopted by the Convention, provision was made " authorizing the exertion of the force of the other States against a delinquent State." The effect of this would be to abridge the rights of the States.

Mr. MADISON observed, " that the more he reflected on the use of force, the more he doubted the practicability, the justice, and the efficacy of it, when applied to a people collectively and not individually. A union of the States, containing such an ingredient, seemed to provide for its own destruction. The use of force against a State would look more like a declaration of war than an infliction of punishment, and would probably be considered by the party attacked as a dissolution of all previous compacts by which it might be bound. He hoped such a system might be framed as would render this resource unnecessary, and moved that the clause be postponed. This motion was agreed to, *nem. con.*"—*Madison Papers*, p. 761.

ALEXANDER HAMILTON used the following language on the same subject. After referring to the case of Shay's rebellion, in which military force could be properly employed, and for which "Massachusetts was making provision," by State authority, he adds : "But how can this force be exerted on the States collectively ? (against State authority.) It is impossible. It amounts to a declaration of war between the parties. Foreign powers also will not be idle spectators. They will interpose; the confusion will increase; and a dissolution of the Union will ensue."—*Idem*, p. 881.

Thus it appears that no State can constitutionally be coerced by the other States by force of arms.

In the Convention, so determined were the advocates of State rights not to give up certain of these to the General Government, that the Convention came to a dead stand, and was in danger of failing entirely to accomplish the object for which they assembled. CHARLES PINCKNEY declared, that for nearly six weeks the small States pertinaciously struggled to obtain equal power in both branches.

The term "United States" was in constant use when the Constitution was framed, with a fixed and definite meaning in the minds of men, namely, the same as in the Articles of Confederation. That document is described as "Articles of Confederation, and perpetual union between the States of New Hampshire, Massachusetts, Rhode Island, &c. Article I. The style of this Confederacy shall be, *The United States of America.*"

Now it is evident that the term "United States," in the Constitution, means the same that it does in the Articles of Confederation, and is equivalent to New Hampshire, Massachusetts, &c., united, or the States united. They formed a union by a compact *between themselves.* Article VII. "The ratification of the conventions of nine States shall be sufficient for the establishment of this Constitution *between the States* so ratifying the same." Here the word is *between*, not *over*. The Constitution is a compact between the States. "We the people of the United States," evidently must mean the same as we the people of New Hampshire, Massachusetts, &c., taken *severally*, and not *collectively;* that is, the people of New Hampshire and the people of Massachusetts, &c. The people who voted for the Constitution by States must have understood the phrase as meaning the same in the Constitution that it does in the Articles of Confederation, namely, the people of the *several* States, and not the people of America, taken *collectively* as one people. It was a majority of the people of *each* State acting by itself that adopted the Constitution, and not a majority of the people of *all* the States taken collectively.

Indeed, the people of all the States have never acted together as one whole. Even in the election of President, the people vote by separate States, not for a President, but for *State electors.* A majority of the people of the whole country do not appoint electors, but a majority of each separate State. If the electors fail to elect a President, then the States as States in Congress assembled appoint the President; Rhode Island having one vote and New York no more. And if the House of Representatives fail of making a choice, the Senate, appointed by the several States, shall elect a Vice-President, who shall act as President of the States.

The Southern States became dissatisfied with. Mr. ADAMS and his measures, and a portion of them looked to the doctrines of State rights for relief.

To JOHN TAYLOR of Virginia, Mr. JEFFERSON addressed a letter, June, 1798. In it he says: "It is true that we are completely under the saddle of Massachusetts and Connecticut, and they ride us very hard, cruelly insulting our feelings, as well as exhausting our strength and subsistence. Their natural friends, the three other Eastern States, join them from a sort of family pride, and they have the art to divide certain other parts of the Union, so as to make use of them to govern the whole."

"If we rid ourselves of the present rulers of Massachusetts and Connecticut, we break the Union; will the work stop there? Suppose the New England States alone cut off, will our nature be changed? Are there not men to the South with all the passions of men? Immediately we shall see a Pennsylvania and Virginia party arise in the residuary Confederacy, and the public mind will be distracted with the same party spirit."

In another place he says : " Mr. NEW showed me your letter on the subject of the protest, which gives me an opportunity of observing what you said as to the effect with you of public proceedings, and that it is not unwise now to estimate the separate map of Virginia and North Carolina, with a view to their separate existence." " Seeing we must have somebody to quarrel with, I had rather keep our New England associates for that purpose, than to see our bickerings transferred to others. They are circumstanced within such narrow limits, and their population so full, that their numbers will soon be in the minority ; and they are marked, like the Jews, with such perversity of character, as to constitute, from that circumstance, the natural division of our parties."

" During the Administration of Mr. ADAMS, Virginia was almost in open revolt against the national authority, merely because a Yankee, and not a Virginian, was President."—*Life of G. Morris*, vol. iii., p. 196.

JOHN ADAMS, when President, wrote as follows: "I have found this Congress like the last. When we first came together, I found a strong jealousy of us of New England, and of Massachusetts in particular."—*Life and Times of John Adams*, vol. i., p. 176.

" You inquire why so young a man as Mr. JEFFERSON was placed at the head of the committee for preparing the Declaration of Independence ; I answer, it was the Frankfort advice to place Virginia at the head of every thing."—*Life and Times of John Adams*, vol. ii., p. 513.

REMARKS.

1. The sectional feeling, which existed during General WASHINGTON's Administration, became intensified, especially in the South, during the Administration of Mr. ADAMS ; he being a Northern man, and sustained chiefly by Northern men, and by several of the Northern States. In the view of the party opposed to him, his policy savored too much of monarchy, and tended to exalt and extend the powers of the General Government towards a conformity to the English government, to the disparagement of the reserved rights of the

States. The Virginia and Kentucky Resolutions were professedly brought forward in order to restrain that policy, and to preserve to the States their Constitutional relations to the Federal Government. But sectional or party feeling had much to do in this matter.

It is somewhat remarkable, that Virginia was, in the Constitutional Convention, opposed to reserving large powers to the several States, on some important points, and yet was the first to place herself on her reserved powers, and, as some would say, to magnify those powers. Thus Virginia voted in favor of giving the Federal Legislature power to negative State laws contravening the articles of union, and voted against giving equal rights to the States in the Senate. PATRICK HENRY, in the Virginia Convention, tauntingly said : " Why are such extensive powers given to the Senate? Because the little States gained their point." The " little States " did, indeed, gain their point as against the large States, but they also gained their point for each of the large States as against the popular vote of the whole Union. In practice, Virginia has enjoyed this advantage.

2. Some of the Northern States, while they had a prevailing influence during the presidency of General WASHINGTON and of Mr. ADAMS, were accused of endeavoring to enlarge the powers of the General Government; and yet those same States, when that influence was impaired during the Administration of Mr. JEFFERSON and of Mr. MADISON, placed themselves on the reserved rights of the States, in their opposition to the General Government. This subject will be resumed in statements concerning Mr. MADISON's Administration.

3. The States were the only parties to the " Constitutional Compact." This phrase, equivalent to the word Constitution, and descriptive of it, is used in the Report of the Hartford Convention, and by eminent statesmen.

4. The Constitution contains only *delegated* powers. " The State Governments may be regarded as *constituent* and essential parties of the Federal Government, while the latter is in no wise essential to the operation of the former."—MADISON, No. 45 of *The Federalist*. The " constituent," by the force or meaning of the term, is superior to the delegate.

CHAPTER V.

Mr. JEFFERSON was friendly to France, rather than to England; was in favor of a strict construction of the Constitution, by which the rights of the several States, and of the people of those States, would be protected against any usurpations of the General Government. He received 73 electoral votes for the presidency, nearly all the Southern States voting for him. Mr. BURR received the same number of votes.

Mr. ADAMS received 65 votes; his strength lying chiefly in the Northern States.

Mr. JEFFERSON and Mr. BURR received an equal number of votes; it remained for the House of Representatives, voting by States, to determine the choice.

A portion of the federal party, which had cast its electoral vote for JOHN ADAMS and CHARLES C. PINCKNEY, had resolved that States represented by that party should throw their votes for AARON BURR, himself a democrat, instead of JEFFERSON, whom the democrats wished to elect President. On the 17th February, 1801, after balloting in the House 36 times, THOMAS JEFFERSON was elected President, *Connecticut, Massachusetts, New Hampshire*, and *Rhode Island* voting to the last for AARON BURR.

· *Commercial Advertiser*, New York, Feb. 23, 1801.—" Our communications from the City of Washington are as late as Thursday, half-past 3 o'clock, A. M. At that time the balloting had been postponed, an hour at a time; when the hour expires and the members are called to proceed again, it is ludicrous to see some of them rushing with anxiety from the committee rooms, with their night caps on. Numbers of them are provided with pillows and blankets; and the contest would seem to be who has the most strength of constitution, or who is most able to bear fatigue. Many of them lie down in their places, resolving (at least to sleep, if not) to die at their posts."

SPIRIT OF THE TIMES.

Washington Federalist, February 12, 1801.

" Unworthy will he be, and consecrated his name to infamy, who, with a view to the permanency of our political system, has hitherto strenuously opposed the exaltation of Mr. JEFFERSON to the Presidential chair, shall now, meanly and inconsistently, lend his aid to promote it. Such conduct will be dishonorable in the extreme. Such conduct, therefore, cannot possibly characterize the Federal party. * * *

" But, say the bold and impetuous partisans of Mr. JEFFERSON, and that, too, in the teeth of the assembled Congress of America, *Dare* to designate any officer whatever, even temporarily to administer the government, in the want of the non-agreement, on the part of the House of Representatives, and we will march and dethrone him as a *usurper*. Dare, in fact, to exercise the right of opinion, and place in the Presidential chair any other than the sage of Monticello, and ten thousand Republican swords will leap from their scabbards in defence of the violated rights of the *people*. * * *

" Are they, then, ripe for civil war, and ready to embrue their hands in kindred blood?

" If the tumultuous meetings of a set of factions foreigners in Pennsylvania, and a few fighting bacchanals in Virginia, mean the people, and are to dictate to the Congress of the United States whom to elect as President; if the constitutional rights of this body are so soon to become the prey of anarchy and faction; if we are already arrived at that disastrous period in the life of nations, when ' liberty consists in no longer reverencing either the laws or the authority; ' if, in short, the scenes that sadden the history of the elective monarchies of Europe are so soon to be reacted in America, it would be prudent at once to prepare for the contest: the woful experiment, if tried at all, could never be tried at a more favorable conjuncture.

"With the militia of Massachusetts, consisting of seventy thousand, (regulars let us call them,) in arms; with those of New Hampshire, united almost to a man; with half the number of the citizens of the other States, ranged under the Federal banner in support of the Constitution, what could Pennsylvania do, aided by Virginia? the militia of the latter, untrained and farcically performing the manual exercise with *cornstalks* instead of muskets, burdened besides with a formidable internal foe, whose disposition has been shown in not very agreeable colors, a foe, too, in contest against whom, Mr. JEFFERSON declares, the Almighty has no attribute which could induce him to take a part; what, may it be asked, would be the issue of the struggle? Let these madmen reflect on these things. Let them forbear their menaces. Let them respect the decision of the constituted authorities."

In the *Connecticut Courant*, Hartford, September 22, 1800, a writer, signing himself BURLEIGH, after speaking of the evils of slavery, uses the following language:

"To avoid sharing in these calamities, and, perhaps, with the hope of saving the Government, the Northern States will probably be disposed to separate the Union. This, though an evil of mighty magnitude, is less, far less, than anarchy or slavery. Should such an event take place, where the border States will be is not for me to say. Perhaps the Potomac, the Delaware, or the Hudson, like the Rhine, may part rival hostile nations, and the shores of one of them be perpetually crimsoned with the blood of the inhabitants."

Boston Gazette, December 24, 1801: "IT WAS A GOOD THING, in the District Court of Connecticut, to let Mr. JEFFERSON know, that when he attempted to restore *by his order* to his good friends the French, the prize-money of a French schooner, which was captured and legally condemned as a lawful prize in the court, that he was feeling power and forgetting right. Mr. JEFFERSON has so long been accustomed to govern *slaves*, that he hardly knows how to act in the government of freemen.

But, however implicitly his commands in a *land of slavery* may have been obeyed, he must be careful how he *orders* without authority in New England, as he will surely get himself affronted."

From the *Boston Gazette*, December 28, 1801, and credited to the *American Minerva*: " New England people turned aristocrats ! say the Southern gentlemen. This is very odd. Let us examine the fact, and compare New England aristocracy with Southern democracy. An Eastern aristocrat is a New England farmer. Nine out of ten of all these people are men of small landed estates, consisting of from fifty to two hundred acres of land, and worth one thousand to three thousand dollars. There is not *one* in twenty of them that ever owned a slave : and those who have them are getting rid of them as fast as they can, without injury to the slaves. The farmer himself, his wife, his sons and daughters, all labor in person on the farm or at the spinning-wheel. A farmer in New England who does *not* labor in person, is no more to be found than a planter in Virginia or Carolina who *does*. If they have occasion to hire laboring men, they associate with them and eat at the same table. In the whole village there is little or no distinction of rank ; the farmers and mechanics, the justice of the peace, and the blacksmith, all associate on equal terms. There is no such thing as a farmer's *commanding* his workmen ; he treats them all as his equals. These people are generally very civil and obliging : they make bows to each other, and teach their children to do the same. This is New England aristocracy.

" Virginia *democracy* is a very different thing. A democrat, in the Southern States, is a planter or other person who owns a large number of slaves—who is above labor himself, and not only so, but is above the drudgery of overseeing his own business. He commits it to a steward and a negro driver. He establishes all the ranks of the feudal system in his own family. The planter is king or lord paramount ; his children are nobles : the tutor, the steward, and clerk, are the commons ; and the laboring people and the blacks are the vassals. Yet this planter is a mighty *democrat*, a warm stickler for the *rights* of man, for liberty, and, what is more, *equality*. This little domestic monarch writes and spouts incessantly about the *funding system*.

and the *danger of power*. He will not labor—not he; this is the business of slaves. He will not associate with the laboring people; he will not eat at the same table. His sons must not labor; this would disgrace them. They are seen at a tavern from morning to night, sawing a fiddle or playing at billiards.

" A New England *Aristocrat*, on Sunday, puts saddle and pillion on a team horse, takes his wife behind him and his child on a pillow before him, and rides to church; and when he gets home, he reads a sermon, or a chapter in the Bible, and teaches his children some catechism.

" The Southern *Democrat*, on Sunday, gets into his coach, if he has it, or can borrow one, and, accompanied by two or three dirty, ragged, half-naked slaves, rides to some friends or to some amusement. It is idle to deny these things; thousands of witnesses can attest them. Let the truth, then, be acknowledged. Let the charge of Aristocracy fall where it ought. The Northern people are the most *Republican* in the universe; equality reigns among them in reality; but they expect law and order, and when they have a government they wish to keep it."

RESTRICTIONS UPON COMMERCE.

In opposition to British encroachments, a memorial was presented to Congress by the Boston merchants, dated January 20, 1806, urging that " such measures should be promptly adopted as will tend to disembarrass our commerce, assert our rights, and support the dignity of the United States." Similar memorials were presented, about the same time, by the merchants of New York and of Philadelphia.

The " Berlin Decree," by Napoleon, was declared November 1, 1806. The " British Orders in Council " were declared November 11, 1807. The "Milan Decree," by Napoleon, was declared December 17, 1807.

To meet these decrees and orders in council, ruinous as they were to American commerce, the embargo was laid on the 23d of December, 1807.

" It was generally believed, at the North, that the embargo was the result of a combination between Southern and Western States, to ruin the Eastern." In a memorial from the town of

Boston to the Legislature of Massachusetts, January 25, 1809. requesting the "interposition" of that body to relieve the citizens from their "grievances," is the following: "Our hope and consolation rest with the Legislature of our State, *to whom it is competent to devise means of relief against the unconstitutional measures of the General Government;* that your power is adequate to this object, is evident *from the organization of the Confederacy.*" Other towns in Massachusetts expressed the same sentiments to the Legislature in more decided terms, pointing to resistance to the Federal Government.

"If petitions do not produce a relaxation or removal of the embargo, the people ought immediately to assume a higher tone. The Government of Massachusetts has also a *duty* to perform. *The State is still sovereign and independent.*"—*Boston Centinel,* September 10, 1808.

In the same spirit Northern statesmen spoke: "To my mind the present crisis excites the most serious apprehensions. *A storm seems to be gathering,* which portends not a tempest on the ocean, but *domestic convulsions.* I feel myself bound in conscience to declare, lest the blood of those who should fall in executing this measure (enforcing the embargo) may lie on my head, that I consider this to be an act which directs a mortal blow at the liberties of my country—an act containing unconstitutional provisions, to which *the people are not bound to submit,* and to which, in my opinion, they will not submit."—*Speech of* Mr. HILLHOUSE, *of Connecticut, in the Senate of the United States,* January, 1809.

The embargo was repealed March 1, 1809.

THE PURCHASE OF LOUISIANA.

To the proposal of Mr. JEFFERSON to purchase Louisiana the Eastern States were strongly opposed, though the great importance of preserving the free navigation of the Mississippi was acknowledged. To prevent the purchase, ridicule, sarcasm without mercy, menace of the separation of the States, as well as argument, were employed by their representatives in Congress, and by the editors of newspapers.

The ground of this violent opposition was the apprehension that the Southern and Western States would, by the admission

5

of Louisiana, acquire an undue influence in the General Government. In the debate upon the admission of Louisiana, Mr. Quincy, of Massachusetts, used the following language in Congress, January 15, 1811 : " If this bill passes, it is my deliberate opinion " (which he committed to writing to prevent misapprehension) " that it is virtually *a dissolution of the Union;* that it will free the States from their moral obligation ; and, as it will be *the right of all,* so it will be the *duty of some* to *prepare* for separation, amicably if they can, VIOLENTLY IF THEY MUST." These were the sentiments of a large number in New England at that time. Most of them lived to adopt more patriotic views, when they saw the relation and value of Louisiana to the whole country. A committee of the Legislature of Massachusetts, 1813, reported the following :

"*Resolved,* that it is the interest and duty of the people of Massachusetts to oppose the admission of such States (Louisiana) into the Union, as a measure tending to dissolve the Confederacy."

REMARKS.

1. By the election of Mr. JEFFERSON, the Eastern States had lost much of their influence in the General Government. They accused him of being unfriendly to the interests of commerce, and of not taking energetic measures for its protection against the encroachments of England and France, and of laying the embargo in disregard of their interests.

2. Several of the Eastern States made a great mistake in voting for AARON BURR in opposition to Mr. JEFFERSON, on sectional grounds, when the election came into the House of Representatives. They had the constitutional right to do so ; but it was not to their honor to endeavor to thwart the wishes of the people of the several States, who had voted for electors who were in favor of Mr. JEFFERSON for President, and of Mr. BURR for Vice-President. They voted for Mr. BURR, who proved to be a bad man, on sectional grounds.

3. The opposition to the purchase of Louisiana was largely sectional, springing as it did from the apprehension that the introduction of new States made from it would still further diminish the influence of the Eastern States. The purchase was, confessedly, unconstitutional.

CHAPTER VI.

MR. MADISON had acted with the North in framing the Constitution ; but he had acted with the South generally in the interpretation of its powers.

The foreign policy adopted by Mr. JEFFERSON in the administration of the Government, was continued by MADISON, injurious though it was to the interests of the commercial States. The commerce of the country was crushed between the upper and the nether millstones of the British orders in council, and the Berlin and Milan decrees. By the one, American ships were excluded from Great Britain ; and by the other, from France, to the ruin of our commerce. Mr. MADISON, like Mr. JEFFERSON, was accused of favoring France rather than England, and thus of increasing the evil, first by a commercial contest with the latter nation, by a non-intercourse act, and by an embargo of ninety days, in the way of reprisal, and then by the declaration of war.

To these measures the Northern States, and especially New England, were violently opposed. And their opposition was manifested in newspapers, speeches, and conventions, in bitter and determined language. During the embargo, their ships were rotting at the wharves or on the stocks. Their seamen were idle, and restless, and unhappy. Grass grew in the streets of cities which had been marts of commerce. Bankruptcy was felt or feared. Their harbors were no longer whitened by the sails of successful commercial adventure. Thousands could say, " My occupation is gone."

The Southern States, on the other hand, generally sustained these anti-commercial measures, and thus provoked the resentment of the North, and the fiercest denunciations. As a specimen of the feelings that prevailed, read the following, originally published in the *Connecticut Journal*, 1812, from an article entitled, "*Slave Representation*," by BOREAS:

"'Awake! O spirit of the North.'

" The article authorizing the Southern negroes to be represented in Congress is *the rotten part of the Constitution, and must be amputated*. Since the commencement of the Government, its whole undivided influence has been only putrefactive and deadly, although before the fatal change of men and measures on the fourth of March, 1801, its effects were not perceptibly felt on the sounder members of the body politic. That change was wholly effected by slave representation. The slave *electoral votes* first brought Mr. JEFFERSON into the Presidency ; and the *slave votes in Congress* have turned the majority in favor of many of the worst measures which the Virginia faction have dared to bring forward. * * *

" If this stain upon the face of the Constitution, this impress of mischief and dishonor, is ever to be blotted out, it must be done at a time when the NORTH, roused by repeated injuries, and provoked by galling oppression, shall appeal directly to *her own strength*, and to the *fears* and *weakness* of the COUNTRY OF SLAVES.

" At a time when these injuries are deeply felt, and these oppressions are boldly resisted, would we call upon all the men of the *North* to unite as one man, and that a strong man, *armed* to take a solemn view of the magnitude and injustice of the grievance, and then at *every hazard* to apply the needed remedy. * * *

" On this subject, all the North have a common interest. To the MEN OF THE NORTH we would boldly and directly make the solemn appeal : Will you suffer the *slave country* to triumph any longer in this palpable fraud ? Will you still look coolly on and witness this foul blot on the page of the Constitution, this deep stigma on the national honor? If you will, go, and for *twelve long, weary years* see the commerce of the nation bound, her agriculture blasted, her coffers lavished, and her glory trampled in the dust, by the very man whom Southern slaves have lifted into office."

SECTIONAL OPPOSITION TO THE WAR OF 1812.

The Northern States, having adopted the Federal Constitution mainly for promoting their *commercial interests*, were very indignant at the passage of the embargo act of 1807, on recommendation of Mr. JEFFERSON ; and threats were uttered, first in undertones and then loudly, that they would secede—at least a portion of them—from the Union, and form a new confederacy. On the first of March, 1809, just before the accession of Mr. MADISON, the embargo act was repealed, " to appease the New England States."

War was declared against Great Britain, in due form, on the 18th of June, 1812, by a vote of 72 to 49 in the House of Representatives, and 19 to 13 in the Senate. To this war there was a strong opposition manifested in the Eastern States, in the pulpit, the press, in public speeches, and private conversation. Ministers of the Gospel called it an " unholy war," an " unrighteous war." At the time when our armies were invading Canada, some of them prayed " that all invading armies might be cut off," and " that they who take the sword might perish by the sword." The Rev. Mr. GARDINER, in a sermon preached July 23, 1812, in Boston, uses the following language : " The Union has long since been dissolved, and it is full time that this part of the United States should take care of itself." Rev. Dr. PARISH, in Byfield, Mass., delivered a sermon April 7, 1814, in which he uses the following language : " The Israelites became weary of yielding the fruit of their labor to pamper tyrants. They left their political woes. They separated. *Where is our Moses ?* Where is the rod of his miracles ? Where is our Aaron ? Alas ! no voice from the burning bush has directed him here." These are only specimens.

The press teemed with similar sentiments. " My plan is to withhold our money, and make a separate peace with England."—

Boston Advertiser. "That there will be a revolution, if the war continues, no one can doubt who is acquainted with human nature, and is accustomed to study cause and effect. The Eastern States are marching steadily and straightforward up to the object."—*Federal Republican.* These are specimens.

"We call upon our State Legislature to protect us in the enjoyment of those privileges, to assert which our fathers died, and to defend which we profess ourselves *ready to resist unto blood.*"—*Memorial of the citizens of Newburyport, Mass., January 13, 1814.* "Resolved, that we place the fullest confidence in the Governor and Legislature of Massachusetts, and in the State authorities of New England; and that to them, under God, the chief Governor of the universe, we look for aid and direction; and that, for the present, until public opinion shall be known, we will not enter our carriages, *pay our Continental taxes,* or aid, inform, or assist any officer in their collection."—*Passed by the inhabitants of Reading, Mass., January 5, 1815.* "*A separation of the States* will be an inevitable result. Motives, numerous and urgent, will demand that measure. As they originate in oppression, the oppressors must be responsible for the momentous and contingent events arising from the *dissolution* of the present Confederacy, and erection of *separate governments.* It will be their work."—*Northern Grievances, p. 4, May, 1814.* These are specimens.

"Yes, sir, I consider this Administration as alien to us, so much so, that New England would be justified in declaring them like all foreign nations, enemies in war, in peace friends." "The States of New England can never be satellites in any system; but, like the primary planets, they will revolve round the sun of Federalism, until the Almighty hand, which created them, shall dash them from their orbits forever."—CYRUS KING, of Massachusetts, in Congress, October 22, 1814.

"On or before the fourth of July next, if JAMES MADISON is not out of office, a new form of government will be in operation in the *Eastern section of the Union.* Instantly after, the contest in many of the States will be, whether to adhere to the old, or to join the new Government."—*Federal Republican, November 7, 1814.*

THE HARTFORD CONVENTION.

"Early in the year 1814, memorials from a great many towns in Massachusetts, were forwarded to the Legislature of that State, praying that body to exert their authority to protect the citizens in their Constitutional rights and privileges, and suggesting the expediency of appointing delegates to meet delegates from such other States as may choose to appoint them, for the purpose of devising proper measures to procure the united efforts of the commercial States to obtain such amendments and explanations of the Constitution as will secure them from further evils."

Accordingly, on the 16th of October, 1814, by a large majority of the Legislature—260 yeas, 90 nays—twelve men were appointed as delegates from Massachusetts to meet in convention other delegates from the other New England States.

The Convention met in Hartford on the 15th of December, 1814. There were twelve members from Massachusetts; seven from Connecticut; four from Rhode Island; three from New Hampshire; one from Vermont. They were gentlemen of the highest character for intelligence, wisdom, and patriotism. After a session of three weeks, they made a report of the result of their conference.

In order to remove the evils under which they were suffering, and prevent their recurrence, the Convention proposed certain amendments to the Federal Constitution; by which the slave States would be deprived of the slave representation, as at present provided; and by which, new States would be prevented from coming into the Union, except by a vote of two-thirds of both Houses; and by which, Congress would be deprived of power to lay an embargo for more than sixty days; and by which, Congress shall not have power, without the concurrence of two-thirds of both Houses, to interdict the commercial intercourse between the United States and any foreign nation; and by which, Congress shall not have power to make or declare war against a foreign nation, without the concurrence of two-thirds of both Houses; and by which, persons naturalized hereafter shall not be eligible to certain offices; and by which, no person shall be a second time elected President.

It was also resolved by the Convention, that in the event of the continuance of the present evils, without a prospect of relief, it will, in the opinion of the Convention, be expedient for the Legislatures of the several States to send delegates to another Convention, to meet in June next. Provision was also made for calling another meeting of the Convention, if it should be desirable, before new delegates shall be chosen.

In that report, drawn up with great ability, they discuss the subject of the *dissolution of the Union*, to which public attention had been earnestly turned, and the formation of a new Confederacy, as the means of escaping the evils under which the commercial States were suffering. Such a dissolution, they say, should "be the work of peaceable times and deliberate consent;" "some new form of Confederacy should be substituted among those States which shall intend to maintain a Federal relation to each other." "Whenever it shall appear that these causes (of our calamities) are radical and permanent, a separation, by mutual arrangement, will be preferable to an alliance, by constraint, among nominal friends but real enemies." They argue, at length, against the claims of the General Government upon the militia of the States, and justify Massachusetts and Connecticut in refusing to place the militia in the regular army and under United States officers. They complain that the "Constitutional Compact," as they term the Constitution, has been extensively violated by the General Government, and that so many abuses have been practised, under color of its authority, that the time for change is believed to be at hand. They declare that "acts of Congress in violation of the Constitution are *absolutely void.*" And, as the Governors of Massachusetts and Connecticut had refused to place the militia of those States in the regular army, and under the officers of the General Government, they propose that a portion of the national tax, raised by the State, should be paid into its treasury, to be used for its defence, for which the General Government had neglected to provide, in the case of those States. They declare that they are "solicitous for the continuance of the Union as well as the sovereignty of the States."

The first amendment proposed, namely, to take from the South the representation of slaves, was designed to lessen the political power of the South. The object of the second amendment proposed was substantially the same ; or, in the language of HARRISON GRAY OTIS, " the object of the amendment was to diminish what the decision of the Missouri question is calculated to increase—the representation of slaves." This referred to the admission of Louisiana.

The Legislatures of Massachusetts and Connecticut, on receiving the report of the Hartford Convention, sent commissioners to Washington ; the former, HARRISON GRAY OTIS, THOMAS H. PERKINS, and WILLIAM SULLIVAN; the latter, NATHANIEL TERRY and CALVIN GODDARD.

CONTEMPORANEOUS VIEWS OF NORTHERN MEN.

JOHN LOWELL.

In an ably-reasoned pamphlet, written by JOHN LOWELL, of Massachusetts, and published in 1812, the writer asked : " Is there no Constitutional right in the executive, judiciary, and people of the several States, to judge whether the militia are, or are not, Constitutionally called into service ? In whom, from the very nature of the limitation in the Constitution, reposes the ultimate right to judge whether either of the three cases, (to execute the laws of the Union ; suppress insurrections ; and repel invasion.) provided by the Constitution, does exist ?

" We answer, generally in the constituent, not in the delegate ; in the master, not in the servant ; *ultimately* in the people, (of the several States ;) *principally* from the necessity of the case in the commanders-in-chief of the several States. The very idea of limitation excludes the possibility that the delegate should be the judge. If he were, his powers would be limited only by his own judgment, or, in other words, by his own arbitrary will, which is no limitation at all." The General Government is regarded here as the *delegate*, and the people of the several States as the *constituent*, acting by their constituted authorities as Governors, Judges, or Legislatures. We have the distinct declaration of the doctrine of State rights, from one of the ablest and best men of the times. If carried to its logical results it comes fully up to the Virginia resolutions of 1798, fully up to the teachings of JEFFERSON and MADISON.

GOUVERNEUR MORRIS was the very man in the Constitutional Convention who revised the language of the Constitution before its final adoption by that body, and must therefore have understood what was its meaning and its bearings and the nature of the compact, and who were the parties to it. He declared that it was a compact between the States, and not a compact between individuals scattered over the whole Union. These are his words : " That the Constitution was a compact, not between solitary individuals, but between political societies, the people, not of America, but of the United States—each (State) enjoying sovereign power, and of course equal rights." Thus it differs from a State Constitution, which is a compact, so far as it can be called a compact, between individuals. It is a *compact between sovereignties.*

"New England will, I trust, continue true to herself. The appropriate course, pertinaciously pursued, must open the eyes even of the wilfully blind. You will unite with Massachusetts, and New York must connect herself, whether she will or no, with New England. The question of boundary to be solved, therefore, is the Delaware, Susquehanna, or Potomac."—*Letter of Gouverneur Morris to Lewis Sturgis, Connecticut, Nov. 1, 1814.*

"I supposed, also, that to such as would charge you with meditating a breach of the Union, you would calmly reply : 'The Union is already broken by this Administration. Should we now rely upon it, we should forfeit all claim to common sense.'"—*Idem, to Harrison Gray Otis, Nov. 8, 1814.*

Having in the first extract stated what is the nature of the Constitutional Compact, and who are the parties to it, namely, the States, he then, in the next two, shows in what way the meditated separation of the States can be justified, and where might be the line of separation.

JOHN ADAMS, in a letter to THOMAS JEFFERSON, July, 1813, says: "The Northern States are now retaliating upon the

Southern States, their conduct from 1797 to 1800." He al-
ludes to the opposition to his own administration by the Southern States, especially by Virginia and Kentucky.

DE WITT CLINTON.

" The opposition, now excited, is not an ordinary opposition.
It does not merely aim a blow at a rival party. Nor is it confined to the destruction of an individual. It takes a more
daring and adventurous attitude. It bids defiance to our laws,
and threatens the dissolution of the Union. It is, perhaps,
known to but few, that the project of the dismemberment of
this country is not a novel plan growing out of recent measures
of the Government, as has been pretended. It has been cherished by a number of individuals for a series of years ; and a
few months before the death of a *distinguished citizen*, whose
death so strongly excited the public sensibility, it was proposed
to him to enlist his great talents in the formation of this nefarious
scheme ; and, to his honor be it spoken, it was repelled by him
with disdain. Some of the newspapers of New England have,
at various times, inculcated the treasonable doctrines in elaborate essays, and the match appears to be now lighted, to produce an explosion, which will overwhelm us with all the evils
of civil war.

" Look at the storm that is gathering in the east ; its clouds are
black, heavy, and portentous. Look at the resolves of several
of the towns, and even of the capital of Massachusetts. Observe
the disorganizing, jacobinical, seditious, and traitorous spirit
which pervades them. The Legislatures of the several States
are incited to array themselves against the General Government. The very men who a few years since were the strenuous
advocates for putting down the State Governments, for a strong
National Government, that would maintain the union of the
States ; for an energetic, absorbing National Government, that
would control and regulate the centrifugal force of the local
Government, these men are now warm partisans of a State supremacy, the devoted friends of the State Legislatures."—*Speech
of De Witt Clinton, in Senate of New York*.

John Quincy Adams fully sustains the declarations of Mr.
Clinton, and refers to the " distinguished citizen," who, it was

hoped, would lead the armies of the North, in a possible contest with the Federal Government, and who was no other than
ALEXANDER HAMILTON.

The sentiments of disunion were in existence at the North
at an early period, certainly as early as 1796, not long after the
ratification of JAY's treaty was opposed by Mr. MADISON, Mr.
GILES, and other leading men of the South, and just before the
election of Mr. ADAMS, who was destined to meet with opposition to his election from the Southern States, and then with
embarrassments during his administration, and finally with defeat when candidate a second time.

The following is an extract from a very able series of papers,
signed PELHAM, and published in the *Connecticut Courant*, in
Hartford, 1796 :

"I shall, in the future papers, consider some of the great
events which *will lead to a separation of the United States ;*
show the importance of retaining their present Constitution,
even at the expense of a separation ; endeavor to prove the responsibility of a Union for a long period in future, both from the
moral and political habits of the citizens of the Northern States ;
and finally, examine carefully to see whether *we have not already approached to the era when they must be divided.*"

These sentiments gathered strength during Mr. JEFFERSON's
administration, from the purchase of Louisiana and the restrictions upon commerce, until, in 1809, they became so well known,
that an agent, JOHN HENRY, was sent by the Governor-general
of Canada, Sir JAMES CRAIG, into New England, in reference to
a co-operation with England, and a union with Canada. These
sentiments still gathered strength during Mr. MADISON's administration, until they culminated in the appointment of the Hartford Convention, and brought the Eastern States to the very
verge of disunion. For this the General Government was held
responsible. " If, by your violence and oppression, you drive
off New England from the Confederacy, you must answer for
it. And you have already driven them to the very brink.
One step more, and the union of these States is severed."—*Federal Republican.*

This was a matter of general notoriety throughout the country. The following is an extract from a letter addressed to

ELBRIDGE GERRY, of Massachusetts, dated June 11, 1812, from Mr. JEFFERSON:

"What then does this English faction with you mean? Their newspapers say, rebellion, and that they will not continue united with us, unless we will permit them to govern the majority. * * They count on British aid. But what can that avail them by land? They would separate from their friends, who alone furnish employment for their navigation, to unite with their only rival, for that employment. * * But I trust that such perverseness will not be that of the honest and well-meaning mass of the Federalists of Massachusetts; and that when the question of separation and rebellion shall be nakedly proposed to them, the GORES and the PICKERINGS will find their levees crowded with silk stocking gentry, but no yeomanry; an army of officers, but no soldiers."

REMARKS.

1. When the North was the dominant section in the General Government, Southern statesmen placed themselves on the reserved rights of the States, to resist the encroachments of federal power, under the first two Presidents; as in the case of the assumption of State debts, and of the charter of the United States Bank; and of the alien and sedition laws.

When the South became the dominant section in the General Government, the Northern States placed themselves on the same reserved rights of the States, to resist the encroachments of federal power, under Presidents JEFFERSON and MADISON; as in the case of the purchase of Louisiana, and of the restrictions upon commerce; and of the requisition to place the militia of the States under federal officers.

In each case the dominant party was opposed to the doctrines of State rights. The North was opposed to the Virginia and the Kentucky resolutions. The South was opposed to the doctrines of the Hartford Convention.

2. The doctrine of State rights was asserted in 1798 by Virginia, and in 1814 by Massachusetts, in a manner corresponding with the character of the people of the two States. In a letter, dated Dec. 18, 1814, addressed to JAMES LLOYD, of Massachu-

setts, JOHN RANDOLPH writes : " A Virginia and a New England Republican are about as much alike as an English whig and a French democrat." And yet the doctrines of State rights, as enunciated by Northern statesmen and by Southern statesmen, are substantially the same. The Northern view and the Southern in these cases were nearly the same.

a. That the Constitution is federal, namely, a compact between the States, and was made by the States, namely by the people of each State, acting for the State, and not by solitary individuals, each acting for himself.—*See Gouverneur Morris's Declaration, Dr. S. Johnson's Remarks, &c.*

b. That the Constitution was formed for the States, and for individuals only as a citizen of a State.

c. That all powers not distinctly given to the General Government, are reserved to the States; and that it is just as important that the reserved powers should remain unimpaired, as that the granted powers should be unimpaired.

d. That each State, as a party to the compact, must judge as to the powers granted, and of any violation of the compact.

e. That if a dispute should arise between a State and its co-States, in respect to what powers are granted and what powers are reserved, an amendment to the compact by a Convention of the States, or otherwise, must settle the doubtful point.

f. That if the compact be broken by the States " on one side. it is broken on all sides."

3. Violent resistance was, during the War of 1812, threatened against some of the requisitions of the Federal Government. Governor TRUMBULL of Connecticut, took the ground, that on great emergencies, when the National Legislature had been led to overstep its Constitutional powers, it became the right and the duty of the State Legislatures " to interpose their protecting shield between the rights and the liberties of the people. and the assumed power of the General Government." Governor CHITTENDEN, of Vermont, had issued his proclamation, recalling the Vermont militia. And when a member of Congress proposed to instruct the Attorney-general to prosecute Governor CHITTENDEN, " Mr. OTIS laid on the table of the Massachusetts senate a resolve expressive of the duty and readiness of Massachusetts, to aid with her whole power the Governor of Ver-

mont, and the people of any other State, in support of Constitutional rights, by whomsoever infringed." By a legislative act, the authorities of the United States were forbid "to use the gaols in Massachusetts for the confinement of prisoners committed by any other than judicial authority; and the gaolers were directed, at the end of thirty days, to discharge all British officers, prisoners of war, committed to them for close confinement."

A Bill for the enlistment of minors having passed Congress. the Legislatures of Connecticut and Massachusetts "proceeded to pass an act requiring the State judges to discharge, on habeas corpus, all minors enlisted without the consent of their parents or guardians, and subjecting to fine and imprisonment any persons concerned in any such enlistment, who should remove any minor out of the State, so that he could not be then discharged."

4. Mr. Madison was greatly disturbed and annoyed by the meeting of the Hartford Convention, and by the necessity of meeting the commissioners appointed by Massachusetts and Connecticut. But the tidings of peace came, just as they arrived in Washington, and relieved him from the necessity of receiving them in the character of commissioners, and of entering into negotiations with them on the subject of their mission; but placed them in a very awkward position.

On the arrival of the intelligence that a treaty of peace had been signed, the people of Washington hastened to the President's levee, in the fulness of their joy. One, who was present. told me, that the hilarity exceeded all common bounds; that. not satisfied with congratulating one another once, they would. many of them, repeat the congratulations. Mr. Madison acted as if a great load had been removed from his mind. Mrs. Madison was more of a queen than ever.

When the mirth was at the highest, the commissioners were announced. Immediately, from the shock, there was a universal stillness, like that in a church. They were received by Mr. and Mrs. Madison with all due courtesy; but it was some minutes before the assembly relapsed into its former hilarity. and before the commissioners were restored to their natural dignity and self-possession.

5. What course would have been taken in New England, if

peace had not been declared, it is impossible to say. How far the General Government might have been disposed to comply with the proposals or demands of the Hartford Convention, it is impossible to say. But this much can be said, that the men who were concerned in this sectional movement, in the State Legislatures and the Convention, were men of the highest character for intelligence, virtue, and patriotism; as also were those concerned in the Virginia and Kentucky resolutions in 1798--'9. In each case they knew their rights, and knowing, they dared to maintain them.

6. The reserved rights of the States need to be constantly kept before the minds of those who are called to act in the legislative, the executive, and the judicial departments of the General Government, lest they should lose their influence, and the granted powers become, in practice, too much enlarged. There is a strong centralizing tendency, arising from that love of power which is inherent in human nature, from a desire to carry out certain measures deemed useful, but which the Constitution does not authorize; and especially from the great patronage of the Government, which it can use to induce men to support its usurpation.

7. The relations of the Federal Government to the State Governments are not well understood. The following are the remarks of Mr. JEFFERSON:

"With respect to our State and Federal Governments, I do not think that their relations are correctly understood by foreigners. They generally suppose the former to be subordinate to the latter. But this is not the case. They are co-ordinate departments of one simple and integral whole. But you may ask, if the two departments should claim each the same subject of power, where is the common umpire to decide between them? In cases of little importance and urgency, the prudence of both parties will keep them aloof from the questionable ground; but if it can neither be avoided, nor *compromised, a Convention of the States must be called to ascribe the doubtful power to that department which they may think best.*"

KOSSUTH, it is said, formed an exception to this general remark respecting foreigners; for he understood at once the nature of the American Confederacy. "It is," said he, "a Republic, composed of republics."

But the relations of the Federal Government to the State Governments are not well understood, even by the native-born citizens. The Virginia and Kentucky resolutions on the one hand, and on the other the doctrines taught in Massachusetts and Connecticut during the war, and, indeed, some years before that era, if carefully studied, will assist a citizen of the States to understand our double Government; and to learn what are the powers granted to the Federal Government, and what are the rights reserved to the States.

8. While New England was meditating the separation of the States in certain contingencies, the general feeling in that section was, that a peaceful separation ought to take place, if at all ; or, in the language of the Hartford Convention, that " a separation by mutual arrangement will be preferable to an alliance by constraint among nominal friends, but real enemies." JOHN QUINCY ADAMS, in a speech delivered in the city of New York, in 1839, just fifty years after the Federal Constitution went into operation, expressed the same sentiments :

" But the indissoluble link of union between the people of the several States in this Confederation is, after all, not in the *right* but in the *heart*. If the day should ever come—may heaven avert it !—when the affections of the people in these States shall be alienated from each other—when the fraternal feeling shall give way to cold indifference, or collisions of interest shall foster into hatred—the bonds of political association will not long hold together parties no longer attracted by the magnetism of conciliated interests and friendly sympathies ; and *far better will it be for the people of the disunited States to part in friendship from each other*, than to be held together by constraint. Then will be the time for reverting to the precedents which occurred at the formation and adoption of the Constitution, to form again a more perfect union by dissolving that which could no longer bind, and to leave the separate parts to be united by the law of political gravitation to the centre."

6

CHAPTER VII.

MARCH 4, 1817—MARCH 4, 1825.

THE period of Mr. MONROE's administration has been styled the " era of good feeling." The war had, with some reverses, been triumphantly sustained. Old sectional feuds had died out. The Federal party having ceased to exist, new political friendships had been formed. Mr. CLAY had brought from abroad an admiration of some of the institutions of Great Britain. Some of the old difficulties with that nation had been settled. The manufactures of the North had, to some extent, been protected by the tariff law of 1816, passed partly by Southern votes. The commercial interests of the North had been favored by the establishment of the United States Bank ; the bill having been signed by a Southern President, who had been opposed to a bank. Business revived. Internal improvements were projected. Hopes of general prosperity were rife in the land. President MONROE made a tour through the Northern and Eastern States, and was everywhere received with demonstrations of cordiality and good will. And yet in his administration, a sectional contest arose of the most bitter and dangerous character, threatening at once the unity and peace of the country.

RESTRICTION OF SLAVERY IN MISSOURI.

February 13, 1819.—The bill, enabling Missouri to form a State Government, was taken up in the House of Representatives; the question being on the following amendment, moved by Mr. TALLMAGE of New York:

"*And provided*, That the further introduction of slavery or involuntary servitude be prohibited, except for the punishment of crimes, whereof the party has been duly convicted; and that all children born within the said State, after the admission thereof into the Union, shall be free at the age of twenty-five years."

Mr. TAYLOR, of New York, in favor of the amendment, after speaking on the importance of the question, said there were two points at issue: 1. Has Congress the constitutional power to prohibit slavery as the condition of admission; 2. If the power exists, is it wise to exercise it?

His arguments were drawn from that article in the Constitution, which declares that "the Congress shall have power to dispose of, and make all needful rules respecting the territory and other property belonging to the United States;" from the fact that slavery is wrong, being contrary to the Declaration of Independence, which asserts "that all men are created equal;" from the fact that slavery is incompatible with republican institutions.

Mr. P. P. BARBOUR, of Virginia, opposed the amendment, on the ground that the Congress has no constitutional power to impose the restriction; that Congress has power to "admit new States into the Union." "The term State has a fixed and determinate meaning. It imports the existence of a political community, free and independent, and entitled to exercise the rights of sovereignty, such as the original States enjoyed. Virginia has slaves; Pennsylvania has no slaves, but she has power to have them; ought not Missouri to have the same power in this respect that Pennsylvania has?" Other gentlemen who engaged in the discussion took similar grounds.

The amendment passed in the Committee of the Whole, 79 to 67.

On the 16th of February, the House proceeded to consider the restriction. After an able discussion, the amendment was passed by a vote of 87 to 76, on the first branch; and by a vote of 82 to 78, on the second branch.

The Senate passed the bill to admit Missouri *without the re-*

striction, March 2d. On the motion to concur with the Senate, the vote was 76 yeas, 78 nays. Thus the bill failed, the Houses having failed to agree.

"This," says Benton, in the "Debates in Congress," "was the end of the bill, and it left the Houses *geographically* divided, and the same division extending itself, with electric speed, to the States. It was a period of deep apprehension, filling with dismay the hearts of the steadiest patriots. It would be nine months before Congress would sit again. The agitation, great as it was, was to become greater, and no one could foresee its bounds. The movement to put the slavery restriction on Arkansas greatly aggravated the Missouri question, and seemed to menace the slave States with total exclusion from Louisiana."

It was during the agitation and suspense of the public mind, that Mr. MADISON wrote a letter to ROBERT WALSH, dated Nov. 27, 1819, just before the meeting of Congress, from which the following is an extract: "Parties, under some denomination or other, must always be expected in a free government like ours. When the individuals belonging to them are intermingled in every part of the whole country, they strengthen the union of the whole, while they divide every part. Should a state of parties arise, founded on geographical boundaries, and other physical and permanent distinctions which happen to coincide with them, what is then to control those great repulsive masses from awful shocks against each other?"

The Southern States deeply felt, that by the action of the House, their constitutional rights had been denied to them, and that language had been used and arguments employed, derogatory to their character. It was in reference to this state of things, and while the country was in a blaze of excitement, that Mr. JEFFERSON wrote, that the notes of alarm fell upon his ear like a "fire bell in the night."

"The Missouri question," he says, "is the most portentous one that ever threatened our Union. In the gloomiest moments of the Revolutionary War, I never had any apprehensions equal to what I feel from this source."

In the early part of the next session in Congress, Jan. 3, 1820, it was proposed in the Senate to couple Missouri with Maine in one bill, the latter having applied to be admitted as a State into the Union. To this there was great opposition on the part of Northern members, and very extensive discussion, in which the evils of slavery formed an important part of the staple of a portion of the speeches. To show the absurdity of coupling them together, Mr. ROBERTS of Pennsylvania said: "What do we find in the front of the Constitution of Maine? Article I. Section 1: 'All men are born free and equal, and are free to worship God in their own way.' Here is a substantial pledge to the good old faith. To her we may say, Come, sister, take your place in this constellation: the lustre of your countenance will brighten the American galaxy. But do not urge us to admit Missouri under a pretence of congeniality—with the visage of a savage, deformed with the hideous cicatrices of barbaric pride, with her features marred as if the finger of Lucifer had been drawn across it."

Mr. PINKNEY, of Maryland, in his speech on the other side, said: "New States may be admitted by Congress into this Union. What is that Union? a confederation of States equal in sovereignty, capable of every thing which the Constitution does not forbid, or authorize Congress to forbid. It is an equal union between parties equally sovereign. * * By acceding to it, the new State is placed on the same footing as the original States. * * If it comes in shorn of its beams, crippled and disparaged beyond the original States—it is not into the original Union that it comes, for it is a different sort of union. The first was union *inter pares;* this is a union between disparates, between giants and a dwarf, between power and feebleness, between full-proportioned sovereignties and a miserable image of power, a thing which that very union has shrunk and shrivelled from its past size, instead of preserving it in its true dimensions."

In the Senate, the vote for uniting the two bills was 23 in favor, and 21 against; Feb. 16, 1820.

At this stage of the business, it became evident, that though the Senate was willing to receive Missouri upon an equal footing with the other States, the House would persist in excluding her, unless she would consent to come into the Union with impaired sovereignty, and unable to determine what some of her internal institutions should be.

What was to be done? What was done?

THE COMPROMISE.

Mr. Thomas, of Illinois, proposed in the Senate to amend the bill, by striking out the restrictive clause, to pass the bill for the admission of Maine, and to prohibit slavery in all of the territory north of 36° 30', that the Northern members might in this way allow Missouri to come into the Union without restriction, upon the same footing as the other States. His proposal was acceded to, and the amendment was passed in the Senate, March 2, 1820, by a vote of 22 in favor, and 15 against it. In the House the amendment passed by a vote of 134 in favor, and 42 against it. Still Missouri did not obtain admittance into the Union.

At the next session of Congress, for the third time Missouri presented herself for admission into the Union. Maine had been admitted, and her representatives were on the floor of Congress. Slavery was prohibited north of 36° 30'. But strange to say, the compromise was not carried out by the Northern members, with some honorable exceptions!

On the question in the House, Shall Missouri be admitted on the compromise of 1820? the vote stood, Feb. 13, 1821, 88 against admission, 67 in favor of admission. From Maine, 5 against, 2 in favor; from New Hampshire 6, all against; from Massachusetts 13, all against; from Rhode Island 1, and in favor; from Connecticut, 6 against, and 1 in favor; from Vermont 6, all against; from New York, 17 against, and 7 in favor; from New Jersey, 1 against, and 3 in favor; from Pennsylvania, 22 against, and 1 in favor; from Ohio 6, all against; from Indiana 1, and against; from Illinois 1, and against.

Thus the North rejected the compromise which had been made March 2, 1820, nearly a year before.

Were the Northern States faithful to the compromise? Candor must admit, as the above votes show, that they were not. They had got their share, and it was the lion's share. Maine had been admitted into the Union. Slavery had been prohibited by a stretch of power, north of 36° 30', upon the compromise by which Missouri was to be admitted, but they still refused to admit her into the Union. One of their number, Mr.

CLARK of New York, who had voted against the compromise, did say: " I consider myself bound by the *pledge*. I cannot for a moment consent, as a member of this House, to observe a *punic faith* even with Missouri." Others did not faithfully keep good faith, but punic faith.

After the Northern members had thus refused to carry out the compromise, Mr. BROWN, of Kentucky, proposed to repeal the act prohibiting slavery north of 36° 30'. But they would not consent; they would keep the consideration, but would not carry out the compromise by which they obtained the consideration.

The Southern States regarded the compromise of 1820 as an agreement between their members and the Northern members, and they looked to the latter, with upbraiding or imploring eyes, to carry it out by the admission of Missouri. Yet still the latter refused. Proofs on both points are abundant.

Hear Mr. CHARLES PINCKNEY's testimony. He was, it will be recollected, a leading member of the Convention that formed the Constitution, and was at the present time a member of Congress from South Carolina who voted for the compromise. " I feel authorized to express this fear (of the dissolution of the Union) by the fact, that gentlemen in opposition now throw off the veil, and expressly declare that it is their intention to leave, if possible, this question to the next Congress, to leave to them, if possible, unfettered by any act of ours, the power to decide how far the true interests of the Union may then make it necessary to produce anew, and struggle for the imposition of the restriction on slavery, which has, during the three last sessions, shaken the Union to the very foundations. They openly avow that they do not consider themselves bound by the *compact of the last year*, confining the restriction to the north of 36° 30', but *aver if they have the strength to do so, their intention to leave the next Congress free to decide it as they please.*"

Months had passed away, between the time when the compromise bill had been passed and the succeeding session, and yet at this session the North still refused to admit Missouri !

What was the real motive for this apparently treacherous conduct on the part of the North? *It was the desire to retain political power.* This was the temptation to the political sin of still refusing to admit Missouri upon the same footing as the original States.

What was the pretext for this delay and this shirking the responsibility? It was that Missouri had, in her constitution, made provision to exclude free negroes and mulattoes from the State. It was but a pretext, because other States have been admitted without resistance or objection, in whose constitutions there were similar provisions; and Massachusetts had placed similar provisions on her statute book as early as 1788, just after the ratification of the Constitution.

Missouri was finally admitted February 28, 1821. Petitions for the admission of Missouri were presented March 16, 1818. A bill was introduced into the House to enable Missouri to form a State government, February 13, 1819. The restriction was moved February 17, 1819. It thus took more than three years from the first-mentioned date, and more than two years from the second date, to procure the admission of Missouri. She was finally admitted upon a vote of 86 in favor and 82 against. Of the Northern States, New Hampshire cast no vote in favor; Massachusetts, two votes; Connecticut, one vote; Vermont, no vote in favor; New York, seven; New Jersey, two; Pennsylvania, four votes. Not a single Northern State gave its vote in favor of the admission of Missouri. Of the Northern votes cast in favor of the admission of Missouri upon the final vote, some were due to the sense of constitutional right which Missouri had to admission upon the original footing of other States, expressed in the early part of the debates; others were due to the compromise, to which they remained faithful; others still were due to political considerations of a patriotic or party character.

"For a while," says Benton, in his "Thirty Years' View," "this formidable Missouri question threatened the total overthrow of all political parties or principles, and the substitution of geographical parties, discriminated by a slave line, and of course destroying the first and proper action of the Federal Government, and leading eventually to a separation of the States. It was a Federal movement, accruing to the benefit of that party, and at first was overwhelming, sweeping all the Northern Democracy into its current, and giving the supremacy to its adversaries. When this effect was perceived, the Northern Democracy became alarmed, and only wanted a turn in the popular feeling at home, to take the first opportunity to get rid of the question by admitting the State, and reëstablishing party lines upon the basis of political principles. This was the decided feeling when I arrived at Washington, and many of the old Northern Democracy took early opportunity to declare themselves to me to that effect, and showed that they were ready to vote for the admission of the State in any form that would answer the purpose, and save themselves from going so far as to lose their own State, and give the ascendant to their political adversaries."

But patriotic considerations also operated upon another class of minds to induce them to vote for the admission of Missouri. The whole country was agitated and threatened with disunion. By voting to admit, the agitation would cease, and the danger of disunion be removed.

Members of Congress from Northern States, who voted for the admission of Missouri, were influenced : 1, by a regard for the constitutional right of Missouri to come into the Union upon the same footing as the original States ; or 2, by a regard for the Democratic party ; or 3, by a regard for the peace and union of the country ; or 4, by a regard to the compromise. There was at least one, Mr. CLARK, of New York, who was influenced by the last consideration, though he did not vote for the compromise. How many are to be classed with him it is difficult to say.

It is remarkable that every man belonging to New England, in the Lower House, who voted to admit Missouri, was ostracized from the confidence of the public, by the intolerant or unforgiving spirit which prevailed. It was said of Mr. SHAW, one of them, that he was killed by the negroes, and that Mr. DWIGHT, of the same State, was killed by the Indians, (in the Georgia case.)

I have seen no proof that New England was ever reconciled to the admission of Missour'

REMARKS.

1. Mr. MONROE was the last of the Virginia dynasty. When he went out of office in 1825, the Government under the Con-

stitution had been in operation thirty-six years, during which period a Virginian had been at the head of the Government thirty-two years. WASHINGTON, JEFFERSON, MADISON, and MONROE, were each worthy of the place. But there grew up, naturally, in the breasts of Northern men, a bitter jealousy of the South, and especially of Virginia, whose sons had for so long a time occupied the Presidential chair. These men had been elected to office by controlling Southern votes, aided, indeed, in each case, by votes of the North, and in one case, by all the electoral votes of the North. At six successive elections, Northern men had brought forward their Presidential candidates only to suffer defeat and mortification. As a consequence, there grew up a strong desire to lessen the influence of the slaveholding States, and to prevent the increase of their number. The Northern States were under the influence of a great political temptation to do a great political wrong to Missouri and the slave States.

The people of the North, generally, were prepared to enter into the feelings of their political leaders, in opposing the increase of the political power of the South; and, in their desire to extend to all men the enjoyment of their natural rights, they were ready to overlook the constitutional rights of Missouri.

2. In order to show the true state of the case, in the estimation of enlightened statesmen, I quote the following extract from a speech of JOHN QUINCY ADAMS, delivered in Congress, 1835, in favor of the admission of Arkansas, whose constitution was offered for acceptance; it being of the same character as that of Missouri, both of them permitting slavery: "Mr. Chairman,—I cannot, consistently with my sense of obligation as a citizen of the United States, and bound by oath to support their Constitution, I cannot object to the admission of Arkansas into the Union as a slave State. I cannot propose or agree to make it a condition of her admission into the Union, that a convention of her people shall expunge this article from the Constitution. She is entitled to admission as a slave State." The argument against the admission of Missouri, from the Declaration of Independence, that "all men are created equal," is irrelevant. The argument from the power of Congress to make "needful rules and regulations in respect to the Territory and other prop-

erty," is irrelevant, for this " power " relates to *property*. The argument from the clause, " New States may be admitted by Congress into the Union," is all on the other side, from the very meaning of the terms. The House, therefore, was wrong in imposing the restriction as the condition of admitting Missouri, and the Senate was right in voting to admit her without this restriction. Thus much in regard to RESTRICTION.

3. But did the North act honorably in respect to the COMPROMISE? This compromise was proposed by a Northern man, and was accepted by Southern men and by Northern men ; and yet it was not adhered to by Northern men, after the North had received the advantage of admitting the State of Maine, and after slavery had been prohibited north of 36° 30'. When Missouri a third time had presented herself for admittance with this compact or compromise in her hand, she was again rejected by a vote of 87 against admission, and 67 in favor of it.

4. The difference between the " restriction " and the " compromise," has not been well understood. " No words," says BENTON, in his " Debates," " have been more confounded than those of the restriction and the compromise ; so much so, that some of the eminent speakers of the time have had their speeches against the restriction quoted as being against the compromise, of which they were zealous advocates. Though confounded, no two measures could be more opposite in their nature and effects. The restriction was to operate on a State, the compromise on a Territory. The restriction was to prevent the State of Missouri from admitting slavery ; the compromise was to admit slavery there, and to divide the rest of Louisiana about equally between free and slave soil. The restriction came from the North, the compromise from the South. The restriction raised the storm, the compromise allayed it."

5. One of the most unfortunate circumstances attending the debate was, that some of the Northern members used intemperate and insulting language towards the Southern men and Southern institutions, which were not soon forgotten. Instead of discussing constitutional questions, by referring to the Constitution as the sole ground of argument, they uttered the language of invective and sarcasm against slavery itself, if not against slaveholders. Such men as RUFUS KING and HARRISON GRAY OTIS

were not guilty of these improprieties. But there were others who drew from their quiver arrows envenomed by hatred, and sent them, at random or with deliberate aim, to rankle in the breast of the South. And the effect of their speeches upon the North was to kindle up a bitter and intolerant spirit. The present writer remembers that, in a most respectable Northern city, during the discussions respecting the admittance of Missouri, a small company of boys were employed to carry through the streets, on a flag, the picture of a chained African, uttering the words, "Am I not a man and a brother?" and also another, in which the "noble Virginians" were represented, with up-raised whips, driving the negroes at their field work. In this way, but more especially by speeches and inflammatory articles in newspapers, the passions of the people of the North were kindled into indignation.

6. To men of this generation it may seem strange, that worthy men in both Houses should refuse to vote for the admission of Missouri upon the grounds alleged, and for the reasons given. But it should be borne in mind that the real reason was the fear of increasing the political power of the South. Under the influence of this fear, on the part of demagogues in Congress, the evils of slavery were magnified, and the constitutional powers of Congress were distorted, until the members, in given cases, felt that they should commit political suicide by voting for the measure of admitting Missouri. It was easier to excite the masses than it was to calm the excitement. In some cases they did commit political suicide. They voted for the measure, but their constituents never forgave them. Some of the State Legislatures passed resolutions against the measure, which might operate to prevent the members from those States from acting in the premises, according to their own judgment.

7. Did Congress act Constitutionally in prohibiting slavery north of 36° 30'? This question did not come up in a very distinct form for discussion, though there were those, Mr. RANDOLPH among them, who refused to vote for the compromise on that ground. His penetrating mind saw the constitutional objection. But the Senate and the House were in an awkward relation to each other, each insisting on its own bill. Missouri, with great reason, complained of the treatment she had experi-

enced. Maine was clamoring for admission. The whole country was agitated. The power of Congress was greater over Territory than over States. The ordinance of 1787, which excluded slavery, was remembered, while the difference between the two cases was not insisted on. Congress was tired of the subject. Some thought, perhaps, that it was best to do a great right and a little wrong. The bill, as amended, came from the Senate without very much discussion in that body, into the House, March 2, 1820, and was passed the same day.

The subject has since been more carefully examined, and the conviction has been produced upon some of the ablest statesmen of the land, that the Constitution gives no power to interdict slavery in the Territories.

The restriction of slavery in Missouri as the condition of admission into the Union, with the delay, after the restriction was struck out, of the bill, on the ground of an invidious distinction between the States, opened a fountain of sectional feeling, the bitter waters from which at the time deluged the land. These waters from that fountain have not yet ceased to flow.

CHAPTER VIII.

Mr. ADAMS was elected by the House of Representatives over General JACKSON, there having been a failure to make an election of President by the electoral votes. The friends of Mr. CLAY united with the friends of Mr. ADAMS in placing the latter in the Presidential chair; though General JACKSON had the largest vote of the electors.

Mr. ADAMS had large experience and undoubted honesty as a statesman, but was inclined to a broad interpretation of the Constitution; and, like Mr. CLAY, was in favor of a high tariff, as was supposed. It was very natural that Mr. CLAY should unite his political fortunes with him, in preference to General JACKSON; but by doing so, they both lost some share of the public confidence, especially from the circumstance that Mr. CLAY accepted of the office of Secretary of State under him. Sectional feelings were strongly excited during the Presidential contest, and especially during the administration of Mr. ADAMS. The *protective* policy, sanctioned by the tariff act of 1824, entered now, for the first time, into a Presidential contest.

THE TARIFF OF 1828.

Previous to the year 1816, protection to American manufactures had been incidental. The Constitution gave Congress power to raise a *revenue*, but not to encourage one branch of industry to the injury of another. As the powers granted by that instrument do not allow Congress to protect manufactures directly, they were forced to depend on such an amount of protection as they could incidentally receive from the imposition of duties for revenue. By a judicious discrimination as to what imported articles should be dutied, and what should be the duty on each class, the American manufacturer had the advantage of the foreign manufacturer of the same class of articles, by the amount of the duty paid added to the expense of transportation; while the consumer could not complain, because what he paid additional to what he would have to pay for the same articles if imported duty free, he paid only as revenue for the support of the Government.

But in 1816 a new policy was adopted. It had been found by the experience of the war, that the country had suffered great inconvenience from depending on foreign manufactures. Accordingly, patriotism was appealed to for the support of domestic manufactures, which would render the country more independent of foreign nations. Besides, a large amount of capital had been embarked in manufactures, which, at peace prices, with foreign competition, could not be sustained. The national debt must be paid. In this state of things the tariff law of 1816 was enacted, the opposition to it being based chiefly on the ground that it would produce an injurious effect upon commerce.

In 1824 a bill was passed, giving still further protection to manufactures. It was in support of this bill that Mr. CLAY made his celebrated speech in favor of what, by a strange misnomer, he called "an American system." It was the privilege of the present writer to hear that speech, and, indeed, all the speeches of importance delivered that session on the subject of the tariff. In a very taking and persuasive statement of the present distress of the country and the necessity of a change of policy in favor of manufactures, he presented the general and special arguments in favor of a protective tariff. He was aided by manufacturers or their agents, who were present to furnish him, and others united with him, with facts which would operate on the minds of members to induce them to favor domestic industry employed in the manufacturing business. A political party, if not formed already, was about to be formed on this issue among others. Mr. CLAY was still regarded as a democrat; and such was his patriotism and his eminent personal qualities, such were his eloquence and powers of reasoning, that he had great influence in carrying the bill through the House, notwithstanding the vigorous opposition against it.

Mr. WEBSTER was opposed to the bill, and, in his reply, was more than equal to Mr. CLAY in his arguments, and hardly inferior in eloquence. Massachusetts went against the bill with the South; but it was carried by a vote in the House of 107 to 102, and in the Senate of 25 to 20. With other distinguished men who were opposed to the "new policy," inaugurated by Mr. CLAY, and so characterized by him, was RUFUS KING.

Mr. CLAY saw clearly that it would be opposed by Southern members, because it sacrificed the interests of their constituents for the benefit of other States. He spoke of the importance of preserving the harmony of the whole Union. He remarked that "if the North, the East, and the West formed an independent State, unassociated with the South, can there be a doubt that the restrictive system would be carried to the point of prohibition of every foreign fabric of which they produce the raw material, and which they could manufacture? Such would be their policy if alone; but they are fortunately connected with the South, which believes its interest to require a free admission of foreign manufacture." Mr. CLAY evidently intended to act in the most conciliatory manner towards the South; but he also was determined to carry the measure.

Mr. McDUFFIE, in one of his speeches, said "that the honorable Speaker had remarked that, in the legislation of this country, the most scrupulous regard should be had to the general harmony. But he put it to the Speaker whether it was not the introduction of such a bill which was likely to disturb that harmony, rather than its discussion." He went on to show that it is a question distinctly arraying against each other the two different sections of the Confederacy. All the arguments by which the proposed duty is supported have been, therefore, and necessarily must be, of a sectional character. "When gentlemen are attempting by legislation to affect the interests of the two sections of the Union relatively to each other, how can they throw upon us the responsibility of that feeling, which the discussion may excite?"

Mr. WEBSTER replied to Mr. CLAY on another point, in a manner equally triumphant. "On the general question, sir, allow me to ask if the doctrine of prohibition, as a general doctrine, be not preposterous? Suppose all nations to act upon it, they would be prosperous then precisely in proportion as they abolished intercourse with one another. The less of mutual commerce they had the better, upon this hypothesis. Protection and encouragement may be, and are, doubtless, sometimes wise and beneficial, if kept within proper limits; but when carried to an extravagant height, or the point of prohibition, the absurd character of the system manifests itself."

Notwithstanding the very able argumentation against the bill, it passed as already stated, by a small majority. Mr. CLAY became identified with the protective system. It became a settled matter that he should promote the interests of the manufacturers, and that they should act politically under his leadership.

In 1828, the manufacturers applied to Congress for still further protection. They previously held a convention in Harrisburg, which met July 30, 1827, in which the subject of protection was discussed with great earnestness; and having settled that question to their own satisfaction, they addressed Congress in a memorial, in which they asked for a large increase of duties.

In the mean time Massachusetts, and New England generally, though extensively opposed to the tariff of 1824, had experienced a change in their interests or in their political purposes, so that they were disposed to go for higher protective duties. Mr. WEBSTER, who had supported the interests of commerce, in opposition to the interests of manufactures, was now ready to vote for a high tariff bill, for the benefit of corporate capital.

The Southern States, thus deserted by New England, became greatly alarmed at the impending additional burdens which were to be imposed on their industry. The President, and the Secretary of State, Mr. CLAY, were in favor of protection, as were a majority of both Houses in Congress. But such men as JOHN RANDOLPH, Mr. McDUFFIE, General HAMILTON, P. P. BARBOUR, and others, made very able speeches against the bill,

7

showing up the fallacies of the Harrisburg address, and the wrong of taxing one part of the country for the benefit of another part, beyond what is necessary for the purposes of revenue. The bill, however, was passed April 22, 1828, by a vote of 105 to 94.

On the passage of the bill, Mr. WILDE moved to amend the title, by adding the words, "and for the encouragement of domestic manufactures." Mr. RANDOLPH opposed the amendment, and said if the bill had its true name, it should be called, "A bill to rob and plunder nearly one-half of the country for the benefit of the residue." Mr. DRAYTON proposed to strike out all after "An act," and to insert, "to increase the duties upon certain imports, for the purpose of increasing the profits of certain manufactures." It would not have been decorous to propose the additional amendment, "and to make a certain man President."

PROTEST OF GEORGIA.

Like the tariff act of 1824, but with much greater emphasis, this tariff act of 1828 was passed in opposition to the determined opposition of the Southern States, an opposition which continued to manifest itself during its operation. A protest against it by the Legislature of Georgia, was introduced into the Senate of the United States, through the Vice-President, January 12, 1829, of which the following is an extract: "In her sovereign character, the State of Georgia protests against the act of the last session of Congress, entitled, 'An act in alteration of the several acts imposing duties on imports,' as deceptive in its title, fraudulent in its pretexts, oppressive in its exactions, partial and unjust in its operation, unconstitutional in its well-known objects, ruinous to commerce and agriculture, to secure a hateful monopoly to a combination of importunate manufacturers.

"Demanding the repeal of an act which has already disturbed the Union and endangered the public tranquillity, weakened the confidence of the whole States in the Federal Government, and diminished the affection of large masses of the people to the Union itself, and the abandonment of the degrading system which considers the people as incapable of wisely directing

their own enterprise, which sets up the servants of the people in
Congress as the exclusive judges of what pursuits are most ad-
vantageous and suitable for those by whom they were elected,
the State of Georgia expects that, in perpetual testimony thereof, the deliberate and solemn expression of her opinion will be
carefully kept in the archives of the Senate ; and in justification
of her character to the present generation and to posterity, if,
unfortunately, Congress, disregarding the protest, and continuing to pervert powers granted for clearly defined and well-un-
derstood purposes, to effectuate objects never intended by the
great parties by whom the Constitution was framed, to be intrusted to the controlling guardianship of the Federal Government, should render necessary measures of a more decisive character, for the protection of the people of the State, and the vindication of the Constitution of the United States."

Mr. BERRIEN, on the occasion of its presentation, made,
among other remarks, the following : " Forty years of successful experiment have proved the efficiency of this Government to
sustain us in an honorable intercourse with the other nations of
the world.   Externally in peace and in war, amid the fluctua-
tions of commerce and the strife of arms, it has protected our
interests and defended our rights.   One trial, one fearful trial,
remains to be made.   It is one, under the apprehension of which
the bravest may tremble, which the wise and the good will
anxiously endeavor to avoid.   It is that experiment which shall
test the competency of this Government to preserve our internal
peace, whenever a question, vitally affecting the bond which
unites us as one people, shall come to be solemnly agitated between the sovereign members of this Confederacy.   In proportion to its dangers should be our solicitude to avoid it, by abstaining on the one hand from acts of doubtful legislation, as
well as by the manner of resistance on the other, to those which
are deemed unconstitutional.   Between the independent members of this Confederacy, sir, there can be no common arbiter.
They are necessarily remitted to their own sovereign will, deliberately expressed, in the exercise of those reserved rights of
sovereignty, the delegation of which would have been an act of
political suicide.   The designation of such an arbiter, sir, was,
by the force of invincible necessity, *casus omissus* among the

provisions of a Constitution conferring limited powers, the interpretation of which was to be confided to the subordinate agents, created by those who were intrusted to administer it.

"I earnestly hope that the wise and conciliatory spirit of this Government, and of those of the several States, will postpone to a period far distant, the day that will summon us to so fearful a trial. If, indeed, we are doomed to encounter it, I as earnestly hope that it may be entered upon in the spirit of peace, and with cherished recollections of former amity."

PROTEST OF SOUTH CAROLINA.

February 10, 1829.—Mr. W. SMITH, Senator, presented to the Senate the protest of South Carolina against the tariff act of 1828, for the following reasons :

"1. Because the good people of this commonwealth believe the powers of Congress were delegated to it in trust for the accomplishment of certain specified objects, which limit and control them, and that every exercise of them for any other purpose is a violation of the Constitution, as unwarrantable as the undisguised assumption of substantive powers, not granted or expressly withheld.

"2. Because the power to lay duties on imports is, and in its very nature can be, only the means of effecting the objects specified in the Constitution ; since no free Government, and, least of all, a Government of enumerated powers, can of right impose any tax (any more than a penalty) which is not at once justified by public necessity, and clearly within the scope and province of the social compact ; and since the right of confining appropriations of the public money to such legitimate and constitutional objects is as essential to the liberties of the people, as their unquestionable privilege to be taxed only by their own consent.

"3. Because they believe that the tariff law, passed by Congress at its last session, and all other acts of which the principal object is the protection of manufactures, or any other branch of domestic industry—if they be considered as the exercise of a supposed power in Congress to tax at its own good will and pleasure and to apply the money raised to objects not specified in the Constitution—is a violation of these fundamental principles, a breach of a well-defined trust, and a perversion of the high powers vested in the Federal Government for Federal purposes only.

" 4. Because such acts considered in the light of a regulation of commerce, are equally liable to objection ; since, although the power to regulate commerce may, like other powers, be exercised so as to protect domestic manufactures, yet it is clearly distinguished from a power to do so *co nomine*, both in the nature of the thing, and in the common acceptation of the terms ; and because the confounding of them would lead to the most extravagant results ; since the encouragement of domestic industry implies an absolute control over all the interests, resources, and pursuits of a people, and is inconsistent with the idea of any other than a simple consolidated Government.

" 5. Because, from contemporaneous expositions of the Constitution in the numbers of the Federalist, (which is cited only because the Supreme Court has recognized its authority,) it is clear that to regulate commerce was considered by the Convention as only incidentally connected with the encouragement of agriculture and manufactures ; and because the laying imposts and duties on imports was not understood to justify, in any case, a prohibition of foreign commodities, except as a means of extending commerce by coercing foreign nations to a fair reciprocity in their intercourse with us, or for some other *bona fide* commercial purpose.

" 6. Because, whilst the power to protect manufactures is nowhere expressly granted to Congress, nor can be considered as necessary and proper to carry into effect any specified power, it seems to be expressly reserved to the States by the tenth section of the first article of the Constitution.

" 7. Because, even admitting Congress have a constitutional right to protect manufactures by the imposition of duties, or by regulations of commerce, designed principally for that purpose, yet a tariff, the operation of which is grossly unequal and oppressive, is such an abuse of power as is incompatible with the principles of a free Government and the great end of civil society, and equality of rights and protection.

" 8. Finally, because South Carolina, from her climate, situation, and peculiar institutions, is, and must ever continue to be, wholly dependent upon agriculture and commerce, not only for her prosperity, but for her very existence as a State ; because the valuable products of her soil, the blessings by which Divine Providence seems to have designed to compensate for the disadvantages under which she suffers in other respects, are among the very few that can be cultivated by slave labor ; and if, by the loss of her foreign commerce, those products should be confined to an inadequate market, the fate of this fertile State would be poverty and utter desolation ; her citizens, in despair, would emigrate to more fortunate regions, and the whole frame of her civil polity be impaired and deranged, if not dissolved entirely.

" Deeply impressed with these considerations, the representatives of the good people of this commonwealth, anxiously desiring to live in peace with their fellow-citizens, and to do all that in them lies to preserve and perpetuate the union of the States, and the liberties of which it is the surest pledge ; but feeling it to be their bounden duty to expose and resist all encroachments upon the true spirit of the Constitution, lest an apparent acquiescence in the system of protecting duties should be drawn into precedent, do, in the name of the commonwealth of South Carolina, claim to enter upon the journals of the Senate their protest against it, as unconstitutional, oppressive, and unjust."

Mr. SMITH, who was a distinguished member of the first Congress, and enjoyed the confidence and friendship of ALEXANDER HAMILTON, in presenting the protest, among other things said : " South Carolina believed that when, as a sovereign State, she surrendered a portion of her authority, it was for certain and specified objects ; and that, when those objects were accomplished, the authority ceded to the General Government was at an end ; that any measures pursued beyond the objects just contemplated was a violation of the compact : it belonged to the States to resume their authority. South Carolina did not assent to the postulate that the authority was ever delegated to the Government, which the Government had assumed over individuals and property composing the State.

" We had been told that the high duties would be reduced ;

but so far from this, the manufactories had increased; the prosperity of one had induced others to embark in the business, and there had been constant application for new duties, which had been granted. South Carolina has protested against these duties; he did not know that the Constitution acknowledged this principle; he did know that the Constitution had not lately been looked to. Constitutional arguments had been used which had never been replied to."

Mr. HAYNE, the other Senator, among other things said: "One of the most unhappy circumstances connected with the present condition of the Southern States, is the great, he might perhaps say, the insuperable difficulty of causing their sentiments and feelings to be made known, so as to be understood and appreciated by their fellow-citizens in other quarters of the Union. Viewing the United States as one country, the people of the South might almost be considered as strangers in the land of their fathers. The fruits of their industry had, from the policy pursued by the Federal Government, been flowing to the North, in a current as steady and as undeviating as the waters of the great Gulf; and as the sources of our prosperity were drying up, that reciprocal intercourse, which had softened asperities and bound the different parts of the Union together in the bonds of sympathy and affection, had in a great measure ceased.

"That close and intimate communion, necessary to a full knowledge of each other, no longer existed, and in place of it there was springing up, (it is useless to disguise the truth,) among the people in opposite quarters of the Union, a spirit of jealousy and distrust, founded on the settled conviction, on the one part, that they are the victims of injustice, and on the other, that our complaints, if not groundless, may be safely disregarded. The people of the South are well aware of the evils growing out of this unhappy state of things, and of none are they more deeply sensible than that (from causes to which I shall now advert) the eyes of our brethren have been closed to our true condition, and their hearts shut against our just complaints. Although South Carolina, in common with several of her sister States, had, on former occasions, avowed the principles contained in the protest, yet it may well be doubted (if we can judge from

what we see and hear around us) whether it is believed north
of the Potomac that she really entertains them : for, in the face
of the solemn declarations of her people and their representatives, denouncing the policy pursued by the Federal Government as involving them in ruin, we find the public ear abused
and the public mind deluded by exaggerated statements of our
uninterrupted prosperity and happiness. It has even been insinuated here, at the very seat of Government, that the enlightened public of the South is in favor of this policy, and that the
excitement which prevails there is merely ' artificial,' if it has
not been ' got up for party purposes.' "

North Carolina also protested against the law ; and Alabama
denied the power of Congress to lay duties for protection.

REMARKS.

1. Tariff laws, from 1789 until 1816, had been enacted for
the raising *revenue* for the support of the Government, and paying off the national debts ; while the protection afforded by
them to manufactures had been purely incidental.

2. In 1816, mainly from patriotic motives, the rates of tariff
were raised, for the purpose of affording protection to manufacturers, who could not maintain a competition with foreign manufacturers at peace prices. To this there was no sectional opposition. It was generally felt to be desirable that the country
ought to be more independent of foreign nations than it had
been during the war, for the supply of manufactures.

3. In 1824 it became evident that politicians and manufacturers had united their efforts to promote what Mr. CLAY
called the "American system," by which the former class
might the better rise to political power in the country, and by
which the latter might accumulate large fortunes by the indirect
bounty paid by their countrymen in the shape of a tariff for
protection. Mr. CLAY, having left the Democratic party, united
his political fortunes with the Northern manufacturers. The
interests of the Southern States lay in free trade. Party politics
and the hopes of politicians likewise became connected with the
doctrines of free trade.

4. The tariff of 1828 was not a "judicious tariff." Like the

tariff of 1824, it was established immediately before the Presidential election, which it was designed to influence and control. The address of the Harrisburg manufacturers' Convention was a strange medley of ideas, and yet it had a powerful influence ·in certain quarters upon party politics of the time. It was designed, probably, among other things, to promote the election of some politician to the Presidency who was in favor of a high tariff, and who would satisfy the cravings of the manufacturers for large gains.

5. The Southern States naturally became very hostile to the strangely so-called "American system," which they viewed as adopted to enrich Northern manufacturers, and exalt to office its patrons. From the increasing demands of manufacturers, they came to regard the tariff for protection as a "daughter of the horse-leech which cries 'Give, give.'"

It was not strange that the Southern States should have the same repugnance to Federal legislation in 1828, which imposed ruinous burdens upon their agricultural industry, which the Northern States manifested during and some years before the war of 1812, towards Federal legislation, which imposed severe restrictions upon their commerce. However injudicious, it is not strange that they should look to nullification or secession as a relief from what they deemed unconstitutional burdens, just as some of the Northern States then did.

6. Northern manufacturers, like Northern men generally, were not acquainted with the agricultural interests of the South; just as Southern planters were not acquainted with Northern interests. They did not apprehend the real operation of the tariff upon the planting States. Politicians and manufacturers persuaded themselves that they understood the interests of the South better than Southern men did. They seriously attempted in Congress, in editorials, and in conversation, to show that it was for the benefit of Southern planters that they should pay high duties to the Government, or high prices to Northern manufacturers. They wrote or talked as if the Northern States were justified in forcing upon the South a high tariff for its benefit.

CHAPTER IX.

GENERAL JACKSON was elected President by 178 electoral votes against 83 votes which were cast for Mr. ADAMS. Every State south of the Potomac cast its electoral vote for General JACKSON. Every electoral vote of the New England States, except one from Maine, was cast for Mr. ADAMS. At his second election he received 219 votes; Mr. CLAY received 49 votes.

He was in favor of a strict construction of the Constitution, by which the States would practically retain their reserved rights. He was opposed to that broad or large construction of the Constitution, by which a United States Bank had been chartered, and by which a system of internal improvements had been adopted or projected, and by which high protective tariffs had been established.

In his inaugural address, he has the following paragraph in reference to the position of South Carolina and Georgia and other States in respect to the tariff of 1828. "In such measures as I may be called on to pursue, in regard to the rights of the separate States, I hope to be animated by a proper respect for those sovereign members of our Union; taking care not to confound the powers they have reserved to themselves, with those they have granted to the Confederacy." In his first annual message, after speaking of the tariff and any attempts that may be made to connect it with the party politics of the day, he adds: "Legislation, subjected to such influences, can never be just, and cannot long retain the sanction of a people whose active patriotism is not bounded by sectional limits, nor insensible to that spirit of concession and forbearance which gives life to our political compact, and still sustains it. Discarding all calculations of political ascendency, the North, the South, the East, the West, should unite in diminishing any burthen of which either may justly complain." "I cannot, therefore, too strongly warn you against all encroachments upon the legitimate sphere of State Sovereignty."

SPEECHES ON NULLIFICATION.

In January, 1830, during the first session of Congress in General JACKSON's Administration, the celebrated dispute upon Mr. FOOT's Resolution concerning the public lands took place in the Senate. In this debate, Mr. HAYNE and Mr. WEBSTER made their sectional speeches, into which the subject of Nullification largely entered. Mr. HAYNE opened the debate on the subject of the public lands, and was followed by Mr. WEBSTER, in a speech in which he combated opinions on the Union, held by some of Mr. HAYNE's friends, among whom was the Vice-President, (Mr. CALHOUN,) then in the chair. This unexpectedly called out Mr. HAYNE to defend these opinions, from which Mr. WEBSTER had exonerated him, which he generously did, in a speech of great ability and eloquence. To this Mr. WEBSTER replied, in a speech of equal or greater ability and eloquence. This produced a rejoinder by Mr. HAYNE, which produced a surrejoinder by Mr. WEBSTER.

These speeches were eminently sectional, and have had an influence to increase the strength of sectional feeling in the North and in the South. Mr. WEBSTER's eulogy upon Massachusetts and upon the Union, in his most elaborate speech on the occasion, are familiar as declamations to the colleges and schools of the North. In the speeches, both of Mr. HAYNE and Mr. WEBSTER, there were fallacies which were shown up by other speakers who addressed the Senate on the subject of Nullification, among whom were Mr. ROWAN, Mr. GRUNDY, Mr. CLAYTON, Mr. WOODBURY, and Mr. EDWARD LIVINGSTON. In the course of his speech, Mr. LIVINGSTON spoke as follows :

"My learned and honorable friend, the Senator near me, from South Carolina, (Mr. HAYNE,) comes, in the eloquent arguments he has made, to the conclusion, that whenever, in the language of the Virginia resolutions, (which he adopts,) there is, in the opinion of any one State, " a palpable, deliberate, and dangerous violation of the Constitution by a law of Congress," such State may, without ceasing to be a member of the Union, declare the law to be unconstitutional, and prevent its execution within the State; that this is a constitutional right, and that its exercise will produce a constitutional remedy, by obliging Congress either to repeal the law, or to obtain an explicit grant of the power which is denied by the State, by submitting an amendment to the several States, and that, by the decision of the requisite number, the State, as well as the Union, would be bound. It would be doing injustice, both to my friend and to his argument, if I did not add, that this resort to the nullifying power, as it has been termed, ought to be had only in the last resort, when the grievance was intolerable, and all other means of remonstrance and appeal to the other States had failed.

"In this opinion, I understand the honorable and learned Chairman of the Judiciary Committee (Mr. ROWAN) substantially to agree, particularly in the constitutional right of preventing the execution of the obnoxious law.

"The Senator from Tennessee, (Mr. GRUNDY,) in his speech, which was listened to with so much attention and pleasure, very justly denies the right of declaring the nullity of a law, and preventing its execution, to the ordinary Legislature, but erroneously, in my opinion, gives it to a convention.

"My friend from New Hampshire, (Mr. WOODBURY,) of whose luminous argument I cannot speak too highly, and to the greatest part of which I agree, does not coincide in the assertion of a constitutional right of preventing the execution of a law believed to be unconstitutional, but refers opposition to the unalienable right of resistance to oppression.

"All these Senators consider the Constitution as a compact between the States in their sovereign capacity; and one of them (Mr. ROWAN) has contended that sovereignty cannot be divided; from which it may be inferred that no part of the sovereign power has been transferred to the General Government.

"The Senator from Massachusetts, (Mr. WEBSTER,) in his very eloquent and justly admired address on this subject, considers the Federal Constitution as entirely popular, and not created by compact, and from this position, very naturally shows that there can be no constitutional right of actual resistance to a law of that Government, but that intolerable and illegal acts may justify it on first principles.

" However these opinions may differ, there is one consolatory reflection, that none of them justify a violent opposition given to an unconstitutional law, until an extreme case of suffering has occurred. Still less do any of them suppose the actual existence of such a case.

" But the danger of establishing, on the one hand, a constitutional veto in each of the States, upon any act of the whole, to be exercised whenever, in the opinion of the Legislature of such State, the act they complain of is contrary to the Constitution ; and on the other, the dangers which result to the State Governments by considering that of the Union as entirely popular, and denying the existence of any compact ; seem, both of them, to be so great, as to justify, and indeed demand, an expression of my dissent from both.

" The arguments on the one side, to show that the Constitution is the result of a compact between the States, cannot, I think, be controverted ; and those which go to show that it is founded on the consent of the people, and, in one sense, a popular government, are equally incontrovertible. Both of these propositions, seemingly so contradictory, are true, and both of them are false—true, as it respects one feature in the Constitution ; erroneous, if applied to the whole.

" By a popular consolidated Government, I understand one that is founded on the consent, express or implied, of the people of the whole nation ; and which operates directly upon the people.

" By a Federative Government, as contradistinguished from the former, I mean one composed of several independent States, bound together for specific purposes, and relying for the efficacy of its operations on its action upon the different States in their political capacity, not individually upon their citizens.

" The old Confederation was a compact between the States ;

but among a number of stipulations strictly federative, it contained others which gave to the Congress powers which trenched upon the State sovereignties; to declare war and to make peace; to enter into treaties binding on the whole; to establish Courts of Admiralty, with power to bind the citizens of the States individually in cases coming under that jurisdiction; to raise armies, equip fleets, coin money, emit bills of credit, and other similar powers.

"In the Federal Constitution, this combination of the two characteristics of Government is more apparent. It was framed by delegates appointed by the States; it was ratified by conventions of the people of each State, convened according to the laws of the respective States. It guarantees the existence of the States, which are necessary to its own; the States are represented in one branch by Senators, chosen by the Legislatures; and in the other, by Representatives taken from the people, but chosen by a rule which may be made and varied by the States, not by Congress—the qualifications of electors being different in different States. They may make amendments to the Constitution. In short, the Government had its inception with them: it depends on their political existence for its operation; and its duration cannot go beyond theirs. The States existed before the Constitution; they parted only with such powers as are specified in that instrument; they continue still to exist, with all the powers they have not ceded; and the present Government would never, itself, have gone into operation, had not the States, in their political capacity, consented. That consent is a compact of each one with the whole; not, as has been argued, (by Mr. WEBSTER, in order to throw a kind of ridicule on this convincing part of the argument of my friend from South Carolina,) with the Government which was made by such compact. It is difficult, therefore, it would appear, with all these characters of a federative nature, to deny to the present Government the description of one founded on compact, to which each State was a party; and a conclusive proof, if any more were wanted, would be in the fact, that the States adopted the Constitution at different times, and many of them on conditions which were afterwards complied with by amendments. If it were strictly a popular Government, in the sense that is contended for, the moment a majority of the people of the United States had consented, it would have bound the rest; and yet, after all the others, except one, had adopted the Constitution, the smallest still held out; and if Rhode Island had not consented to enter into the Confederacy, she would, perhaps, at this time, have been unconnected with us.

"But with all these proofs (and I think them incontrovertible) that the Government could not have been brought into being without a compact, yet I am far from admitting that, because this entered so largely into its origin, therefore there are no characteristics of another kind, which impress on it strongly the marks of a more intimate union and amalgamation of the interests of the citizens of the different States, which gives to them the general character of citizens of the United nation. * * The Government, also, for the most part, (except in the election of Senators, Representatives, and President, and some others,) acts in the exercise of its legitimate powers directly upon individuals, and not through the medium of State authorities. This is an essential character of a popular Government.

"I place little reliance on the argument which has been mostly depended on, to show that this is a popular Government: I mean the preamble, which begins with the words, 'We, the people.' It proves nothing more than the fact, that the people of the several States had been consulted, and had given their consent to the instrument. To give these words any other construction, would be to make them an assertion directly contrary to the fact. We know, and it never has been imagined or asserted, that the people of the United States, collectively, as a whole people, gave their assent, or were consulted in that capacity; the people of each State were consulted, to know whether that State would form a part of the United States, under the Articles of the Constitution, and to that they gave their assent, simply as citizens of that State."

The discussion, as already stated, came up unexpectedly to Mr. HAYNE and Mr. WEBSTER, certainly to the former, on a subject, namely the public lands, which had no necessary connection with the subject of *Nullification;* probably the mind of each was full of the latter subject; and hence the facility with which both entered on the discussion, after it had been distinctly introduced by Mr. WEBSTER.

President JACKSON, in his annual message, at the opening of Congress, 1831, recommended the abolition of duties on numerous articles of necessity or comfort not produced at home. On the 9th of January, 1832, Mr. CLAY submitted a Resolution in relation to the tariff, and in a speech of three days' duration he supported his "American system," in subordination to which he proposed to make any reduction of duties which should be necessary.

In opposition to Mr. CLAY's resolution, General SAMUEL SMITH of Maryland spoke as follows :

"We have arrived at a crisis. Yes, Mr. President, a crisis more appalling than a day of battle. I adjure the Committee on Manufactures to pause ; to reflect on the dissatisfaction of the South. South Carolina has expressed herself strongly against the tariff of 1828, stronger than the other States are willing to speak. But, sir, the whole South feel deeply the oppression of this tariff. In this respect there is no difference of opinion. The South, the whole Southern States, all consider it as oppressive. They have not yet spoken ; but when they do speak, it will be in a voice that will not implore, but will demand redress.

"I am, Mr. President, one of the few survivors of those who fought in the War of the Revolution. We then thought we fought for liberty, for equal rights. We fought against taxation, the proceeds of which were for the benefit of others. Where is the difference if the people are to be taxed by the manufacturers or by any others? I say manufacturers, and why do I say so? When the Senate met, there was a strong disposition with all parties to ameliorate the tariff of 1828 ; but now I see a change, which makes me almost despair of any thing effectual being accomplished. Even the small concessions made by the Senator from Kentucky, (Mr. CLAY,) have been reprobated by the lobby members, the agents of the manufacturers. I am told they have put their fiat on any change whatever, and hence, as a consequence, the change in the course and language of gentlemen that precludes all hope. Those interested may hang on the Committee of Manufactures like an incubus. I say to that Committee, depend upon your own good judgment, discard sectional interests, and study only the common weal. Act with these views, and thus retain the affections of the South."

Mr. CLAY was deeply and anxiously sensible of the discontent in the Southern States in respect to a protective tariff. He would, if possible, avert the danger to the Union from that quarter, but he felt that there was a greater danger from another quarter if the "American system" should be given up. In his speech he expresses himself in the following terms :

"And now, Mr. President, I have to make a few observations on a delicate subject, which I approach with all the respect that is due to its serious and grave nature. They have not, indeed, been rendered necessary by the speech of the gentleman from South Carolina, (Mr. HAYNE,) whose forbearance to notice the topic was commendable, as his argument throughout was characterized by an ability and dignity worthy of him and of the Senate. * * But it is impossible to conceal from our view the fact that there is a great excitement in South Carolina, that the protective system is openly and violently denounced in public meetings, and that the Legislature itself has declared its purpose of resorting to counteracting measures ; a suspension of which has only been submitted to, for the purpose of allowing Congress to retrace its steps with respect to this Union. Mr. President, the truth cannot be too generally proclaimed, nor too strongly inculcated, that it is necessary to the whole and to all the parts—necessary to those parts in different degrees, but vitally necessary to each.

"The danger to our Union does not lie on the side of persistence in the American system, but on that of its abandonment. If, as I have supposed and believe, the inhabitants of all north and east of James River, and all west of the mountains, including Louisiana, are deeply interested in the preservation of that system, would they be reconciled to its overthrow? Can it be expected that two-thirds or three-fourths of the people of the United States would consent to the destruction of a policy believed to be absolutely necessary to their prosperity ? When, too, the sacrifice is made at the instance of a single interest, which they verily believe will not be promoted by it. * * *

8

What would be the condition of this Union, if Pennsylvania and New York, those mammoth members of our confederacy, were firmly persuaded that their industry was paralyzed and their prosperity blighted, by the enforcement of the British Colonial system, under the delusive name of free trade? They are now tranquil, and happy, and contented, conscious of their welfare, and feeling a salutary and rapid circulation of the products of home manufactures and home industry throughout all their great arteries. But let that be checked, let them feel that a foreign system is to predominate, and the sources of their subsistence and comfort are to be dried up; let New England and the Middle States all feel that they too are the victims of a mistaken policy, and let those vast portions of our country despair of any favorable change, and then, indeed, might we tremble for the continuance of the Union."

Here we are presented with the picture of disunion coming from the North, if the protective system should be abandoned. Mr. CLAY thus intimates that if the North should not have the advantages of protection to their manufactures, it would adopt a course to destroy the Union.

On January 23, 1832, Mr. DRAYTON, of South Carolina, presented a memorial of the members of the Legislature of South Carolina, *opposed* to nullification. They state "that they are exceedingly aggrieved by the laws of the United States, imposing high duties on foreign merchandise for the protection of manufactures;" "that the policy, the justice, and the constitutionality of the present system of high protective duties have been strenuously denied." "The objections to the restrictive system are of the gravest character, and the sense of oppression and injustice, which it has excited, are widely diffused and deeply felt." Thus there appears to have been no difference of opinion in South Carolina, in respect to the injurious effects of the tariff laws then in force.

While this bill was under consideration, Mr. CHOATE, of Massachusetts, in an able and characteristic speech, said : " Still the difficulty recurs. There is a great sectional excitement, and that, whether groundless or not, is, *per se*, a case to act on. It is desirable to allay the excitement. Yes, certainly; but how? Sir, my humble scheme is this: I think, in the language of

medical men, the case requires topical treatment, local applications. Search out the sectional grievance, if you can find it.
Find what are the articles exclusively of Southern consumption,
and important in the economy of the South, and relieve them
of all protective duty. Strike them out of the statute. For so
much let there be no tariff, and let them be fabricated in England, that the American Union may be preserved; and let all
others be as they are now effectually protected." He evidently
was for concession and conciliation.

The bill was passed in the House, June 27, 1832, and in the
Senate, July 9, 1832, and was entirely unsatisfactory to the
Southern States.

In the next annual message, President JACKSON, and in his
report, the Secretary of the Treasury, recommended a change in
the tariff laws.

The ORDINANCE of the Convention of South Carolina was
issued November 24, 1832, declaring the revenue laws of the
United States null and void, and enjoining the Legislature to
carry the decree into effect. The Legislature met and passed
the necessary laws. The State authorities were now placed in
opposition to the Federal laws. The militia of the State were
organized and armed, to be ready for action. General SCOTT
was sent to Charleston with Federal troops and two vessels of
war, to be prepared to enforce the laws of the Federal Government for the collection of the revenue. The proclamation of
General JACKSON, in view of that ordinance, was issued December 11, 1832. His message was sent into the Senate and the
House of Representatives, in which he asked for authority and
means to enforce the collection of revenue in South Carolina.
A bill for that purpose was introduced into the Senate from the
Committee on the Judiciary, January 28, 1833.

But before that bill was passed, Mr. CLAY introduced his
compromise bill, February 12, 1833. This bill was passed in
the House, February 22, 1833, and in the Senate, March 1,
1833. The revenue collection bill was passed in Senate, February 18, 1833, and in the House, February 28, 1833. The
compromise bill satisfied South Carolina so far, that Governor
HAMILTON called the Convention together, and communicated
to it the modification of the tariff. The Convention then passed

an ordinance repealing the nullification law. Thus the sectional difficulty was settled for the time.

REMARKS.

1. The tariff laws of 1824, 1828, 1832, were carried against the opinions and interests of the Southern States, by the combined influence of manufacturers and politicians. In 1824, a portion of the Eastern members were opposed to the tariff act, from a regard to the commercial interests of the States or districts which they represented. With some exceptions, the tariff laws of 1828 and 1832 were Northern measures, for the benefit of the North. With some few exceptions, these laws were vigorously opposed by the South, because they would operate injuriously upon Southern interests. Louisiana, from a regard to her sugar crop, which was protected by the tariff laws, went in favor of those laws. The greed of gain and the greed of office conspired to pass those laws for the evident benefit of the North, for the doubtful benefit of the whole country, and to the manifest injury of the South, which had no manufactures to be benefited.

2. The Southern States felt that they were oppressed by these burdensome tariffs. According to the intimation of GEORGE MASON in the Constitutional Convention, they found themselves "bound hand and foot" in the power of the Eastern States. And if these did not exclaim, "The Lord hath delivered them in our hands," still they talked about the "general welfare" as they understood it, and not about the rights of the States, or the provisions of the Constitution which secured those rights. As "a gift destroyeth the heart," so "oppression maketh a wise man mad." As the profits derived from protected manufactures produced narrow and sectional feelings at the North, so the burdens imposed by extravagant tariff laws led the State of South Carolina to the madness or folly of nullifying those laws, on the ground that they were oppressive and unconstitutional.

To relieve herself from the operation of these tariff laws, South Carolina passed the ordinance of nullification, which, whatever may be true in the theory of the relationship of the

States, involves the practical absurdity that a State may, at one and the same time, be in the Union for the enjoyment of its benefits, and out of the Union in bearing its burdens. South Carolina, in the ordinance, declares that in case of the application of physical force, on the part of the General Government, to execute the tariff laws, she will secede and set up a separate Government. To meet this threat, Senator CLAYTON declared and proved that State secession is a less evil than State nullification.

The country was in a very unhappy condition. South Carolina had passed the ordinance of nullification, and was threatening secession. The Southern States sympathized with her. Virginia had passed a resolve that she expected both the General Government and South Carolina to keep the peace.

3. General JACKSON was the man for the occasion ; and yet his action in the premises and his motives have been misunderstood.

a. He was opposed to high tariffs, and thus agreed with Southern men in regard to the cause of the difficulty.

b. He earnestly advised the repeal, or rather a modification of the tariff laws, which had created the difficulty. This he did repeatedly in his messages to Congress, and just before the ordinance was passed.

c. He claimed to be a native of South Carolina, and could, therefore, address the inhabitants of that State in a manner that would inspire confidence, in his endeavors to win them back into the Union. While he thus claims kindred with them, they would feel inclined to allow his claims, and yield to his persuasion.

Listen to his language of kindness which he addresses to them in his proclamation : " Fellow-citizens of my native State ! Let me not only admonish you, as the first magistrate of our common country, not to incur the penalty of its laws, but use the influence that a father would have over his children, whom he saw rushing to ruin. In that paternal language, with that paternal feeling, let me tell you, my countrymen, that you are deluded by the men who are either deceived themselves, or wish to deceive you."

d. He asked authority from Congress to use force, if it should be necessary, in the collection of duties in South Carolina. Congress gave him this authority, but it also passed the compromise bill, which would render the application of force unnecessary. He was resolute to execute the laws, even upon his native State, but he preferred a peaceful settlement of the difficulties, such as was accomplished by his own wisdom, and that of the very able men in the Cabinet, and in the Senate and House of Representatives.

4. Mr. CLAY must have been greatly disappointed in the result of the election of 1832; General JACKSON receiving 219 votes, and he only 49. Besides losing his election, which his friends hoped to carry by means of his " American system," he saw that the system itself was in danger. That system was made by his party one of the important issues in that election, and the decision of the Presidential electors seemed to be against that system as well as against himself. General JACKSON, too, in his recent message, had recommended an alteration of the tariff laws, a recommendation that would be very apt to take effect.

Moreover, Mr. CLAY, noble-spirited as he was, must have had some " compunctious visitings of nature," in view of the sectional difficulties which had been brought about by the introduction of his favorite system into the legislation of the country. He had left the Democratic party, of which he was an ornament, to form a party of his own, which had been successful in carrying his favorite measure, but which had not been successful in the late Presidential campaign. Self-reliant as he was, he could hardly fail to have some misgivings as to the wisdom of his course, which had helped to bring the country into its present perilous condition. He was, without doubt, anxious to settle the sectional difficulties in a way honorable to both sections.

When Mr. CLAY introduced his compromise bill for the settlement of these difficulties, he accompanied it with the declaration " that, whether rightfully or wrongfully, the tariff stands in imminent danger. If it should even be preserved during this session, it must fall at the next session."

In the course of his speech, he said: " I wish to see the tariff separated from the politics of the country, that business men may go to work in security, with some prospect of stability in our laws, and without every thing being staked on the issue of our elections, as it were on the hazards of the die."

In reference to the state of sectional feeling for and against the tariff, he said : " I am anxious to find out some principle of mutual accommodation, to satisfy, as far as practicable, both parties; to increase the stability of our legislation; and, at some distant day, not too distant when we take into view the magnitude of the interests which are involved, to bring down the rate of duties to that revenue standard for which our opponents have so long contended."

Mr. Forsyth, of Georgia, in his reply to Mr. Clay, remarked : " The avowed object of the bill would meet with universal approbation. It was a project to harmonize the people, and it could come from no better source than from the gentleman from Kentucky ; for to no one else were we more indebted than to him, for the discord and the discontent which agitate us." " The Senator from Kentucky says the tariff is in danger : aye, sir, it is at its last gasp. It has received the irremediable wound ; no hellebore can cure it."

Mr. John Davis, of Massachusetts, in the House of Representatives, said, in reference to this bill : " But I do object to a compromise which destines the East to the altar. No victim, in my judgment, is required—none is necessary ; and yet you propose to bind us hand and foot, to pour out our blood on the altar, and sacrifice us as a burnt-offering to appease the unnatural and unfounded discontent of the South—a discontent, I fear, having deeper root than the tariff, and will continue when that is forgotten."

5. Mr. Calhoun, like Mr. Clay, was worthy of the highest office in the gift of the nation, and, like him, he aspired after it. He was a leading member of the Democratic party, and had acted with Mr. Clay in promoting the war of 1812. To the " American system," which Mr. Clay had labored during three Presidential campaigns to establish, he was strongly opposed. He was an advocate of free trade, except for the purposes of a revenue, and was in favor of only incidental protection to manufactures. He enjoyed the confidence of the Democratic party, and, indeed, of the whole country, as an able statesman and an

honest man. It was predicted of him at an early period, that if he would bide his time, he would certainly be President of the United States.

But now in 1833, both he and Mr. CLAY seemed to be as far off as ever from the position they both coveted. They need not, therefore, now be jealous of each other. They were both patriots; they both hated General JACKSON; they were both willing to unite and save the country, and to thwart any military schemes for the subjugation of South Carolina. On the introduction of the compromise bill, Mr. CALHOUN said: "He who loved the Union must desire to see this great agitating question brought to a termination. Until it should be terminated, we could not expect the restoration of peace and harmony, or a sound condition of things throughout the country. He believed that to the unhappy divisions which had kept the Northern and Southern States apart from each other, the present entirely degraded condition of .the country was solely attributable."

To Mr. CLAY, and Mr. CALHOUN, and General JACKSON, it was principally owing that these sectional difficulties connected with the tariff were settled, and the land had rest for a time and a season.

It is a remarkable fact that Massachusetts, Connecticut, and Rhode Island, States that had great difficulties with the General Government, during the Administration of Mr. JEFFERSON and Mr. MADISON, on account of their commercial interests, as set forth in the doings of the Hartford Convention, did not give a single vote for the settlement of the sectional difficulties, by the passage of the compromise bill proposed by Mr. CLAY.

CHAPTER X.

Mr. Van Buren being regarded as a Northern man with Southern principles, was not elected upon sectional issues; though both before and after his election such issues were pressed upon the attention of the people, both North and South.

In the latter part of General Jackson's Administration, and while the politicians were looking out upon the country for available Presidential candidates, the subject of slavery was forced upon the attention of Congress, in the shape of petitions for the abolition of slavery in the District of Columbia.

One of these, signed by 800 ladies from the State of New York, was presented in the House of Representatives in February, 1835. And another in the same month was presented from Massachusetts, signed by 1,249 male citizens, and by 2,643 ladies. Petitions like these from different portions of the Northern States were pressed on the attention of both Houses of Congress for the space of four years, or until the session of Congress immediately before the next Presidential campaign. One of the last was presented by Mr. Clay, Feb. 13, 1840, as he said " in deference to the right of petition, which he admitted in its full force. He thought the crisis of this unfortunate agitation was passed; it was certainly passed when Congress convened in December last. Whether the political uses which have since been made of it may not revive it, and revive it in a more imposing form, he was not prepared to say." The abolition of slavery was provided for in this petition.

The ground taken in the petitions generally, was, that slavery is wrong or improper, and that as by Article 1st, section 8th, Congress has power "to exercise exclusive legislation in all cases whatsoever over the District of Columbia," it is bound to abolish slavery in the District. It was in Congress declared to be "the Great National Question."

The grounds of opposition to the abolition of slavery in the District of Columbia are the following: "The District was ceded, not to the United States, but to Congress, which can claim no rights of sovereignty, whatever the United States may: it was ceded by the ordinary Legislatures of Maryland and Virginia, which never pretended to sovereignty. We know that the sovereignty of each State resides in the people. The principle agreed on both hands, from which we are arguing, is, that Congress, in exclusive legislation over the territory, property, and people of this District, are competent to do in respect to territory, property, and people of this District, whatever the Legislatures of Maryland and Virginia are competent to do in respect to the territory, property, and people of those States respectively ; and (I add and insist) no more. Therefore, in order to show that Congress has Constitutional power to abolish the rights of slave property in this District, it must first be shown that the Legislatures of those two States have, and had, at the time of their cession, Constitutional power to abolish the rights of slave property within their limits.

"I can venture to say that the great body of the jurists of Virginia, as well as of the people, have always denied, and do yet deny, the Constitutional power of the ordinary Legislature to abolish the rights of slave property, without the consent of the individual owners. I do not know what opinion has been entertained in Maryland. I only know that the same reasoning is equally applicable to the legal institutions of both States.

"I presume it can hardly be imagined that Congress can have derived from the acts of cession of Maryland and Virginia, that is, by virtue of those acts alone, any other or greater powers of legislation over the District, than those Legislatures themselves had at the time of the cession ; in other words, that the grantee has acquired by the grant more power than the grantor had to cede."

"If the provision of the Constitution of the United States, giving power to Congress 'to exercise exclusive legislation, in all cases whatsoever, over such District as may, by the cession of particular States, and acceptance of Congress, become the seat of Government of the United States,' is to be taken as the only source and the only measure of the power of Congress; if this provision is to be construed as conferring on Congress absolute, sovereign, despotic authority over the people of the District, and their private rights of property, unlimited by the just measure of authority that belonged to the State Legislatures by which the territory was ceded, unlimited by any consideration of the nature, purposes, and exigencies of the trust for which the power of exclusive legislation was given, then it will follow that Congress may, in its wisdom, or in its folly, abolish property in lands as well as in slaves; may enact an agrarian law; nay, more, may abolish the principle of property entirely, and establish a community of goods. Now, certainly, I do not apprehend any such absurd and mischievous legislation; but it is fair, it is even necessary, to pursue this claim of power to its consequences in order to test its justice. The truth is, sir, that a grant of power of 'exclusive legislation in all cases whatsoever,' over a territory and the people in it, does not, in the just sense of that language, as used by American law-givers, import a grant of absolute, despotic, sovereign authority, or of any authority at all to assume, abolish, or impair private rights of property. It imports a grant of the power of ordinary legislation. The proper as well as ordinary business of legislation is to regulate and secure the rights of property, never to annihilate them."—*Speech of Mr. Leigh in the Senate*, Jan. 19, 1836.

PINCKNEY'S RESOLUTIONS.—HOUSE OF REPRESENTATIVES, MAY 25, 1836.

1. *Resolved*, That Congress possesses no Constitutional authority to interfere, in any way, with the institution of slavery in any of the States of this Confederacy; *passed by a vote of*

182 *to* 9; *of which* 6 *were from New England*, and 3 from Pennsylvania.

2. *Resolved*, That Congress ought not to interfere in any way with slavery in the District of Columbia; *passed by a vote of* 132 *yeas, and* 45 *nays. All the votes given by Massachusetts, Vermont, and Rhode Island, in the negative.*

And whereas it is extremely important and desirable that the agitation of this subject should be finally arrested, for the purpose of restoring tranquillity to the public mind, your committee respectfully recommend the adoption of the following resolution, viz. :

3. *Resolved*, That all petitions, memorials, resolutions, and papers, relating in any way, or to any extent whatever, to the subject of slavery or the abolition of slavery, shall, without being either printed or referred, be laid upon the table, and that no farther action whatever shall be had thereon.

This was passed by a vote of 117 to 68. All the votes given by Massachusetts, Vermont, and Rhode Island were in the negative.

VERMONT ANTI-SLAVERY RESOLUTIONS.—SENATE.

Mr. SWIFT, of Vermont, presented, Dec. 19, 1837, a memorial and resolutions from the Legislature of Vermont in relation to " Texas and slavery in the District of Columbia."

Mr. KING, of Alabama, said " he considered it an infamous libel and insult upon the South, let it come from what quarter it would; it was a false statement in relation to the people of the South, when it charged them with disregard for the laws, and he expressed his surprise that gentlemen should present papers which they could not but feel were untrue." The memorial was withdrawn for future presentation.

It was again presented January 16. Mr. SWIFT said " he would offer no other apology than the duty he owed to the State. The Resolutions spoke for themselves; nor did Vermont require him to vindicate them on this floor. He expressed his regret, however, that they should have been so harshly assailed as they had been. Not only the sentiments contained in them, but the motives of those who adopted them, had been subjects of unjust censure and reproach."

Mr. Preston, of South Carolina, "presumed the document would not have been presented unless under authority of command in obedience to higher power, where the servant could exercise no discretion. Coming from a sovereign State, we were, he presumed, bound to treat it with respect and deference. Here was a report wantonly presented, characterized by language which, if used by an individual or senator of this body, would be rejected with disdain. In it the South is charged with immorality and irreligion; and when with becoming dignity we repel the charge, we are 'uncourteous' and 'offensive' in our language; while we are stigmatized as debauched, sensual, immoral, sinful, God-offending creatures; and when we speak of fanatics and incendiaries, we are rebuked and chidden. Was this fair? Was this proper?"

HOUSE.—DECEMBER 20, 1837.

The most angry and portentous debate which had yet taken place in Congress occurred at this time in the House of Representatives. It was brought on by Mr. William Slade, of Vermont, who, besides presenting petitions of the usual abolition character, and moving to refer them to a committee, moved their reference to a select committee, with instructions to report a bill in conformity to their prayer. This motion, inflammatory and irritating in itself, and without practical legislative object, as the great majority of the House was known to be opposed to it, was rendered still more exasperating by the manner of supporting it. The mover entered into a general disquisition on the subject of slavery, all denunciatory, and was proceeding to speak upon it in the State of Virginia, and other States, in the same spirit, when Mr. Legare, of South Carolina, interposed, and—

"Hoped the gentleman from Vermont would allow him to make a few remarks before he proceeded further. He sincerely hoped that gentleman would consider well what he was about before he ventured on such ground, and that he would take time to consider what might be its probable consequences. He solemnly entreated him to reflect on the possible results of such a course, which involved the interests of a nation and a continent. He would warn him, not in the language of defiance, which all brave and wise men despised, but he would warn him in the language of a solemn sense of duty, that if there was ' a spirit aroused in the North in relation to this subject,' that spirit would encounter another spirit in the South full as stubborn. He would tell them that, when this question was forced upon the people of the South, they would be ready to take up the gauntlet. He concluded by urging on the gentleman from Vermont to ponder well on his course before he ventured to proceed."

Mr. SLADE continued his remarks, when Mr. DAWSON, of Georgia, asked him for the floor, that he might move an adjournment—evidently to carry off the storm which he saw rising. Mr. SLADE refused to yield it; so the motion to adjourn could not be made. Mr. SLADE continued, and was proceeding to answer his own inquiry, put to himself—*what was slavery ?* when Mr. DAWSON again asked for the floor, to make his motion of adjournment. Mr. SLADE refused it : a visible commotion began to pervade the House—members rising, clustering together, and talking with animation ; Mr. SLADE continued, and was about reading a judicial opinion in one of the Southern States which defined a slave to be a chattel, when Mr. WISE called him to order for speaking beside the question—the question being upon the abolition of slavery in the District of Columbia, and Mr. SLADE's remarks going to its legal character, as property in a State.

The Speaker, Mr. JOHN WHITE, of Kentucky, sustained the call, saying it was not in order to discuss the subject of slavery in any of the States. Mr. SLADE denied that he was doing so, and said he was merely quoting a Southern judicial decision as he might quote a legal opinion delivered in Great Britain. Mr. ROBERTSON, of Virginia, moved that the House adjourn. The Speaker pronounced the motion (and correctly) out of order, as the member from Vermont was in possession of the floor and addressing the House. He would, however, suggest to the member from Vermont, who could not but observe the state of the House, to confine himself strictly to the subject of his motion. Mr. SLADE went on at great length, when Mr. PETRIKIN, of Pennsylvania, called him to order; but the Chair did not

sustain the call. Mr. SLADE went on, quoting from the Declaration of Independence, and the Constitutions of the several
States, and had got to that of Virginia, when Mr. WISE called
him to order for reading papers without the leave of the House.
The Speaker decided that no paper objected to could be read
without the leave of the House. Mr. WISE then said :

" That the gentleman had wantonly discussed the abstract
question of slavery, going back to the very first day of the crea-
tion, instead of slavery as it existed in the District, and the
powers and duties of Congress in relation to it. He was now
examining the State Constitutions to show that as it existed in
the States it was against them, and against the laws of God and
man. This was out of order."

Mr. SLADE explained, and argued in vindication of his course,
and was about to read a memorial of Dr. FRANKLIN, and an
opinion of Mr. MADISON on the subject of slavery, when the
reading was objected to by Mr. GRIFFIN, of South Carolina ;
and the Speaker decided they could not be read without the
permission of the House. Mr. SLADE, without asking the permission of the House, which he knew would not be granted,
assumed to understand the prohibition as extending only to himself personally, said : " Then *I send them to the clerk ; let him
read them.*" The Speaker decided that this was equally against
the rule. Then Mr. GRIFFIN withdrew the objection, and Mr.
SLADE proceeded to read the papers, and to comment upon them
as he went on, and was about to go back to the State of Virginia, and show what had been the feeling there on the subject
of slavery previous to the date of Dr. FRANKLIN's memorial :

Mr. RHETT, of South Carolina, inquired of the Chair what
the opinions of Virginia fifty years ago had to do with the case ?
The Speaker was about to reply, when Mr. WISE rose with
warmth, and said : " He has discussed the whole abstract
question of slavery ; of slavery in my own district ; and I now
ask all my colleagues to retire with me from this hall." Mr.
SLADE reminded the Speaker that he had not yielded the floor :
but his progress was impeded by the condition of the House,
and the many exclamations of members, among whom Mr.
HALSEY, of Georgia, was heard calling on the Georgia delegation to withdraw with him ; and Mr. RHETT was heard pro-

claiming that the South Carolina members had already consulted together, and agreed to have a meeting at three o'clock
in the committee room of the District of Columbia. Here the
Speaker interposed to calm the House, standing up in his place
and saying:

"The gentleman from Vermont had been reminded by the
Chair that the discussion of slavery, as existing within the
States, was not in order; when he was desirous to read a paper
and it was objected to, the Chair had stopped him; but the
objection had been withdrawn, and Mr. Slade had been suffered
to proceed; he was now about to read another paper, and objection was made; the Chair would, therefore, take the question on permitting it to be read."

Many members rose, all addressing the Chair at the same
time, and many members leaving the hall, and a general scene
of noise and confusion prevailing. Mr. Rhett succeeded in
raising his voice above the roar of the tempest which raged in
the House, and invited the entire delegations from all the slave
States to retire from the hall forthwith, and meet in the committee room of the District of Columbia. The Speaker again
essayed to calm the House, and again standing up in his place,
he recapitulated his attempts to preserve order, and vindicated
the correctness of his own conduct, seemingly impugned by
many: "What his personal feelings were on the subject (he
was from a slave State) might easily be conjectured. He had
endeavored to enforce the rules. Had it been in his power to
restrain the discussion, he should promptly have exercised the
power; but it was not." Mr. Slade, continuing, said the paper
which he wished to read was of the Continental Congress of
1774. The Speaker was about to put the question on leave,
when Mr. Cost Johnson, of Maryland, inquired whether it
would be in order to force the House to vote that the member
from Vermont be not permitted to proceed? The Speaker
replied it would not. Then Mr. James J. McKay, of North
Carolina—a clear, cool-headed, sagacious man—interposed the
objection which headed Mr. Slade. There was a rule of the
House, that when a member was called to order he should take
his seat; and if decided to be out of order, he should not be
allowed to speak again, except on leave of the House. Mr.

McKay judged this to be a proper occasion for the enforcement of that rule; and stood up and said :

"That the gentleman had been pronounced out of order in discussing slavery in the States; and the rule declared that when a member was so pronounced by the Chair, he should take his seat, and if any one objected to his proceeding again, he should not do so unless by leave of the House. Mr. McKay did now object to the gentleman from Vermont proceeding any further."

Redoubled noise and confusion ensued, a crowd of members rising and speaking at once, who eventually yielded to the resounding blows of the Speaker's hammer upon the lid of his desk, and his apparent desire to read something to the House, as he held a book (recognized to be that of the rules) in his hand. Obtaining quiet so as to enable himself to be heard, he read the rule referred to by Mr. McKay; and said that, as objection had now for the first time been made under that rule to the gentleman's resuming his speech, the Chair decided that he could not do so without the leave of the House. Mr. SLADE attempted to go on : the Speaker directed him to take his seat until the question of leave should be put. Then Mr. SLADE, still keeping on his feet, asked leave to proceed as in order, saying he would not discuss slavery in Virginia. On that question, Mr. ALLEN, of Vermont, asked the yeas and nays. Mr. RENCHER, of North Carolina, moved an adjournment. Mr. ADAMS, and many others, demanded the yeas and nays on this motion, which were ordered, and resulted in 106 yeas and 63 nays—some fifty or sixty members having withdrawn. This opposition to adjournment was one of the worst features of that unhappy day's work; the only effect of keeping the House together being to increase irritation, and multiply the chances for an outbreak. From the beginning, Southern members had been in favor of it, and essayed to accomplish it, but were prevented by the tenacity with which Mr. SLADE kept possession of the floor; and now, at last, when it was time to adjourn any way —when the House was in a condition in which no good could be expected, and great harm might be apprehended, there were sixty-three members—being nearly one-third of the House— willing to continue it in session. They were :

9

"Messrs. Adams, Alexander, H. Allen, J. W. Allen, Ay-crigg, Bell, Biddle, Bond, Borden, Briggs, W. B. Calhoun, Coffin, Corwin, Cranston, Curtis, Cushing, Darlington, Davies, Dunn, Evans, Everett, Ewing, J. Fletcher, Fill-more, Goode, Grennell, Haley, Hall, Hastings, Henry, Herod, Hoffman, Lincoln, Marvin, S. Mason, Maxwell, McKennan, Milligan, M. Morris, C. Morris, Naylor, Noyes, Ogle, Parmenter, Patterson, Peck, Phillips, Potts, Potter, Rariden, Randolph, Reed, Ridgway, Russel, Sheffer, Sibley, Slade, Stratton, Tillinghast, Toland, A. S. White, J. White, E. Whittlesey—63.

"The House then stood adjourned; and as the adjournment was being pronounced, Mr. Campbell, of South Carolina, stood up on a chair, and calling for the attention of the members, said:

"He had been appointed, as one of the Southern delegation, to announce that all those gentlemen who represented slave-holding States, were invited to attend the meeting now being held in the District Committee room."

Members from the slaveholding States had repaired in large numbers to the room in the basement, where they were invited to meet. Various passions agitated them—some violent. Extreme propositions were suggested, of which Mr. Rhett, of South Carolina, in a letter to his constituents, gave a full account of his own—thus:

"In a private and friendly letter to the editor of the Charleston Mercury, amongst other events accompanying the memorable secession of the Southern members from the hall of the House of Representatives, I stated to him, that I had prepared two resolutions, drawn as amendments to the motion of the member from Vermont, whilst he was discussing the institution of slavery in the South, 'declaring that the Constitution having failed to protect the South in the peaceable possession and enjoyment of their rights and peculiar institutions, it was expedient that the Union should be dissolved; and the other, appointing a committee of two members from each State to report upon the best means of peaceably dissolving it.' They were intended as amendments to a motion, to refer with instructions to report a bill, abolishing slavery in the District of Columbia.

" I expected them to share the fate which inevitably awaited the original motion, so soon as the floor could have been obtained, viz., to be laid upon the table. My design in presenting them was to place before Congress and the people, what, in my opinion, was the true issue upon this great and vital question ; and to point out the course of policy by which it should be met by the Southern States.

" But extreme counsels did not prevail. There were members present who well considered that although the provocation was great, and the number voting for such a firebrand motion was deplorably large, yet it was but little more than the one-fourth of the House, and decidedly less than one-half of the members from the Free States ; so that, even if left to the Free State vote alone, the motion would have been rejected. But the motion itself, and the manner in which it was supported, was most reprehensible ; necessarily leading to disorder in the House, the destruction of its harmony and capacity for useful legislation, tending to a sectional segregation of the members, the alienation of feeling between the North and the South, and alarm to all the slaveholding States. The evil required a remedy, but not the remedy of breaking up the Union ; but one which might prevent the like in future, while administering a rebuke upon the past. That remedy was found in adopting a proposition to be offered to the House, which, if agreed to, would close the door against any discussion upon abolition petitions in future, and assimilate the proceedings of the House in that particular to those of the Senate. This proposition was put into the hands of Mr. PATTON, of Virginia, to be offered as an amendment to the rules at the opening of the House the next morning. It was in these words :

" 'Resolved, That all petitions, memorials, and papers, touching the abolition of slavery, or the buying, selling, or transferring of slaves in any State, District, or Territory of the United States, be laid on the table, without being debated, printed, read, or referred, and that no further action whatever shall be had thereon.'

" Accordingly, at the opening of the House, Mr. PATTON asked leave to submit the resolution, which was read for information. Mr. ADAMS objected to the grant of leave. Mr.

PATTON then moved a suspension of the rules, which motion required two-thirds to sustain it; and, unless obtained, this salutary remedy for an alarming evil (which was already in force in the Senate) could not be offered. It was a test motion, and on which the opponents of abolition agitation in the House required all their strength; for, unless two to one, they were defeated. Happily, the two to one were ready, and on taking the yeas and nays, demanded by an abolition member, (to keep his friends to the track, and to hold the free State anti-abolitionists to their responsibility at home,) the result stood 135 yeas to 60 nays; the full two-thirds and fifteen over."—BENTON's *Thirty Years' View*, vol. ii., p. 150.

MR. CALHOUN'S RESOLUTIONS—FRIDAY, JANUARY 12, 1838.

1. *Resolved*, That, in the adoption of the Federal Constitution, the States adopting the same acted, severally, as free, independent, and sovereign States; and that each for itself, by its own voluntary assent, entered the Union with the view to its increased security against all dangers, *domestic* as well as foreign, and the more perfect and secure enjoyment of its advantages—natural, political, and social.

2. *Resolved*, That, in delegating a portion of their powers to be exercised by the Federal Government, the States retained, severally, the exclusive and sole right over their own domestic institutions and police, to the full extent to which those powers were not thus delegated, and are alone responsible for them; and that any intermeddling of any one or more States, or a combination of their citizens, with the domestic institutions and police of the others, on any ground, political, moral, or religious, or under any pretext whatever, with the view to their alteration or subversion, is not warranted by the Constitution, tending to endanger the domestic peace and tranquillity of the States interfered with, subversive of the objects for which the Constitution was formed, and, by necessary consequence, tending to weaken and destroy the Union itself.

3. *Resolved*, That this Government was instituted and adopted by the several States of this Union as a common agent, in order to carry into effect the powers which they had dele-

gated by the Constitution for their mutual security and prosperity, and that, in fulfilment of this high and sacred trust, this Government is bound so to exercise its powers, as not to interfere with the stability and security of the domestic institutions of the States that compose the Union ; and that it is the solemn duty of the Government to resist, to the extent of its constitutional power, all attempts by one portion of the Union to use it as an instrument to attack the domestic institutions of another, or to weaken or destroy such institutions.

4. *Resolved*, That domestic slavery, as it exists in the Southern and Western States of this Union, composes an important part of their domestic institutions, inherited from their ancestors, and existing at the adoption of the Constitution, by which it is recognized as constituting an important element in the apportionment of powers among the States, and that no change of opinion or feeling on the part of the other States of the Union in relation to it, can justify them or their citizens in open and systematic attacks thereon, with the view to its overthrow ; and that all such attacks are in manifest violation of the mutual and solemn pledge to protect and defend each other, given by the States respectively, on entering into the Constitutional compact which formed the Union, and as such are a manifest breach of faith, and a violation of the most solemn obligations.

5. *Resolved*, That the interference by the citizens of any of the States, with the view to the abolition of slavery in this District, is endangering the rights and security of the people of the District, and that any act or measure of Congress designed to abolish slavery in this District, would be a violation of the faith implied in the cessions by the States of Virginia and Maryland, a just cause of alarm to the people of the. slaveholding States, and have a direct and inevitable tendency to disturb and endanger the Union.

6. *And Resolved*, That any attempt of Congress to abolish slavery in any Territory of the United States in which it exists, would create serious alarm and just apprehension in the States sustaining that domestic institution ; would be a violation of good faith towards the inhabitants of any such Territory who have been permitted to settle with, and hold slaves therein, because the people of any such Territory have not asked for the

abolition of slavery therein, and because, when any such Territory shall be admitted into the Union as a State, the people thereof will be entitled to decide that question exclusively for themselves.

The final vote upon the adoption of these resolutions, was :

YEAS—Messrs. ALLEN, BAYARD, BENTON, BLACK, BROWN, BUCHANAN, CALHOUN, CLAY of Alabama, CLAY of Ky., CRITTENDEN, CUTHBERT, FULTON, GRUNDY, HUBBARD, KING, LUMPKIN, LYON, MERRICK, NICHOLAS, NILES, NORVELL, PIERCE, PRESTON, RIVES, ROANE, ROBINSON, SEVIER, SMITH of Connecticut, STRANGE, TIPTON, WALKER, WHITE, WILLIAMS, WRIGHT, YOUNG—35.

NAYS—Messrs. CLAYTON, of Delaware, DAVIS, KNIGHT, McKEAN, of Pennsylvania, PRENTISS, ROBBINS, SMITH, of Indiana, SWIFT, and WEBSTER—9.

Massachusetts, Vermont, and Rhode Island were the only States that voted in the negative.

REMARKS.

1. At the period of which this chapter treats, the sentiments of the people in the several Northern States had undergone a great change on the subject of slavery, since the formation of the Federal Constitution, and especially since the Declaration of Independence. While the people of those States possessed slaves, they could form an estimate of the advantages and disadvantages, the rectitude or the impropriety of slavery, from their own observation of its practical workings. Before the American Revolution, some of the best Christians in the Northern section owned slaves, as now some of the best Christians at the South do. Slavery was sanctioned by the British Government, and by the Colonial Legislatures ; by statesmen and by clergymen. The relations of " superiors, inferiors, and equals," and the correlative duties of masters and servants were recognized, not only in catechisms, but in the public instructions of the sanctuary. In 1749, the celebrated WHITEFIELD thus wrote: " One negro has been given me ; some more I propose to purchase this week." " This confirms me in the opinion that Georgia never can be a flourishing province, without negroes are allowed."

But at this period in Vermont, and in Massachusetts, where it had ceased to exist for nearly sixty years or for two generations, and in other Northern States, there were those who believed that they understood the subject of slavery better than those in the Southern States who had seen its practical workings.

2. There were at the time several classes of abolitionists, who urged Congress to emancipate the slaves in the District of Columbia:

a. Those who were under the influence of a generous, yet unreflecting philanthropy, and who, from their disregard of constitutional rights and obligations, were characterized as having " hearts larger than their heads."

b. Those who believed that the Constitution authorized the abolition of slavery in the District of Columbia, and who felt disposed to use all constitutionl means to abolish slavery throughout the land.

c. Those who would free the slaves on the ground of natural rights as stated in the Declaration of Independence, which they placed on a level with the Constitution, or above it. Such declared that the " Federal Constitution has neither any moral nor political right to tolerate slavery in any of the States belonging to the Federal Union, for a single day."

d. Those who, from a real or a pretended regard for the right of petition, signed petitions to vindicate that right; while they professed to care very little about the object petitioned for.

e. Those who wished to promote political agitation for party purposes.

f. Those who hated slavery and slaveholders ; and who, by memorials and petitions, could vent their wrath in the language of vituperation.

Petitioning was the fashion of the times in some of the States. JOHN QUINCY ADAMS, the champion of the North, declared on one occasion in Congress, that he had before him 350 petitions on which were from 34,000 to 35,000 names.

3. In opposition to these petitions and memorials, it was said in Congress and elsewhere :

a. That they were an abuse of the right granted by the Constitution " peaceably to assemble and petition for the redress of grievances," viz., their own grievances. Slavery was no new thing, but the existence of slavery as an institution recognized by the Constitution, and the right of property in slaves as recognized in the Constitution, is not a grievance under the Constitution to the people of Vermont. "The oppressed subject has a right to petition Government for the redress of grievances." But the existence of slavery in the District of Columbia is not a grievance to the people of Vermont; but the abolition of slavery, in opposition to the wishes of slaveholders in the District of Columbia, would be a grievance to them. In the early days of the Republic, the existence of slavery in the South was not thought of as a " grievance."

b. That a petition for a general object like that is impertinent, inasmuch as Congress is better acquainted with the subject than the men, women, and children, who have never been in the District. Such a petition implies that Congress will not attend to its duties without admonition.

c. That the arguments used against slavery in the District of Columbia are covertly or openly intended to operate against slavery elsewhere; and that the abolition of slavery in the District would be the entering wedge to the abolition of slavery in the States, as soon as Congress could get the power, by altering the Constitution.

d. That the arguments or denunciations against slavery have the effect to create prejudice against slaveholders and slaveholding States.

e. That some of these petitions contain falsehoods, and slanders, and insulting statements, concerning slaveholders, and are therefore adapted to produce a spirit of disunion.

f. That some of the petitions were got up in order to place certain members of Congress in the awkward position of presenting petitions to which they were opposed.

4. At the first presentation of these petitions in Congress, the general sentiment in both Houses was opposed to them, as was the sentiment of the great Northern community Abolitionists were regarded with distrust or abhorrence. But in time antislavery sentiments so far prevailed, that candidates found an appeal to sectional feelings an effectual way to secure an elec-

tion. And after they had secured an election by such an appeal, they felt themselves obliged to carry out in Congress the principles upon which they were elected.

5. In Congress, there was a great diversity of opinion as to what course should be taken with those petitions:

a. Some of the petitions were received and reported on adversely without producing any beneficial effect, or lessening the number of petitions.—*See Mr. Rives' speech, Dec.* 1837.

b. Some of them were received and laid on the table.

c. Some of them were disposed of by a motion to lay the question of reception on the table.

None of these modes satisfied the anti-slavery views of the Northern delegations in Congress; and many even of the members who were opposed to the prayer of the petitioners, were disposed to complain that the right of petition was restricted by the latter course.

6. In February, Mr. John Quincy Adams, who, like some others in or out of the House, was disposed to magnify the right of petition above some other rights, presented a petition from " some ladies in Fredericksburg, Virginia," of whom Mr. Patton, member from that place, declared that he believed all of them to be free negroes of a bad character. Mr. Adams also tendered a petition from twenty-two persons, who declared themselves to be slaves. And (June, 1838) he referred to his tendering such a petition. This act of his was severely condemned by individuals in the House. He escaped a vote of censure which was threatened. But the House voted " That slaves do not possess the right of petition, secured to the people of the United States by the Constitution." The vote was 162 in the affirmative and 18 in the negative.

7. A portion of the multitude of petitions offered during the Administration of Mr. Van Buren, were got up at the instigation of members of Congress, who for one reason and another took pleasure in presenting them. It was supposed that Mr. Adams, under the influence of a deep resentment against the South, took a pleasure in presenting petitions for objects for which he himself would not vote.

While the abolitionists were thus spreading their arguments and denunciations against slavery before the representatives of the nation at Washington, and also before the State Legislatures at the North, they were sending *incendiary publications* through the Southern States by mail and otherwise. As these publications sprang from bitter sectional feelings at the North, so they created bitter sectional feelings at the South. President JACK-SON, in his message, Dec. 1835, thus introduced the subject to the notice of Congress : "I must also invite your attention to the painful excitement produced in the South, by attempts to circulate through the mails inflammatory appeals addressed to the passions of the slaves, in prints and in various publications calculated to stimulate them to insurrection, and to produce all the horrors of a civil war."

The effect of these petitions signed by hundreds of thousands of petitioners was disastrous in producing a bitter sectional spirit throughout the country.

In justice to the North it ought to be added, that some of the ablest and best men in that section were utterly opposed to the movement, as wrong in the end aimed at, wrong in the means used, and wrong in the spirit with which it was conducted. And some of them took the ground that they were wrong as a violation of the principles of international law which ought to control the several States in their relations to each other as sovereignties.

There were those who felt that the abolition societies in the several States ought to be suppressed by State authority. They had the same opinion of them which General WASHINGTON expressed concerning the self-constituted societies in 1794. They considered their influence upon the country through their lectures and publications as malign.

CHAPTER XI.

GENERAL HARRISON was elected by the Whig party, and by the votes of Northern States. There was a wide-spread enthusiasm in his favor, created, it was said, to some extent, by log cabins, coon-skins, hard cider, and the influence of banks. So strong were the party feelings, that sectional considerations were, for the time, ignored. Both General HARRISON and Mr. TYLER were natives of Virginia. On the death of the former, about a month after his inauguration, the latter constitutionally became President.

During his administration, sectional differences of opinion manifested themselves both in Congress and in the country at large. The bankrupt bill, an increase of the tariff, the distribution of the proceeds of the public lands, the establishment of a national bank, the repeal of the sub-treasury, were generally favored by Northern members and opposed by Southern.

ANNEXATION OF TEXAS.

But the principal source of sectional feeling during the administration of President TYLER, was the annexation of Texas, of which he was strongly in favor. Texas had belonged to the United States from 1803, when Louisiana was ceded, until 1819, when, by a great political mistake, it was dismembered from the United States, and attached to Mexico. The people of Texas were in favor of annexation. It would add to the strength of the United States, and give them, with some exceptions, the monopoly of the cotton trade of the world. It would help to keep the slave States on an equality with the non-slave States. It would prevent the existence of a dangerous rival on our borders, who might make treaties with Great Britain to our injury. Mr. ADAMS, when President, aided by Mr. CLAY, Secretary of State, in 1825, and then again in 1827, endeavored to secure the annexation of Texas. General JACKSON, aided by Mr. VAN BUREN, Secretary of State, in 1829; and again in 1833, aided by his Secretary of State, Mr. LIVINGSTON; and again in 1835, aided by his Secretary of State, Mr. FORSYTH, endeavored to secure the annexation of Texas. For this purpose he offered five millions of dollars. It would be of great commercial advantage to the Union, which otherwise a foreign nation would enjoy. The sentiment of the country, taken as a whole, was in favor of annexation.

In opposition, it was asserted that the measure was unconstitutional; that it would involve the country in war with Mexico; that it would increase the slave population of the country. JOHN QUINCY ADAMS declared in substance that, if Texas were free from slavery, and the consent of Mexico were obtained, he would vote for the annexation.

So high did sectional feeling rise while the question was pending, that, in some of the Southern States, the motto was "Texas or disunion;" while, in some of the Northern States, tens of thousands of names were affixed to petitions against the measure. In Massachusetts, so strong was the opposition, that the Senate passed a resolution censuring their Senators in Congress, Messrs. BATES and CHOATE. Indeed, the spirit manifested in that State came up to the measure of the spirit of disunion on the purchase and admission of Louisiana.

The annexation of Texas was a measure properly belonging to Mr. TYLER's administration, though it was not completed until Mr. POLK was in the Presidential chair, December 16, 1845. The final vote in the Senate was 31 in favor, 14 against; and in the House, 141 in favor and 56 against.

On February 5, 1844, Mr. BEARDSLEY, of New York, presented a petition from sundry citizens of New York, praying for an amendment to the Constitution, so as to effect the abolition of slavery in the Southern States. Mr. ADAMS presented the resolutions of the Legislature of Massachusetts, "asking for an amendment to the Constitution, so as to exclude that portion of the representation of the Southern States which is based on their slave population." In the Senate, Mr. BATES presented the same resolves of the Massachusetts Legislature. The Senate refused to print them..

March 22, 1844.—" Mr. DROMGOOLE, of Virginia, from the select committee on the resolutions of the Legislatures of Virginia and Alabama on the proposed amendment to the Constitution so as to prevent slave representation, which was suggested by resolutions from the Legislature of Massachusetts, made a report, accompanied by several resolutions, on which he called for the yeas and nays, and demanded the previous question."

"*Resolved by the House of Representatives of the United States*, That the rule established in the Constitution as the basis of representation and direct taxation, resulting from a spirit of concession and compromise essential to the formation and preservation of the Union of the States, ought to be held sacred by the friends of the Union." This resolution passed by 158 yeas, 18 nays.

" *Resolved*, That no proposition to alter or amend the Constitution, in relation to representation or direct taxation among the States, ought to be recommended by Congress, but that every such proposition ought to be promptly and decisively condemned." This resolve was passed by a vote of 127 yeas, 41 nays.

In the preamble to the report, the committee say : " This proposition (of Massachusetts) is strongly and unanimously condemned by the General Assembly of Virginia, and is regarded, in truth, as a proposition virtually to dissolve the Union. The committee, believing that the basis of representation and direct taxation, as regulated in the Constitution, was the result of a spirit of concession and compromise which was indispensable to the Union of the States, and to the formation and ratification of that Constitution as ordained and established, are of opinion that the proposed alteration of the compromise would produce a peaceable or violent dissolution of the Union."

REMARKS.

1. After the election of General HARRISON, and during the next four years, petitions for the abolition of slavery in the Dis-

trict of Columbia became comparatively infrequent. Why was this? Was it because the public sensibility had become impaired by being so long wrought upon? Or was it because the anti-slavery leaders in the agitation found a more exciting topic in Texas? Or was it because the Whigs, in Congress and out of Congress, having by the election come into power, no longer found agitation desirable? Mr. CLAY was not in favor of anti-slavery agitation, though some of his party had been.

2. The persistent opposition to the annexation of Texas sprang from opposition to slavery, and the opposition to slavery was, to a greater or less extent, owing to a reluctance to increasing the political power of the Southern section of the country.

3. The resolution of the Massachusetts Legislature, instructing their Senators, and requesting the representatives of that State to vote for such an amendment of the Constitution as will allow only free persons to be represented, or, in other words, to abrogate slave representation, excited deep dissatisfaction in Congress.

Mr. KING, of the Senate, said : " He could not but regret that it had become the duty of the honorable Senator from Massachusetts (Mr. BATES) to present to the Senate a proposition from the Legislature of his State to dissolve the Union. Was there a man within the hearing of his voice that believed, for one moment, that such an amendment could be made? and if it could be, by any possibility, that the Federal Government would last twenty-four hours after it was made? It is a resolution framed almost identically like that which had been concocted by inhabitants of Massachusetts, in another period in the history of this Government. It is such as was during the last war passed by the Hartford Convention. * * That the General Assembly of Massachusetts should take up one of these resolutions, after so many attempts to explain them away, and get clear of the odium connected with them, and to adopt its very words, showed a feeling of hostility to an institution which, if persisted in, was calculated to sap the very foundations of the Government itself."

CHAPTER XII.

MR. POLK was elected President by 170 electoral votes, against 105 cast for Mr. CLAY. The Southern States generally voted for the former. He was in favor of a strict construction of the Constitution in opposition to one that is broad or loose. In his inaugural address, he spoke in the following terms on that point: " It will be my first care to administer the Government in the true spirit of that instrument, and to assume no powers not expressly or clearly implied in its terms. The Government of the United States is one of delegated and limited powers; and it is by a strict adherence to the clearly granted powers, and by abstaining from the exercise of doubtful or unauthorized implied powers, that we have the only sure guarantee against the recurrence of those unfortunate collisions between the Federal and State authorities which have, occasionally, so much disturbed the harmony of our system, and even threatened the perpetuity of our glorious Union." " One great object of the Constitution was to restrain majorities from oppressing minorities, or encroaching on their just rights. Minorities have a right to appeal to the Constitution, as a shield against such oppression."

THE TARIFF OF 1846.

The compromise tariff of 1833, according to the provisions of the bill, continued in operation until 1841. In that year the *Home League* was formed, with the same object in view as the

Harrisburg Convention, namely, restoring high duties. The doctrines of the Home League were approved by Mr. Clay and his political friends. A bill was brought in, which passed in 1842. This bill was denounced by Mr. Calhoun. In his speech he said: "I shall not dwell on the fact that it openly violates the compromise act, and the pledges given by its author and by Governor Davis of Massachusetts, that if the South would adhere to the compromise, while it was operating favorably for the manufacturers, they would stand by it when it came to operate favorably for the South. I dwell not on those double breaches of plighted faith, although they are of a serious character, and likely to exercise a very pernicious influence over our future legislation, by preventing amicable adjustments of questions that may hereafter threaten the peace of the country." Mr. McDuffie characterized the tariff law of 1842 as "a foul and faithless violation of the compromise act." Mr. Clay and the manufacturers defended the measures as necessary to supply the wants of Government, which they regarded as paramount to other considerations.

In his message, Dec., 1845, President Polk recommended a revision of the Tariff laws. He declared that "the object of imposing duties on imports should be to raise a revenue to pay the necessary expenses of the Government. Congress may, undoubtedly, in the exercise of a sound discretion, discriminate in arranging the rates of duty on different articles; but the discriminations should be within the revenue standard, and be made with the view to raise money for the support of Government." "The new Administration proposed three important measures in relation to the duties: The first to abandon the protective theory in favor of a revenue theory, that is, to reduce the rates of duty, to levy them ad valorem, to make the rates uniform, and to make them payable in cash; the warehouse system to facilitate the carrying trade; and the Independent treasury, by which the cash duties were to be collected in gold and silver only." The Secretary of the Treasury, Robert J. Walker, made an elaborate report, recommending a *revenue* tariff in opposition to a *protective* tariff. A bill was introduced of such a character, and was passed in the House, July 2, 1846, by 114 votes in the affirmative, and 95 in the negative; and in the Senate by a vote of 28 in the affirmative, and 27 in the negative. The strength of the South, in both Houses, was in the affirmative, and the strength of the North in the negative.

This change in the tariff was advocated by the Southern members upon constitutional grounds, namely, that it was a change from a tariff for protection which is not authorized by the Constitution, unless that protection is incidental, to a tariff for revision which is the legitimate object of a tariff, and is authorized by the Constitution.

It was opposed by Northern men on the ground, that substantive protection had become the policy of the Government ; and, also, because the tariff of 1846 could not be reasonably expected to produce as large a revenue as the tariff of 1842. Experience proved that the Northern members were mistaken. The average of the tariff of 1842 was twenty-six millions ; the average of the tariff of 1846 was forty-six millions. As an apology for the failure of Northern predictions, it should be said that the unexpected gold discoveries in California averaged at once the exports and the imports, and thus the revenue.

Mr. WEBSTER, in the course of his speech in opposition to the bill, said : "It is not a bill for the people. It is not a bill for the masses. It is not a bill to add to the comfort of those in middle life, or the poor. It is not a bill for employment. It is a bill for the relief of the highest and most luxurious classes of the country, and a bill imposing onerous duties on the great industrial masses, and taking away the means of living from labor, everywhere throughout the land."

Mr. McDUFFIE, in reply said : "The strong language of the Senator from Massachusetts, in characterizing this bill as an aristocratic measure, imposes upon me the duty of saying a few words before the question is taken, to disabuse the public mind of any such impression, if any such impression is made upon it. The honorable Senator has asked, with great confidence, and certainly not in the expectation of being replied to, where is the Democratic feature of this bill ? Where is the provision intended to operate in favor of the laboring classes of the country ? On the contrary he goes on to enumerate certain articles of luxury upon which the duties have been reduced, and leaving it to be inferred that these are the great and principal reduc-

10

tions. Now, Mr. President, I will point out to the Senator the Democratic features of this bill. It has reduced the duty upon salt from eight cents to half a cent. It has reduced the duty upon sugar from two and a half cents to one cent per pound. It has reduced the duty on all that class of cotton manufactures, whether white or printed, which is consumed by the laborers, farmers, and mechanics of the United States, God knows how much! But I sincerely believe that in this bill, on all that class of manufactures consumed by the poor and middle ranks, there is a reduction of duties greater than on any other class of articles contained in the bill ; and I have expressed the opinion, which I sincerely believe, that the repeal of the cotton minimums—an invention which never was known until it was introduced in the bill of 1816, and, I believe, unknown to the custom house laws of any other country, so far as my knowledge extends—I believe that the striking out of that will alone enable the people of the United States to consume an increase importation approaching to ten millions of dollars at prices little more than two-thirds of that which they have now to pay.

I was obliged to the Senator from Massachusetts for some little evidence in favor of the Democratic character of this bill, in certain resolutions passed in Boston, in the year 1820, drawn up, I believe, by the honorable member himself, and supported and sustained by him soon after the commencement of the spirit which has resulted in the establishment of the protective system. The duties then under the act of 1816 were about 20 per cent. or 25 per cent. on the great mass of manufactures made out of cotton, wool, and iron, and all the other duties were corresponding. The proposition was then to enhance the duties in about the degree of enhancement which took place under the tariff of 1824 ; and it was in opposition to this, that a meeting of the merchants of Boston, in which the honorable Senator from Massachusetts bore a distinguished part, passed certain resolutions some of which I now recollect. One of them I distinctly remember, and it affirmed that the effect of this protecting law upon the manufactures of the country would redound to the benefit of great capitalists, and not to that of the labor of the country. That was a great political proposition.

Mr. WEBSTER. Does the Senator happen to have those resolutions in his desk? I have no recollection of that.

Mr. McDUFFIE. I am sorry to say that I have not got a copy of the resolutions, but I believe a copy can be obtained.

Mr. WESTCOTT here laid on the desk of the Senator from South Carolina a file of the "Globe," which was supposed to contain the resolutions referred to.

Mr. WEBSTER. I do not wish to trouble the gentleman now: at his convenience, perhaps, he may be able to furnish the resolutions.

Mr. McDUFFIE proceeded. This, sir, was one of the resolutions. Another was in answer to the allegation that the establishment of these factories would give an increased market to the farmer. One of these resolutions was in these words as far as I can recollect:

"They cannot perceive how the farming interest can be benefited by a law which increases the price of every thing that they have to buy, and diminishes the price of every thing they have to sell."

Now, sir, I quote this resolution simply with the view and for no other purpose than to answer a very confident interrogatory of the Senator—where is the Democratic feature of this measure?

But, Mr President, I did not intend to make a speech, and I will not do so. As, however, the Boston Resolutions to which I referred have been handed to me since I alluded to them, I will ask the Clerk to read them. [The Clerk read the resolutions.] I want to say one word (Mr. McD. added) on this subject of the revenue. I had very strong views on that subject, but my desire to see the vote taken led me to refrain from presenting them to the Senate, and so prolonging the discussion. I will take the article of wool, and present a view which seems to be entirely overlooked. He then went on to show that of woollens and cottons, the increase of importation would be very great under the new law, and the revenue be correspondingly augmented. The amount of increase from the destruction of the minimums it was impossible to calculate.

Mr. WEBSTER rose and said: The resolution read cannot be the one referred to by the Senator. I remember that meeting in Faneuil Hall. I dare say that may be the regular account of the proceedings. If it be it cannot be the full account, because there was another resolution passed at the same time to which my attention has been frequently since called in the Senate, and which has not been read in that series of resolutions. However, I attended a meeting. Whether I drew the resolutions or assented to them I do not know. Whether I made a speech on the occasion I cannot tell. But I yield it all to the honorable member. Consider me as having drawn every word of these resolutions, and as having urged their adoption upon the people assembled. Suppose that to be any way. The first thing I have got to say now is, that the honorable member from South Carolina will admit that such is the infirmity of our nature that an honest man may change his opinion, and he may change it in two or three as well as in twenty years. I think the most powerful argument ever addressed to the people of the United States against the annexation of Texas was from the Governor of South Carolina; and I think the greatest speech in favor of it was made by the Senator from South Carolina—*eandem personam !*

Mr. McDuffie. Texas was then an independent State and so recognized.

Mr. Webster. Yes, and I quote it for the purpose of showing that an honest man may change his opinion. Well, sir, I believe that the honorable member from South Carolina was, at the time I had the honor of being associated with him in the House of Representatives, a most powerful advocate of internal improvements, and raised his voice in favor of that principle.

Mr. McDuffie. Not in favor of the exercise-power.

Mr. Webster. Was the power then to be barren?

Mr. McDuffie. Only to make surveys.

Mr. Webster. Why that was the first step. He that can make a survey for improvements, can make improvements. I believe the honorable gentleman also at one time entertained a very favorable opinion of the Bank of the United States, and at another time quite the contrary. Well, then, I stand before the Senate as a man who has found occasion to change his opinions.

Mr. McDuffie. I made no unkind imputation.

Mr. WEBSTER. Certainly not. A word, sir, about these resolutions of 1821. I remember the state of things very well. The commercial people of New England, in 1821, were in a considerable state of alarm. They had commerce all over the world. They thought that a policy had been begun at Washington which would interfere with their commerce, and it was of that, that they were afraid. How was this great evil, of which they had become afraid, fastened upon them? By the minimums put upon them by South Carolina to cut off the New England India trade—that's all. The minimum principle, so odious now, was moved in Congress by a most respectable and distinguished member from South Carolina not now living. It was carried by South Carolina against every vote of Massachusetts. I do not think there was a vote of Massachusetts, not one in favor of the measure. Well, then, it is not because the minimum principle is bad in itself. Why, sir, minimum is now spoken of here as if it were a Pawnee Indian, or one of the Camanches that eats up and destroys everybody and every thing.

Mr. McDUFFIE. So it does!

Mr. WEBSTER. Well, bad as it is, it was introduced by South Carolina against every vote of Massachusetts. We all now see that the Senator from South Carolina is against it. Well, then, in 1820 or thereabouts, an eminent member of Congress from Pennsylvania introduced a high protective tariff bearing among certain other things especially upon iron. I refer to Mr. BALDWIN, afterwards judge of the Supreme Court. That tariff went to protect every thing out of New England. Well, here was New England between the upper and nether mill-stone; between the South Carolina tariff with its minimums on cottons which cut off the India trade, and the Pennsylvania tariff. I wish the gentleman had dwelt a little more, in his address to the Chair, on the effect of this bill upon the iron and coal of Pennsylvania. But now, sir, I agree, that whether it be owing to change of opinion wrought by circumstances, by a change in the condition of things in the country, or otherwise, I am of opinion that in the present state of things which has existed since 1824, there is no going back from that principle of protection which was established in 1824. The law of 1824 did not pass with the consent of Massachusetts. It received but one vote, I think, in the entire delegation from Massachusetts in both Houses of Congress. As I said the other day, New England had been addicted to commerce. But she supposed the time had come, when she must conform herself to the law of the country and invest her capital—for her labor was her capital—and direct her industry to such pursuits as the country had promised to protect and uphold. Now, sir, if there be any thing inconsistent in that, I admit the inconsistency —take it in the broadest sense and I agree to every word of the resolution of Faneuil Hall of 1821. In the present state of things there is an essential importance—an absolute moral necessity for maintaining those habits, pursuits, business, and employments, into which men entered twenty-two years ago, upon the faith of the declared sentiments and policy of a majority of both Houses of Congress.

OREGON TERRITORY.

August 11, 1848.—Mr. DOUGLAS, of the Committee on Territories, moved to amend the Oregon territorial bill, by extending the line of 36° 30′, agreed upon in the Missouri Compromise, to the Pacific Ocean, and thus settle the slavery question in respect to territories. The vote in the Senate in favor of this amendment was 33, against it 21. Those in the negative were: ALLEN and CORWIN of Ohio, ATHERTON and HALE of New Hampshire, BALDWIN and NILES of Connecticut, BRADBURY and HAMLIN of Maine, BROWN of Illinois, CLARKE and GREENE of Rhode Island, DAVIS and WEBSTER of Massachusetts, DAYTON and WELLS of New Jersey, DIX of New York, DODGE of Iowa, FETCH of Michigan, PHELPS and UPHAM of Vermont, WALKER of Wisconsin.

In the House, this amendment was rejected by a vote of 121 against, and 82 in favor. Northern members refused to carry out the Missouri Compromise in its application to territories lying west of Missouri. This is an historical fact of great significance in its relation to the repeal of the Missouri Compromise.

THE WILMOT PROVISO.

To a bill, proposed by Mr. McKay, of North Carolina, for making peace with Mexico, introduced into the House of Rep resentatives, August 8, 1846, Mr. DAVID WILMOT, of Pennsylvania, proposed the following amendment: *provided*, "That as an express and fundamental condition to the acquisition of any territory from the Republic of Mexico by the United States, by virtue of any treaty which may be negotiated between them, and to the use by the Executive of the moneys herein appropriated, neither slavery nor involuntary servitude shall ever exist in any part of said territory, except for crime, whereof the party shall first be duly convicted."

Mr. WICK moved to amend the amendment by inserting therein, after the word " territory," the words, " north of 36° 30' north latitude."

The amendment to the amendment was disagreed to—ayes 54, noes 89.

The question then recurring on the original amendment of Mr. WILMOT, it was decided in the affirmative—ayes 83, noes 64.

This amendment, with some modifications, came up for consideration in the House, March 3, 1847. It was rejected by a vote of 97 in favor, and 102 against the proviso. The votes of the New England States were in favor of the proviso; the votes of the Southern States were opposed to the proviso.

REMARKS.

1. As Northern views prevailed in Congress, during the Administration of General HARRISON and Mr. TYLER; so Southern views prevailed in regard to political principles and policy during the Administration of Mr. POLK.

2. Mr. VAN BUREN expected the nomination to the Presidency from the Democratic party in 1844, but failed of receiving it on account of his declared opposition to the immediate annexation of Texas, which prevented his receiving the votes of Southern delegates in the Convention. Mr. CLAY, for the same reason, failed of his election. He neither satisfied the South, nor all the free soilers of the North, by his letters in respect to Texas.

3. The adoption of the Wilmot proviso in the House on its first introduction, alarmed and wounded the South. This attempt to exclude Southern men and Southern institutions from

the territories which were won by the common blood and the common treasure of the States, created a deep sense of injury in the hearts of Southern people. On the other hand, the legislatures of several Northern States passed resolves approving of the proviso, while the Northern press and Northern speech-makers were clamorous in its favor, and, to some extent, kindled up a fanatical spirit throughout that section. In opposition to these movements, resolutions were introduced by Mr. CALHOUN into the Senate of the United States, declaring that the territories of the United States belong to the several States as joint property; that Congress, as the joint agent of the States, has no right to discriminate between the States, so as to deprive any of them of its full and equal right in any territory of the United States; that the enactment of any law which should deprive the citizens of any of the States from emigrating with their property into any of the territories of the Union, will make such discrimination, and would be a violation of the Constitution and the rights of the States from which such citizens emigrated. These resolutions, though never pressed to a vote, had their influence in Congress and the country.

4. It should be borne in mind that the Northern States claimed *all of the territories* for themselves, and their citizens, and their institutions.

The Southern States claimed a *part, or half of the territories* for themselves, and their citizens, and their institutions.

Which of the two sections was the more generous and liberal and just?

5. The following is one of a series of resolutions adopted by the Legislature of Virginia, March 8, 1847, and re-affirmed in 1849: "*Resolved unanimously*, That all territory which may be acquired by the arms of the United States, or yielded by treaty with any foreign power, belongs to the several States of this Union, as their joint and common property, in which each and all have equal rights; and that the enactment, by the Federal Government, of any law which should directly, or by its effects, prevent the citizens of any State from emigrating with their property, of whatever description, into such territory, would make a discrimination unwarranted by, and in violation of, the compromises of the Constitution, and the rights of the

States from which such citizens emigrated, and in derogation of that perfect equality which belongs to the several States as members of this Union, and would directly tend to subvert the Union itself." This had a direct reference to the Wilmot proviso, but it had also a wider application.

6. Did those members of Congress who voted against extending the line of the Missouri Compromise from the 36° 30′ to the Pacific Ocean, for the settlement of the sectional disputes in regard to territories, act judiciously and fairly? Could they have foreseen the evils which consequently sprang up afterwards, would they not have given a different vote, and thus have avoided those evils?

In the latter part of the Administration of Mr. POLK, the slave State members held nightly meetings, in which the so-called aggressions of Northern States were dwelt upon, and measures considered for the defence and protection of the South. Out of these meetings grew an address to the people of the slave-holding States, signed by about forty members of Congress. In that address, the following language is used: "We allude to the conflict between the two great sections of the Union, growing out of a difference of feeling and opinion in reference to the relation existing between the two races, the European and the African, which inhabit the Southern section, and the acts of aggression and encroachment to which it has led. The conflict commenced not long after the acknowledgment of our independence, and has gradually increased until it has arrayed the great body of the North against the South on this most vital subject. In the progress of this conflict, aggression has followed aggression, and encroachment encroachment, until they have reached a point when a regard for peace and safety will not permit us to remain longer silent."

CHAPTER XIII.

GENERAL ZACHARY TAYLOR was elected by the Whig party, on the ground of availability, and not on the ground of political experience and qualifications. He was regarded as an honest man, and as "rough and ready" in war. Many of the Democratic party voted for him on the ground of his personal and popular qualities. He was elected on the platform of the Constitution, the subject of slavery being ignored by the Convention which nominated him.

Mr. CASS was nominated on a platform which expressed no opposition to slavery, and was acceptable to the slaveholding States generally.

Mr. VAN BUREN was nominated at Buffalo, by a portion of the Democratic party, in consequence of the rejection of the two sets of delegates from New York, by the Democratic nominating Convention at Baltimore. One of these factions in that State whose delegates had been rejected, determined to assert its claim to being the Democratic party of New York, by nominating a candidate of its own. President DWIGHT once said that the old " Council of Appointment " in New York " was a hornet's nest in the kitchen." That Council had been long since abolished, but still, as late as 1848, difficulties existed connected with the appointing power. The hornet's nest had been removed, but the hornets remained. In the platform adopted at Buffalo, it was declared to be the duty of the Federal Government to abolish slavery wherever it can constitutionally be done; thus pointing to the abolition of slavery in the District of Columbia. It was also declared in that platform that Congress alone can prevent the existence of slavery in the Territories; thus pointing to exclusion of slavery in the Territories. The party assumed the name of " Free soilers," or " Free-soil party," and rejoiced in the watchword, " Free speech," " Free labor," " Free men." The " Liberty party," or " Free-soil party," of New York, might have elected Mr. CLAY in 1844, or Mr. CASS in 1848, by throwing their votes with the Whig party at the one election, or with the Democratic party in the other.

General TAYLOR came into office when there was strong sectional feeling both North and South, excited by the attempt to pass the Wilmot proviso, and by many other aggressive movements of the Northern States. These States, or large numbers in these, were disposed :

1. To exclude slaves from the Territories, and in this way to prevent any more slave States from coming into the Union.

2. To abolish slave representation in Congress, by an amendment to the Constitution. This was limited to a few States.

3. To suppress the slave trade between the States, and in the District of Columbia.

4. To abolish slavery in the District of Columbia.

5. To prevent the capture of fugitive slaves, or at least not to aid in restoring them to their owners.

6. To abolish slavery in the States as soon as can constitutionally be done, by an amendment to the Constitution.

In pressing these subjects upon the attention of Congress, a very bitter feeling was awakened in both the Northern and Southern States, which threatened disunion as a natural consequence.

At this time there was an especial interest in the subject of slavery restriction in the Territories, not only on account of the attempted imposition of the Wilmot proviso, but also on account of the projected admission of California.

DANGER OF DISUNION.

So deeply impressed was Mr. CLAY with the danger of disunion, that he brought forward in the Senate, January 29, 1850, his celebrated Compromise Resolutions, for the settlement of the sectional difficulties. In his own language, " taken together in combination, they propose an amicable arrangement of all questions in controversy between the free and the slave States."

Mr. Calhoun, in a speech prepared by him with great care, but owing to his feeble health read by Mr. Mason, March 4, 1850, asserted that " The agitation has been permitted to proceed, with almost no attempts to resist it, until it has reached a period when it is no longer to be disguised or denied, that the Union is in danger." " What is it that has endangered the Union ? To this question there can be but one answer : that the immediate cause is the almost universal discontent which pervades all the States composing the Southern section of the Union. This widely-extended discontent is not of recent origin. It commenced with the agitation of the slavery question, and has been increasing ever since." He goes on to ask, " What has caused this widely-diffused and almost universal discontent ? " He then proceeds to show that it was not originated by demagogues ; that all the great political influences were arrayed against excitement; that the Southern Whigs wished to keep the peace with their brother Whigs at the North ; that the Southern Democrats wished to keep the peace with their brother Democrats at the North. " One of the causes is found in the long-continued agitation of the slave question on the part of the North, and the many aggressions made on the rights of the South during that time."

" There is another cause lying back of it, with which this is so intimately connected that it may be regarded as the great and primary cause; that is to be found in the fact that the equilibrium between the two sections of the Government, as it stood when the Constitution was ratified, and the Government put in action, is destroyed. At that time there was nearly a perfect equilibrium between the two, which afforded ample means to each to protect itself against the aggressions of the other ; but as it now stands, one section has the exclusive power of controlling the Government, which leaves the other without any adequate means of protecting itself against its encroachment and oppression." The change arising from the increase of States and the increase of population, gives to the North a majority in the House of 50, and in the electoral college of 52.

" The great increase of Senators, added to the great increase of numbers in the House of Representatives and in the electoral college, on the part of the North, which must take place under the next decade, will effectually and irretrievably destroy the equilibrium which existed when the Government commenced.

" Had this destruction been the operation of time, without the interference of Government, the South would have had no reason to complain ; but such was not the fact. It was caused by the legislation of this Government, which was appointed as the common agent of all, and charged with the protection of the interests and security of all. The legislation by which it has been effected may be classed under three heads : The first is that series of acts by which the South had been excluded from the common territory belonging to all of the States, as the members of the Federal Union, and which soon had the effect of extending vastly the portion allotted to the Northern section, and restricting within narrow limits the portion left to the South. The next consists in adopting a system of revenue and disbursements, by which an undue portion of the burden of taxation has been imposed on the South, and an undue proportion of the proceeds appropriated to the North. And the last is a system of political measures, by which the original character of the Government has been radically changed.

" The first of the series of acts by which the South was deprived of its due share of the Territories, originated with the Confederacy, which preceded the existence of this Government. It is to be found in the ordinance of 1787. Its effect was to exclude the South entirely from that vast and fertile region which lies between the Ohio and the Mississippi Rivers, now embracing five States and one Territory. The next of the series is the Missouri Compromise, which excluded the South from that large portion of Louisiana which lies north of 36° 30′, except what is included in the State of Missouri. The last in the series excluded the South from the whole Oregon Territory. All these, in the slang of the day, were what is called slave Territories, and not free soil ; that is, Territories belonging to slaveholding powers, and open to the emigration of masters with their slaves. By these several acts the South was excluded from 1,238,025 square miles. To the South was left the portion of the Territory of Louisiana lying south of 36° 30', and the portion north of it included in the State of Missouri ; the portion lying south of 36° 30', including the States of Louisiana and Arkansas ; and the Territory lying west of the latter and south of 36° 30', called the Indian country. These, with the Territory of Florida, now the State, makes in the whole 283,503 square miles. To this must be added the territory acquired with Texas. If the whole should be added to the Southern section, it would make an increase of 325,520, which would make the whole left to the South 609,023. But a large part of Texas is still in contest between the two sections, which leaves it uncertain what will be the real extent of the portion of territory that may be left to the South.

"I have not included the territory recently acquired by the treaty with Mexico. The North is making the most strenuous efforts to appropriate the whole to herself, by excluding the South from every foot of it. If she should succeed, it will add to that from which the South has already been excluded, 526,078 square miles, and would increase the whole which the North has appropriated to herself to 1,764,023, not including the portion that she may succeed in excluding us from in Texas. To sum up the whole, the United States, since they declared their independence, have acquired 2,373,046 square miles of territory, from which the North will have excluded the South, if she should succeed in monopolizing the newly acquired territories, from about three-fourths of the whole, leaving to the South but about one-fourth.

" Such is the first and great cause that has destroyed the equilibrium between the two sections in the Government.

" The next is the system of revenue and disbursements, which has been adopted by the Government. It is well known that the Government has derived its revenue mainly from duties on imports. I shall not undertake to show that such duties must necessarily fall mainly on the exporting States, and that the South, as the great exporting portion of the Union, has in reality paid vastly more than her due proportion of the revenue ; because I deem it unnecessary, as the subject has on so many occasions been fully discussed. Nor shall I, for the same reason, undertake to show that a far greater portion of the revenue has been disbursed at the North than its due share, and that the joint effect of these causes has been to transfer a vast amount from South to North, which, under an equal system of revenue and disbursements, would not have been lost to her. If to this be added, that many of the duties were imposed, not for revenue, but for protection ; that is, intended to put money, not in the treasury, but directly into the pockets of the manufacturers, some conception may be formed of the immense amount which, in the long course of sixty years, has been transferred from South to North. There are no data by which it can be estimated with any certainty ; but it is safe to say that it amounts to hundreds of millions of dollars. Under the most moderate estimate, it would be sufficient. to add greatly to the wealth of the North, and thus greatly increase her population by attracting emigration from all quarters to that section.

"This, combined with the great primary cause, amply explains why the North has acquired a preponderance over every department of the Government by its disproportionate increase of population and States. The former, as has been shown, has increased in fifty years 2,400,000 over that of the South. This increase of population during so long a period, is satisfactorily accounted for by the number of emigrants, and the increase of their descendants, which have been attracted to the Northern section from Europe and the South, in consequence of the advantages derived from the causes assigned. If they had not existed ; if the South had retained all the capital which has been extracted from her by the fiscal action of the Government; and, if it had not been excluded by the ordinance of '87 and the Missouri Compromise from the region lying between the Ohio and the Mississippi Rivers, and between the Mississippi and the Rocky Mountains north of 36° 30', it scarcely admits of a doubt that it would have divided the emigration with the North, and by retaining her own people, would have at least equalled the North in population under the census of 1840, and probably under that about to be taken. She would also, if she had retained her equal rights in those territories, have maintained an equality in the number of States with the North, and have preserved the equilibrium between the two sections that existed at the commencement of the Government. The loss, then, of the equilibrium is to be attributed to the action of this Government. But while these measures were destroying the equilibrium between the two sections, the action of the Government was leading to a radical change in its character, by concentrating all the power of the system in itself. The occasion will not permit me to trace the measures by which this great change has been consummated. If it did, it would not be difficult to show that the process commenced at an early period of the Government; that it proceeded almost without interruption, step by step, until it absorbed virtually its entire powers. But without going through the whole process to establish the fact, it may be done satisfactorily by a very short statement. That the Government claims, and practically maintains, the right to decide, in the last resort, as to the extent of its powers, will scarcely be denied by any one conversant with the political history of the country. That it also claims the right to resort to force, to maintain whatever power she claims against all opposition, is equally certain. Indeed it is apparent, from what we daily hear, that this has become the prevailing and fixed opinion of a great majority of the community. Now, I ask, what limitation can possibly be placed upon the powers of a Government claiming and exercising such rights? And, if none can be, how can the separate Governments of the States maintain and protect the powers reserved to them by the Constitution, or the people of the several States maintain those which are reserved to them, and among others, the sovereign powers by which they ordained and established, not only their separate State Constitutions and Governments, but also the Constitution and Government of the United States? But, if they have no constitutional means of maintaining them against the right claimed by this Government, it necessarily follows that they hold them at its pleasure and discretion, and that all the powers of the system are in reality concentrated in it. It also follows that the character of the Government has been changed, in consequence, from a Federal Republic, as it originally came from the hands of its framers, and that it has been changed into a great national consolidated Democracy. It has indeed, at present, all the characteristics of the latter, and not one of the former, although it still retains its outward form. The result of the whole of these causes combined is, that the North has acquired a decided ascendency over every department of this Government, and through it a control over all the powers of the system. A single section governed by the will of the numerical majority has now, in fact, the control of the Government, and the entire powers of the system. What was once a constitutional Federal Republic is now converted, in reality, into one as absolute as that of the autocrat of Russia, and as despotic in its tendency as any absolute Government that ever existed.

"As, then, the North has the absolute control over the Government, it is manifest that on all questions between it and the South, where there is a diversity of interests, the interests of the latter will be sacrificed to the former, however oppressive the effects may be, as the South possesses no means by which it can resist through the action of the Government. But if there was no question of vital importance to the South, in reference to which there was a diversity of views between the two sections, this state of things might be endured without the hazard of destruction to the South. But such is not the fact. There is a question of vital importance to the Southern section, in reference to which the views and feelings of the two sections are as opposite and hostile as they can possibly be. I refer to the relation between the two races in the Southern section, which constitutes a vital portion of her social organization. Every portion of the North entertains views and feelings more or less hostile to it. Those most opposed and hostile regard it as a sin, and consider themselves under the most sacred obligation to use every effort to destroy it. Indeed, to the extent that they conceive they have the power, they regard themselves as implicated in the sin, and responsible for suppressing it by the use of all and every means. Those less opposed and hostile, regard it as a crime—an offence against humanity, as they call it ; and although not so fanatical, feel themselves bound to use all efforts to effect the same object ; while those who are least opposed and hostile, regard it as a blot and a stain on the character of what they call the nation, and feel themselves accordingly bound to give it no countenance or support.   On the contrary, the Southern section regards the relation as one which

11

cannot be destroyed without subjecting the two races to the
greatest calamity, and the section to poverty, desolation, and
wretchedness; and accordingly they feel bound by every consideration of interest and safety to defend it.

"This hostile feeling on the part of the North towards the
social organization of the South long lay dormant, but it only
required some cause to act on those who felt most intensely
that they were responsible for its continuance to call it into
action. The increasing power of this Government, and of the
control of the Northern section over all its departments, furnished the cause. It was this which made an impression on the
minds of many, that there was little or no restraint to prevent
the Government from doing whatever it might choose to do.
This was sufficient of itself to put the most fanatical portion of
the North in action for the purpose of destroying the existing
relation between the two races in the South.

"The first organized movement towards it commenced in
1835. Then, for the first time, societies were organized, presses
established, lecturers sent forth to excite the people of the
North, and incendiary publications scattered over the whole
South through the mail. The South was thoroughly aroused.
Meetings were held everywhere, and resolutions adopted, calling
upon the North to apply a remedy to arrest the threatened evil,
and pledging themselves to adopt measures for their own protection, if it was not arrested. At the meeting of Congress,
petitions poured in from the North, calling upon Congress to
abolish slavery in the District of Columbia, and to prohibit
what they called the internal slave trade between the States,
announcing at the same time that their ultimate object was to
abolish slavery, not only in the District, but in the States and
throughout the Union. At this period the number engaged in
the agitation was small, and possessed little or no personal influence.

"Neither party in Congress had, at that time, any sympathy
with them or their cause. The members of each party presented their petitions with great reluctance. Nevertheless, as
small and contemptible as the party then was, both of the great
parties at the North dreaded them. They felt that, though
small, they were organized in reference to a subject which had

a great and commanding influence over the Northern mind. Each party on that account feared to oppose their petitions, lest the opposite party should take advantage of the one who might do so by favoring their petitions. The effect was, that both united in insisting that the petitions should be received, and that Congress should take jurisdiction of the subject for which they prayed. To justify their course, they took the extraordinary ground that Congress was bound to receive petitions on every subject, however objectionable it might be, and whether they had or had not jurisdiction over the subject. These views prevailed in the House of Representatives, and partially in the Senate, and thus the party succeeded in their first movements in gaining what they proposed—a position in Congress from which agitation could be extended over the whole Union. This was the commencement of the agitation, which has ever since continued, and which, as is now acknowledged, has endangered the Union itself. As for myself, I believed, at that early period, if the party who got up the petitions should succeed in getting Congress to take jurisdiction, that agitation would follow, and that it would, in the end, if not arrested, destroy the Union. I then so expressed myself in debate, and called upon both parties to take grounds against assuming jurisdiction, but in vain. Had my voice been heeded, and had Congress refused to take jurisdiction, by the united votes of all parties, the agitation which followed would have been prevented, and the fanatical zeal that gives impulse to the agitation, and which has brought us to our present perilous condition, would have become extinguished from the want of something to feed the flame. *That* was the time for the North to show her devotion to the Union ; but unfortunately both of the great parties of that section were so intent on obtaining or retaining party ascendency, that all other considerations were overlooked or forgotten.

" What has since followed are but the natural consequences. With the success of their first movement, this small fanatical party began to acquire strength ; and with that to become an object of courtship to both the great parties. The necessary consequence was a further increase of power, and a gradual tainting of the opinions of both of the other parties with their doctrines, until the infection has extended over both ; and the

great masses of the population of the North who, whatever may
be their opinion of the original abolition party, which still pre-
serves its distinctive organization, hardly ever fail, when it
comes to acting, to co-operate in carrying out their measures.
With the increase of their influence, they extended the sphere
of their action. In a short time after the commencement of
their first movement, they had acquired sufficient influence to
induce the Legislatures of most of the Northern States to pass
acts which, in effect, abrogated the provision of the Constitution that provides for the delivering up of fugitive slaves. Not
long after, petitions followed to abolish slavery in forts, maga-
zines, and dock-yards, and all other places where Congress had
exclusive power of legislation. This was followed by petitions
and resolutions of Legislatures of the Northern States and popular meetings, to exclude the Southern States from all territories acquired or to be acquired, and to prevent the admission
of any State hereafter into the Union, which by its Constitution
does not prohibit slavery. And Congress is invoked to do all
this expressly with the view to the final abolition of slavery in
the States. That has been avowed to be the ultimate object
from the beginning of agitation until the present time ; and yet
the great body of both parties of the North, with the full knowledge of the fact, although disavowing the abolitionists, have co-
operated with them in almost all their measures.

"Such is a brief history of the agitation, as far as it has yet
advanced. Now, I ask Senators, what is there to prevent its
further progress, until it fulfils the ultimate end proposed, unless some decisive measure should be adopted to prevent it ?
Has any one of the causes, which have added to its increase from
its original small and contemptible beginning until it has at-
tained its present magnitude, diminished in force ? Is the
original cause of the movement, that slavery is a sin, and ought
to be suppressed, weaker now than at the commencement ? Or
are the Abolition party less numerous or influential, or have they
less influence over, or control over the two great parties of the
North in elections ? Or has the South greater means of influ-
encing or controlling the movements of this Government now,
than it had when the agitation commenced ? To all these questions but one answer can be given : No, no, no ! The very re-

verse is true. Instead of being weaker, all the elements in favor of agitation are stronger now than they were in 1835, when it first commenced, while all the elements of influence on the part of the South are weaker. Unless something decisive is done, I again ask what is to stop this agitation, before the great and final object at which it aims—the abolition of slavery in the States—is consummated? Is it, then, not certain, that if something decisive is not now done to arrest it, the South will be forced to choose between abolition and secession? Indeed, as events are now moving, it will not require the South to secede to dissolve the Union. Agitation will of itself effect it, of which its past history furnishes abundant proof, as I shall next proceed to show.

"It is a great mistake to suppose that disunion can be effected by a single blow. The cords which bind these States together in one common Union are far too numerous and powerful for that. Disunion must be the work of time. It is only through a long process, and successively, that the cords can be snapped, until the whole fabric falls asunder. Already the agitation of the slavery question has snapped some of the most important, and has greatly weakened all the others, as I shall proceed to show.

"The cords that bind the States together are not only many but various in character. Some are spiritual or ecclesiastical ; some political ; others social. Some appertain to the benefit conferred by the Union, and others to the feeling of duty and obligation.

"The strongest of those of a spiritual and ecclesiastical nature consisted in the unity of the great religious denominations, all of which originally embraced the whole Union. All these denominations, with the exception, perhaps, of the Catholics, were organized very much upon the principle of our political institutions ; beginning with smaller meetings corresponding with the political divisions of the county, their organizations terminated in one great central assemblage, corresponding very much with the character of Congress. At these meetings, the principal clergymen and lay members of the respective denominations from all parts of the Union met to transact business relating to their common concerns. It was not confined to what appertained to the doctrines and discipline of the respective denominations, but extended to plans for disseminating the Bible, establishing missionaries, distributing tracts, and of establishing presses for the publication of tracts, newspapers, and periodicals, with a view of diffusing religious information, and for the support of the doctrines and creeds of the denomination. All this combined, contributed greatly to strengthen the bonds of the Union. The strong ties which held each denomination together formed a strong cord to hold the whole Union together; but, as powerful as they were, they have not been able to resist the explosive effect of slavery agitation.

"The first of these cords which snapped, under its explosive force, was that of the powerful Methodist Episcopal Church. The numerous and strong ties which held it together are all broke, and its unity gone. They now form separate churches, and, instead of that feeling of attachment and devotion to the interests of the whole Church which was formerly felt, they are now arrayed into two hostile bodies, engaged in litigation about what was formerly their common property.

"The next cord that snapped was that of the Baptists, one of the largest and most respectable of the denominations. That of the Presbyterian is not entirely snapped, but some of its strands have given way. That of the Episcopal Church is the only one of the four great Protestant denominations which remains unbroken and entire.

"The strongest cord of a political character consists of the many and strong ties that have held together the two great parties, which have, with some modifications, existed from the beginning of the Government. They both extended to every portion of the Union, and strongly contributed to hold all its parts together. But this powerful cord has fared no better than the spiritual. It resisted for a long time the explosive tendency of the agitation, but has finally snapped under its force—if not entirely, in a great measure. Nor is there one of the remaining cords which has not been greatly weakened. To this extent the Union has already been destroyed by agitation, in the only way it can be, by snapping asunder and weakening the cords which bind it together.

If the agitation goes on, the same force, acting with increased intensity, as has been shown, will finally snap every cord, when nothing will be left to hold the States together except force. But surely that can, with no propriety of language, be called a union, when the only means by which the weaker is held connected with the stronger portion is *force*. It may, indeed, keep them connected; but the connection will partake much more of the character of subjugation, on the part of the weaker to the stronger, than the union of free, independent, and sovereign States, in one confederation, as they stood in the early stages of the Government, and which only is worthy of the sacred name of union.

"Having now, Senators, explained what it is that endangers the Union, and traced it to its cause, and explained its nature and character, the question again recurs, How can the Union be saved? To this I answer, there is but one way by which it can be, and that is, by adopting such measures as will satisfy the States belonging to the Southern section that they can remain in the Union consistently with their honor and their safety. There is, again, only one way by which that can be effected, and that is, by removing the causes by which this belief has been produced. Do *that*, and discontent will cease, harmony and kind feelings between the sections be restored, and every apprehension of danger to the Union removed. The question then is, By what can this be done? But, before I undertake to answer this question, I propose to show by what the Union cannot be saved.

"It cannot, then, be saved by eulogies on the Union, however splendid or numerous. The cry of ' Union, Union, the glorious Union!' can no more prevent disunion than the cry of ' Health, Health, glorious Health!' on the part of the physician, can save a patient lying dangerously ill. So long as the Union, instead of being regarded as a protector, is regarded in the opposite character, by not much less than a majority of the States, it will be in vain to attempt to conciliate them by pronouncing eulogies on it.

"Besides, this cry of Union comes commonly from those whom we cannot believe to be sincere; it usually comes from our assailants. But we cannot believe them to be sincere; for, if they loved the Union, they would necessarily be devoted to the Constitution. It made the Union, and to destroy the Constitution would be to destroy the Union. But the only reliable and certain evidence of devotion to the Constitution is to abstain, on the one hand, from violating it, and to repel, on the other, all attempts to violate it. It is only by faithfully performing these high duties that the Constitution can be preserved, and with it the Union.

"But how stands the profession of devotion to the Union by our assailants, when brought to this test? Have they abstained from violating the Constitution? ·Let the many acts passed by the Northern States, to set aside and annul·the clause of the Constitution providing for the delivery up of fugitive slaves, answer. I cite this, not that it is the only instance, (for there are many others,) but because the violation in this particular is too notorious and palpable to be denied. Again, have they stood forth faithfully to repel violations of the Constitution? Let their course in reference to the agitation of the slavery question, which was commenced and has been carried on for fifteen years, avowedly for the purpose of abolishing slavery in the States—an object all acknowledged to be unconstitutional—answer. Let them show a single instance, during this long period, in which they have denounced the agitators or their attempts to effect what is admitted to be unconstitutional, or a single measure which they have brought forward for that purpose. How can we, with all these facts before us, believe that they are sincere in their profession of devotion to the Union, or avoid believing their profession is but intended to increase the vigor of their assaults, and to weaken the force of our resistance?

"Nor can we regard the profession of devotion to the Union, on the part of those who are not our assailants, as sincere, when they pronounce eulogies upon the Union, evidently with the intent of charging us with disunion, without uttering one word of denunciation against our assailants. If friends of the Union, their course should be to unite with us in repelling these assaults, and denouncing the authors as enemies of the Union. Why they avoid this, and pursue the course they do, it is for them to explain.

"Nor can the Union be saved by invoking the name of the

illustrious Southerner, whose mortal remains repose on the western bank of the Potomac. He was one of us—a slave-holder and a planter. We have studied his history, and find nothing in it to justify submission to wrong. On the contrary, his great fame rests on the solid foundation that, while he was careful to avoid doing wrong to others, he was prompt and decided in repelling wrong. I trust that, in this respect, we profited by his example.

"Nor can we find any thing in his history to deter us from seceding from the Union, should it fail to fulfil the objects for which it was instituted, by being permanently and hopelessly converted into the means of oppressing instead of protecting us. On the contrary, we find much in his example to encourage us, should we be forced to the extremity of deciding between submission and disunion.

"There existed then, as well as now, a Union—that between a parent country and her then colonies. It was a Union that had much to endear it to the people of the colonies. Under its protecting and superintending care, the colonies were planted, and grew up, and prospered, through a long course of years, until they became populous and wealthy. Its benefits were not limited to them. Their extensive agricultural and other productions gave birth to a flourishing commerce, which richly rewarded the parent country for the trouble and expense of establishing and protecting them. Washington was born and grew up to manhood under that Union. He acquired his early distinction in its service, and there is every reason to believe that he was devotedly attached to it. But his devotion was a rational one. He was attached to it, not as an end, but as a means to an end. When it failed to fulfil its end, and, instead of affording protection, was converted into the means of oppressing the colonies, he did not hesitate to draw his sword, and head the great movement by which that Union was forever severed, and the independence of these States established. This was the great and crowning glory of his life, which has spread his fame over the whole globe, and will transmit it to the latest posterity."

Mr. CALHOUN then went on to say, that neither the plan proposed by the distinguished Senator from Kentucky, (Mr. CLAY,) nor that of the Administration, can save the Union.

"Having now shown what cannot save the Union, I return to the question with which I commenced, How can the Union be saved? There is but one way with which it can with any certainty, and that is by a full and final settlement, on the principles of justice, of all questions at issue between the two sections. The South asks for justice, simple justice, and less she ought not to take. She has no compromise to offer but the Constitution, and no concession or surrender to make. She has already surrendered so much that she has little left to surrender. Such a settlement would go to the root of the evil, and remove all cause of discontent, by satisfying the South that she could remain honorably and safely in the Union, and thereby restore the harmony and fraternal feelings between the sections which existed anterior to the Missouri agitation. Nothing else can, with any certainty, finally and forever settle the questions at issue, terminate agitation, and save the Union. But can this be done? Yes, easily; not by the weaker party, for it can of itself do nothing—not even protect itself—but by the stronger. The North has only to will it to accomplish it; *to do justice by conceding to the South an equal right in the acquired territory, and to do her duty by causing the stipulation in regard to fugitive slaves to be faithfully fulfilled; to cease the agitation of the slave question*, and to provide for the insertion in the Constitution of an amendment, which will restore to the South, in substance, the power she possessed of protecting herself before the equilibrium between the sections was destroyed by the action of the Government."

MR. WEBSTER ON THE COMPROMISE, MARCH 7, 1850.

"Mr. President: I wish to speak to-day, not as a Massachusetts man, nor as a Northern man, but as an American, and a member of the Senate of the United States. It is fortunate that there is a Senate of the United States—a body not yet moved from its propriety, not lost to a just sense of its own dignity, and its own high responsibilities, and a body to which the country looks with confidence for wise, moderate, patriotic, and healing counsels. It is not to be denied that we live in the midst of strong agitations, and surrounded by very considerable dangers to our institutions of government. The imprisoned winds are let loose. The East, the West, the North, and the stormy South, all combine to throw the whole ocean into commotion, to top its billows to the skies, and to disclose its profoundest depth. I do not expect to hold or to be fit to hold the helm in this combat of the political elements; but I have a duty to perform, and I mean to perform it with fidelity—not without a sense of the surrounding dangers, but not without hope. I have a part to act, not for my own security or safety, for I am looking out for no fragment upon which to float away from the wreck, if wreck there must be, but for the good of the whole and the preservation of the whole; and there is that which will press me to my duty during this struggle, whether the sun and the stars shall appear, or shall not appear, after many days. I speak to-day for the preservation of the Union. ' Hear me for my cause.' I speak to-day out of a solicitous and anxious heart, for the restoration to the country of that quiet and that harmony which make the blessings of the Union so rich and so dear to us all."

Mr. WEBSTER then proceeded to give a history of some of the difficulties in respect to slavery; spoke of the conquest of California; of the gold mines there; of the Constitution offered to Congress as the ground of admission into the Union, which Constitution contains the prohibition of slavery, which was not satisfactory to the South; of the existence of slavery in other portions and ages of the world, and of the difference of opinion felt respecting the institution, by the North and the South; of the unhappy division in the Methodist church, growing out of the difference of opinion on this subject. He also spoke of the existence of slavery in this country; of the views entertained of it at the time the Constitution was formed, by both North and South; and of the subsequent change of views in both sections : of the influence of cotton cultivation; of the annexation of Texas; of his opinion on the admission of slavery in the Territories; of the Wilmot proviso; of his opposition to the admission of new territory; of the exclusion of slavery by climate and the laws of nature; of the grievances of the North and of the South; of the complaint of the South, " that there has been found at the North among individuals and among the Legisla-

tures at the North a disinclination to perform fully their constitutional duties in regard to the return of persons bound to service, who have escaped into the free States. In that respect it
is my judgment that the South is right, and the North is wrong."
He also spoke of resolutions emanating from Legislatures at the
North, and sent here to us, not only on the subject of slavery in
this District, but sometimes recommending Congress to consider
the means of abolishing slavery in the States. He said that
" it has become, in my opinion, quite too common a practice for
the State Legislatures to present resolutions on all subjects, and
to instruct us here on all subjects." He said, in regard to abolition societies, that " he does not think them useful." He
spoke of the violent language used in Congress with disappro-
bation ; of slave representation ; of the imprisonment of free
blacks who go South in Northern vessels ; of Mr. Hoar's mission ; of the difficulties in the way of secession ; of the gift of
Virginia to the United States in the cession of territory ; of his
hopes that the Union may continue.

This speech, one of the ablest ever made by Mr. WEBSTER,
was intended by him to be catholic and liberal, and by catholic and liberal men in every part of the country it was well received, but not by the abolitionists. He had voted not to place
in the Territorial bills the Wilmot proviso, and hence he in-
curred the censure of the abolition wing of the Whig party. In
allusion to this in a subsequent speech, delivered June 17, he
said : " When I see gentlemen from my own part of the country,
no doubt from motives of the highest character, and for most
conscientious purposes, not concurring in any of these great
questions with myself, I am aware that I am taking on myself
an uncommon degree of responsibility." He adds : " It is a
great emergency, a great exigency, that this country is placed
in." In relation to this censure, he remarks : " Now, sir, I do
not take the trouble to answer things of this sort that appear in
the public press ; I know it would be useless."

He closed his speech as follows : " Sir, my object is peace.
My object is reconciliation. My purpose is not to make up a
case for the North, or to make up a case for the South. My
object is not to continue useless and irritating controversies. I
am against agitation, North and South. I am against local

ideas North or South, and against all narrow and local contests. I am an American, and I know no locality in America : that is my country. My heart, my sentiment, my judgment demand of me, that I shall pursue such a course as shall promote the good and the harmony of the whole country. This I shall do, God willing, to the end of the chapter."

" Mr. President : In the progress of this debate, it has been again and again argued, that perfect tranquillity reigns throughout the country, and that there is no disturbance threatening its peace, endangering its safety, but that which was produced by busy, restless politicians. It has been maintained that the surface of the public mind is perfectly smooth, and undisturbed by a single billow. I most heartily wish I could concur in this picture of general tranquillity that has been drawn upon both sides of the Senate. I am no alarmist ; nor, I thank God, at the advanced age at which his providence has been pleased to allow me to reach, am I very easily alarmed by any human event. But I totally misread the signs of the times, if there be that state of profound peace and quiet, that absence of all just cause of apprehension of future danger to this Confederacy, which appears to be entertained by some other Senators. Mr. President, all the tendencies of the times, I lament to say, are towards disquietude, if not more fatal consequences. When before, in the midst of profound peace with all the nations of the earth, have we seen a convention, representing a considerable portion of one great part of the Republic, meet to deliberate about measures of future safety in connection with great interests of that quarter of the country ? When before have we seen, not one, but more—some half a dozen—legislative bodies solemnly resolving that if any one of these measures—the admission of California, the adoption of the Wilmot proviso, of the abolition of slavery in the District of Columbia—should be adopted by Congress, measures of an extreme character, for the safety of the great interests to which I refer, in a particular section of the country, would be resorted to ? For years, this subject of the abolition of slavery, even within this District of Co-

lumbia, small as is the number of slaves here, has been a source
of constant irritation and disquiet. So of the subject of the recovery of fugitive slaves who have escaped from their lawful
owners; not as a mere border contest, as has been supposed—
although there, undoubtedly, it has given rise to more irritation
than in other portions of the Union—but everywhere through
the slaveholding country it has been felt as a great evil, a great
wrong, which required the intervention of Congressional power.
But these two subjects, unpleasant as has been the agitation to
which they have given rise, are nothing in comparison to those
which have sprung out of the acquisitions recently made from
the republic of Mexico. These are not only great and leading
causes of just apprehension as respects the future, but all the
minor circumstances of the day intimate danger ahead, whatever
may be its final issue and consequence.

Mr. President, I will not dwell upon other concomitant
causes, all having the same tendency, and all well calculated to
awaken, to arouse us—if, as I hope the fact is, we are all of us
sincerely desirous of preserving this Union—to arouse us to dangers which really exist, without underrating them upon the one
hand, or magnifying them upon the other."

In reply to Mr. HALE, Mr. CLAY, in another speech, July
26, 1850, said: "But I stand up here for this measure, and I
do not want the Senator to deal in declamation. I ask him
what right is sacrificed by the North in this measure? Let him
tell me if the North does not get almost every thing, and the
South nothing but her honor—her exemption from usurped authority to the Texas land, which I have mentioned, together
with the fugitive slave proposition, and an exemption from agitation on the subject of slavery in the District of Columbia. I
do not want general broad-cast declamation, but specifications.
Let us meet them as men, point upon point, argument upon argument. Show us the power here to which Northern sacrifices
are made. Show what sacrifices, *what* is sacrificed by the
North in this bill. That is what I want."

The compromise resolutions of Mr. CLAY, and the report of
the Select Committee of Thirteen, to whom the whole subject
had been referred, were in the main sustained by both Houses
of Congress, but not in form. Instead of one bill, separate bills

were brought in and passed. California was admitted as a State, notwithstanding no territorial government had been established over her, and notwithstanding the Constitution prohibited slavery. Eighteen Southern Senators voted against her admission; and ten Senators presented a protest against it, on the ground that the portion of the inhabitants of California, who acted in the premises, did so without authority, and, in doing so, made an odious discrimination against the property of fifteen slaveholding States; on the ground that the bill defeats the right of the slaveholding States to a common or equal enjoyment of the territory of the Union ; on the ground that " to vote for the bill would be to agree to a principle that may exclude forever, as it does now, the States which we represent, from all enjoyment of the common territory of the Union " ; and also on other grounds. This protest the majority of the Senate refused to admit into its journal, twenty-two voting against admitting it, and nineteen in favor. The bill to establish a territorial government over New Mexico and Utah, with power to be admitted into the Union either with slavery or without slavery, was passed, ten Northern Senators voting against it. The fugitive slave law was passed, twelve Northern Senators voting against it. The Texas boundary bill was passed by a vote of thirty to twenty. The bill for the abolition of the slave-trade in the District of Columbia was also passed.

In urging the Senate to pass these bills, Mr. CLAY, in his great speech, July 26, 1850, said : " Will you go home and leave all in disorder, confusion—all unsettled, all open ? The contentions and agitations of the past will be increased and augmented by the agitations resulting from our neglect to decide them. Sir, we shall stand condemned by all human judgment below ; and, of that above, it is not for me to speak. We shall stand condemned in our own consciences, by our own constituents, and by our own country. * * The bill may be defeated. It is possible that, for the chastisements of our sins or transgressions, the rod of Providence may be applied to us, may be still suspended over us. But if defeated, it will be a triumph of ultraism and impracticability ; a triumph of the most extraordinary conjunction of extremes ; a victory won by abolitionism ; a victory won by free-soilism ; the victory of discord

and agitation over peace and tranquillity; and I pray to Almighty God that it may not, in consequence of the inauspicious
result, lead to the most unhappy and disastrous consequences
to our beloved country."

REMARKS.

1. The South felt injured by the efforts made by the North
to exclude her institutions from the territories and the new
States, on the ground of her unworthiness. She remembered
the efforts of the North to prevent Missouri from being admitted
into the Union upon an equal footing with the other States.
She not only felt injured but also insulted by these efforts,
and by the language used in Congress by Northern men, and
generally by the Northern press. The Southern States could
not find any title-deed by which the landed estate was entailed
upon the North, while the other members of the family were to
be dismissed dowerless, and upbraided.

2. Portions of the North had endeavored to deprive the
South of her slave representation, by proposing an alteration of
the Constitution.

3. Large portions of the people of the North refused to deliver up fugitive slaves on the claim of their masters; and by
thus refusing to perform their part of the stipulation, freed the
South from its full obligations to keep the Constitution in its
relation to them, as violators of the Constitution. Some of the
States passed bills designed to obstruct the recovery of fugitive
slaves. Pennsylvania, in 1780, passed an act of comity, allowing masters to bring their slaves into the State, and sojourn
there six months, without forfeiting them. Pennsylvania in
time became intolerant, and repealed that act. New York also
repealed her sojournment act, by which the master was allowed
to sojourn in the State nine months with his slaves, without
subjecting them to emancipation. The sentiments of the people
had been such in the Northern States, that it was perfectly safe
for an owner of slaves, on visiting the North, to bring such
of them with him as he needed, without any intermeddling to
deprive him of their services. That liberal and national sentiment was now giving place to an intolerant, jealous, and inter-

meddling spirit. The present writer distinctly remembers the time when Southern men brought on their slaves to Connecticut for a temporary sojournment, without experiencing any embarrassment in respect to their slaves, or any indignity to themselves. The present writer also remembers that afterwards, when an intolerant spirit became rife in New England, Southern men who brought their slaves simply on a visit to their friends and relatives for a few weeks, were informed that slaveholders were abhorred of God and despised of men; while arguments and persuasions were dishonorably addressed to their slaves, to entice them away from their masters.

4. Slave-stealing organizations were encouraged in the Northern States, so that by their agency, with the connivance of Northern men, the South lost a large number of slaves and a great amount of property annually, through what was called the underground railroad.

5. Southern clergymen were excluded from Northern pulpits, and Southern Christians from Northern communion tables, and Southern students were made uncomfortable by the intolerance of the abolition spirit of the North. In one of the Northern colleges, a respectable Southern clergyman was invited to preach on the Sabbath in the college chapel. Thereupon certain abolitionists among the students addressed a petition to the president, requesting that the clergyman should be excluded from the pulpit, after he had been invited by the proper authority to occupy it. By this arrogant conduct of these students, who were wise in their own conceits above their teachers, the college was thrown into a state of violent fermentation, and the Southern clergyman felt himself constrained to decline fulfilling his engagement. In justice to that college, it should be added, that the students in all the classes, after discussing the bearing and nature of the petition for something like half a day in a public meeting, passed a vote that the president of the college, who was likewise Professor of Divinity, was authorized to supply the pulpit for the instruction of the students as he should see fit, without being controlled by the intermeddling of the students, thus censuring the petitioners. It should be added, that the invitation to the clergyman was not withdrawn by the president, or the officer whose place the Southern gentleman was to fill on that Sabbath.

12

6. Incendiary publications, adapted to produce insurrection among the slaves, had been sent by Northern abolitionists through the Southern States by mail.

7. While the fugitive slave bill was under consideration in the Senate, Mr. DAVIS, of Massachusetts, moved to amend the bill in such a way as to protect free negroes going to Southern ports, against seizure and imprisonment. Such persons had been seized and imprisoned in Charleston, S. C., and elsewhere, under State laws, much to the dissatisfaction of Northern States, where these imprisoned negroes were considered as citizens of the United States, because they were citizens of some of the Northern States. Massachusetts, the acknowledged champion of the North, resolved to try conclusions with South Carolina on the constitutionality of those acts of the latter by which the negro citizens of the former had been imprisoned. For this purpose, Mr. SAMUEL HOAR was appointed by the Governor of Massachusetts, under the authority of the Legislature, as an agent to collect information concering those citizens of Massachusetts, who had been imprisoned under the laws of South Carolina, and also to prosecute one or more suits in behalf of any citizen thus imprisoned, for the purpose of having the legality of such imprisonment tried and determined in the Supreme Court of the United States. It was declared in the Senate of the United States, " that Massachusetts has been anxious to do one single thing, and nothing else, and that is, to submit this question to the tribunal which the Constitution has provided for its final settlement." If these " laws are decided to be constitutional acts, she will acquiesce in the decision." Massachusetts thus claimed that, by adopting negroes as her own citizens, they should be reckoned elsewhere throughout the country as citizens of the United States.

South Carolina, on the other hand, took the ground, that negroes are not citizens of the United States within the meaning of the Constitution, and that the emissary sent by Massachusetts for the avowed purpose of interfering with her institutions and disturbing her peace, should be expelled from her territory.

The mission of Mr. HOAR, and his expulsion, created bad blood in South Carolina and in Massachusetts. Massachusetts complained bitterly that she was not allowed by South Carolina to try the constitutionality of her claim, that her free negro citizens should be considered as citizens of the United States. When the question was settled by the Supreme Court, in the Dred Scott decision, that negroes are not citizens of the United States within the meaning of the Constitution, did Massachusetts acquiesce in the decision?

S. There was great dissatisfaction in New England with the fugitive law, as there would have been with any law which would be efficacious in restoring fugitive slaves. The people of that section practically refused to obey the fugitive slave law of 1793, and also the law of 1850. When Mr. WEBSTER announced his intention of supporting a law for the more effectual reclamation of fugitive slaves, Mr. CALHOUN is said to have replied : " What if you do enact such a bill ? The people of New England will not submit to it." The fugitive, *Sims*, was recovered by his owner, but at an expense to him, it was said, of $3,000, aided though he was by the General Government, and by some of the most able men of Boston. The fugitive, *Burns*, was recovered, but at an expense to the Government and his owner of as much as $30,000. The law has been practically a dead letter except in a few cases. Thus the South lost nearly all that it expected to gain by the Compromise Measures of 1850. The Northern States, in this respect, were not faithful to the Compromise Measures, as is proved by the personal liberty bills passed by different Legislatures, for the purpose of throwing obstacles in the way of reclaiming fugitive slaves. " The entire moral impossibility of effecting the forcible reclamation of fugitive slaves in New England may therefore be solemnly regarded as a fixed state of things ; and the great problem to be solved by politicians and statesmen is, not how they can remove this state of things, but how they shall adapt the laws and institutions of the country to it." This language from a respectable pamphlet, published in 1850, expresses a sentiment that was common in New England at that time. Mr. WEBSTER exhorted Massachusetts to " conquer her prejudices " on this subject. New England needed the same exhortation, though not generally to the same extent, as Massachusetts.

9. What was the effect of the passage of the Compromise Measures upon the country ? Salutary and quieting, at least for

a season. The Senators, CASS, CLAY, COBB, DICKINSON, FOOTE, and others, who had promoted the compromise, were applauded by the country generally for their efforts to heal the sectional difficulties. Mr. CALHOUN had died, and Mr. WEBSTER had resigned his place for a seat in the cabinet, before the measures were passed. Patriotic and moderate men of both political parties were generally disposed to be satisfied with the compromises. The abolition wing of the Whig party and the abolition wing of the Democratic party at the North were not satisfied with the fugitive slave law, and objected to making the North a " slave-hunting ground," and with some intemperance of language denounced " slave-catchers." By their united efforts they influenced the Legislatures of several Northern States to pass unconstitutional personal liberty bills for the purpose, it would seem, of defeating the object of the fugitive slave bill, and thus violating their constitutional obligations.

The following resolution, with some others, passed by the Common Council of the city of Chicago, shows the temper of the times in certain sections of the Northern States. " *Resolved*, that the Senators and Representatives in Congress from the Free States, who aided and assisted in the passage of this infamous law, (the fugitive slave law,) and those who basely sneaked away from their seats, and thereby evaded the question, richly merit the reproach of all lovers of freedom, and are fit only to be ranked with the traitors, BENEDICT ARNOLD and JUDAS ISCARIOT, who betrayed his Lord and Master for thirty pieces of silver."

As the spirit indicated by this resolution prevailed extensively in the Northern States, so it showed itself in the enactment of personal liberty bills by State Legislatures ; in the organized support of underground railroads for carrying off slaves to Canada ; and in the rescue by Northern mobs of fugitives from the legal officers appointed by the General Government. Such an act of a mob the present writer once witnessed, standing within a few feet of the commissioner from whom the rescue was made.

CHAPTER XIV.

AT the election of General FRANKLIN PIERCE, the Democratic candidate, there was not a very extensive sectional feeling. Both the successful and the unsuccessful candidate, General SCOTT, had supporters in both the Northern and the Southern sections of the country. The Abolition or sectional party threw about 150,000 votes for their candidate. Both the Democratic and the Whig national nominating conventions endorsed the Compromise Measures of 1850.

Still it must be admitted, that in the Northern States there was considerable opposition to one portion of the Compromise Measures, namely, the Fugitive Slave Law; just as there had been to the law of 1793, and just as there would have been to any law that would be effectual in carrying out the provision of the Constitution on this subject. Men were clamorous for its repeal, though they would retain other portions of the Compromise Measures which never could have been carried through Congress, except they had been connected with the fugitive slave law. So strong was the opposition to that law, that communities by mobs or connivance, and State Legislatures by personal liberty bills, practically repealed it, and thus violated not only the Compromise of 1850, but also the Constitution. So strong was this opposition to that law in Boston, that Faneuil Hall was closed against DANIEL WEBSTER, because he had advocated the Compromise Measures. It was on that occasion that he said, " Massachusetts must conquer her prejudices." Northern men were talking about a "higher law," which absolved them from obligation to carry out the provisions of the Constitution. They showed as much opposition to the Compromise of 1850, as Northern men of the preceding generation did to the Missouri Compromise of 1820. There was only wanting an occasion to call forth a general sectional excitement. That occasion was forthcoming.

On the 3d of March, 1854, the bill to organize the Territories of Kansas and Nebraska, was passed in the Senate by a vote of 37 to 14, by which the slavery restriction, passed by the Missouri Compromise, was removed, and the people in those territories were thus permitted to form their own institutions, without the interference of Congress. The intent and meaning of the Bill was, that " Congress should neither legislate slavery into the territories nor out of them."

On the introduction of the bill by Mr. DOUGLAS, the chairman of the Committee on Territories, and before he could have an opportunity for discussing it, and thus showing to the country what were its merits, an " Appeal," in opposition to it, was addressed to the *people of the United States.* This Appeal bore date Jan. 19, 1854, and was signed by Senators CHASE of Ohio, and SUMNER of Massachusetts, and by members of the House, EDWARD WADE and J. R. GIDDINGS of Ohio, GERRIT SMITH of New York, and ALEXANDER DE WITT of Massachusetts. The following is a portion of that appeal :

"SHALL SLAVERY BE PERMITTED IN NEBRASKA ? "

" FELLOW-CITIZENS :—As Senators and Representatives in the Congress of the United States, it is our duty to warn our constituents (?) whenever imminent danger menaces the freedom of our institutions and the permanency of our Union. [Were the people of the United States their constituents ?]

" Such danger, as we firmly believe, now impends, and we earnestly solicit your prompt attention to it. * * *

" We arraign this bill as a gross violation of a sacred pledge : as a criminal betrayal of precious rights ; as part and parcel of an atrocious plot to exclude from a vast unoccupied region emigrants from the Old World, and free laborers from our own

States, and convert it into a dreary region of despotism inhabited by masters and slaves.

"We appeal to the people. We warn you that the dearest interests of freedom and the Union are in imminent peril. Demagogues may tell you, that the safety of the Union can be maintained only by submitting to the demands of slavery. We tell you that the safety of the Union can only be insured by the full recognition of the just claims of freedom and man. The Union was formed to establish justice and secure the blessings of liberty. When it fails to accomplish these ends, it will be worthless; and when it becomes worthless, it cannot long endure.

"We implore Christians and Christian ministers to interpose. Their Divine religion requires them to behold in every man a brother, and to labor for the advancement and regeneration of the human race. * * *

"Let all protest, earnestly and emphatically, by correspondence and through the press, by memorials and resolutions of public meetings and legislative bodies, and in whatever mode may seem expedient, against this enormous crime."

Thus addressed, the people of the Northern States promptly responded to the call, in the very modes pointed out in this proclamation, as the "appeal" was styled in Congress. They were combustible, and this "appeal" supplied the torch. Forthwith, the Northern regions of the Union were in a blaze of excitement. The pen, the press, the pulpit, the political forum, and the halls of legislation, were put in requisition to resist the passage of the bill. As an exponent of the general feeling, the "protest" of the clergymen of New England may be taken. The object of the protest may be found in the circular which was "simultaneously sent to every clergyman in New England," and which was signed by CHARLES LOWELL, LYMAN BEECHER, BARON STOWE, SEBASTIAN STREETER, committee of clergymen of Boston, and was dated Feb. 22, 1854. "It is hoped," that circular declares, "that every one of you will append your names to it, and thus furnish to the nation and the age the sublime and influential spectacle of the *great Christian body of the North* (?) united as one man in favor of freedom and of solemn plighted faith."

"If you have already, either as a private Christian or as a clergyman, signed any similar document, please to sign this also, as it is earnestly desired to embrace in this movement the clerical voice of New England.

"It is respectfully submitted, whether the present is not a crisis of sufficient magnitude and imminence of danger to the liberties and integrity of our nation, to warrant and even demand the services of the clergy of all denominations, in arousing the masses of the people to its comprehension, through the press, and even the pulpit."

CLERICAL PROTEST.

"*To the Honorable the Senate and House of Representatives in Congress assembled :*

"The undersigned, clergymen of different denominations in New England, hereby in the name of Almighty God, and in His presence, do solemnly *protest* against what is known as the Nebraska Bill, or any repeal or modification of the existing legal prohibition of slavery in that part of the national domain which it is proposed to organize into the territories of Nebraska and Kansas. We protest against it as a great moral wrong, as a breach of faith, eminently unjust to the moral principles of the community, and subversive of all confidence in national engagements ; as a measure full of danger to the peace, and even the existence, of our beloved Union, and exposing us to the righteous judgments of the Almighty; and your protestants, as in duty bound, will ever pray.—*Boston, Massachusetts,* March 1, 1854."

My limits do not allow me to quote the remarks made in the Senate respecting the "appeal" and the "protest." The ground taken in the "appeal" in opposition to the bill for the repeal of the slavery restriction north of 36° 30' was, first, that it would be contrary to the "original settled policy of the United States," as proved by the ordinance of 1787, to permit slavery in the territories ; and secondly, that it would be a violation of a "sacred pedge," or compact made in 1820, in the Missouri Compromise.

Mr. Douglas denied that it was the "original settled policy" of the United States to prohibit slavery in the territories, inasmuch as slavery was permitted and protected in the territory of Tennessee; and in the legislation respecting Mississippi, the ordinance of 1787 was adopted, with the *exception of the anti-slavery clause.*

"That the repeal was a gross violation of a sacred pledge," has been extensively denied both before and since its accomplishment. The following are some of the grounds of the repeal, in the words of another:

1. "The South was not bound by that compact or compromise, because it was made without the least consideration; that is, because she received nothing for what she conceded. For Missouri, as our adversaries now admit, had a perfect right to admission without any stipulation on the part of the South; she had a perfect right to admission, says the Supreme Court of the United States, without any such terms or conditions, under and by the Federal Constitution alone. If she had to pay for this right, it was because the dominant party at the North then took their stand against the Constitution of the country, and nothing less, it was believed, would save the Union from shipwreck, dissolution, and ruin. The line of 36° 30' was then obtained, or rather extorted, without a 'valuable consideration.' Here is what is called a *nudum pactum,* a contract that is void, and it imposed no sort of obligation either in law or in conscience.

2. "The South was not bound by the Compromise of 1820, because it was not fulfilled by the North." The facts on this point are to be found in the preceding pages.

3. "The South was not bound by the Compromise of 1820, because it was unconstitutional," as has since been decided by the Supreme Court of the United States. Moreover, some Northern statesmen declared they did not esteem it binding as a compact, inasmuch as there were no competent parties to it.

Mr. Douglas, after having spoken of what he deemed the impropriety of said "appeal" in the circumstances of its presentation, uses the following language: "I do not like, I never did like, the system of legislation on our part, by which a geographical line, in violation of the laws of nature, and climate,

and soil, and of the laws of God, should be run to establish institutions for a people; yet out of a regard for the peace and
quiet of the country, out of respect for past pledges, out of
a desire to adhere faithfully to all pledges, and out of a desire
to adhere faithfully to all compromises, I sustained the Missouri
Compromise so long as it was in force, and advocated its extension to the Pacific. Now when that has been abandoned, when
it has been superseded, when a great principle of self-government has been substituted for it, I choose to cling to that principle, and abide in good faith not only by the letter, but by
the spirit, of the last compromise, (namely, that of 1850, in
which the right of framing their own constitutions, whether by
the admission or prohibition of slavery, was conceded to Utah
and New Mexico.)

"Sir, I do not recognize the right of the Abolitionists of
this country to arraign me for being false to sacred pledges, as
they have done in their proclamation. Let them show when
and where I have ever violated a compact. I have proved that
I stood by the compact of 1820 and 1845, and proposed its continuance in 1848. I have proved that the Freesoilers and
Abolitionists were the guilty parties who violated that compromise then. I should like to compare notes with those Abolition confederates about adherence to compromises. When did
they stand by or approve of any one that was ever made?

"Did not every Abolitionist and Freesoiler in America denounce the Missouri Compromise in 1820? Did they not for
years hunt down ravenously for his blood every man who
assisted in making that compromise? Did they not in 1845,
when Texas was annexed, denounce all of us who went for the
annexation of Texas and for the continuation of the Missouri
Compromise line through it? Did they not in 1848 denounce
me as a slavery propagandist for standing by the principles of
the Missouri Compromise, and for proposing to continue the
Missouri Compromise line to the Pacific Ocean? Did they not
violate and repudiate it then? Is not the charge of bad faith
true as to every Abolitionist in America, instead of being true
as to me and the committee, and those who advocate this
bill?

"They talk about the bill being a violation of the compromise measures of 1850. Who can show me a man in either House of Congress who was in favor of the compromise measures of 1850, and who is not now in favor of leaving the people of Nebraska and Kansas to do as they please upon the subject of slavery according to the provisions of my bill? Is there one? If so, I have not heard of him. This tornado has been raised by the Abolitionists, and the Abolitionists alone. They have made an impression on the public mind in the way which I have mentioned, by a falsification of the law and the facts; and this whole organization against the compromise measures of 1850 is an Abolition movement. I presume they had some hope of getting a few tender-footed Democrats into their plot; and acting on what they supposed they might do, they sent forth publicly to the world the falsehood that their address was signed by the Senators and a majority of the Representatives from the State of Ohio; but when we come to examine the signatures we find no one Whig there, no one Democrat there, none but pure, unadulterated Abolitionists. * *

"Now I ask the friends and the opponents of the measure to look at it as it is. Is not the question involved, the simple one, Whether the people of the territories shall be allowed to do as they please upon the question of slavery, subject only to the limitation of the Constitution? * * *

"When you propose to give them a territorial government, do you not acknowledge that they are capable of self-government? Having made that acknowledgment, why should you not allow them to exercise the rights of legislation? Oh, these Abolitionists are entirely willing to concede all this, with one exception. They say they are willing to trust the territorial legislature, under the limitations of the Constitution, to legislate on the rights of inheritance, to legislate in regard to religion, education, morals, to legislate in regard to the relations of husband and wife, of parent and child, and guardian and ward, upon every thing pertaining to the dearest rights and interests of white men, but they are not willing to trust them to legislate in regard to a few miserable negroes. That is their single exception. They acknowledge that the people of the territories are capable of deciding for themselves concerning white men, but not in relation to negroes. The real gist of the matter is this : Does it require any higher degree of civilization, intelligence, bravery, and sagacity, to legislate for negroes than for white men? If it does, we ought to adopt the Abolition doctrine and go with them against this bill. If it does not, if we are willing to trust the people with the great, sacred, fundamental right of prescribing their own institutions, consistent with the Constitution of the country, we must vote for this bill as reported by the Committee on Territories. That is the only question involved in the bill."

Mr. Cass, while the Nebraska bill was under consideration in the Senate, delivered a speech in which the following paragraphs are found :

"Mr. President, for some years we have heard a great deal about the fundamental articles of compact, by which governments for the territory north-west of the Ohio were originally instituted ; and a good many erroneous impressions have prevailed concerning them. What were they? Having lived under a territorial government in that region many years of my life, the history of the organizations of these political communities is perfectly familiar to me. The Congress of the old Confederation, in 1787, passed a law establishing the north-western territory. It was styled an ordinance, and many have supposed that it derived peculiar solemnity from the use of this term. But this is a mistake. "Be it ordained," &c., was the formula of enactment before the Constitution, and this ordinance had no more validity than the usual acts of the old Congress. It has been supposed, too, that the whole of this act constituted a compact. That is an equal error.

"Now, sir, what is a compact? I have just adverted to the dictionary, to the old and standard English lexicographer, to ascertain its meaning, and here it is: 'A compact is a contract, an accord, or agreement between two or more to do or forbear something.' Now, sir, in applying this definition to the case before us, let us inquire who were the 'two or more' parties or persons by whom this contract was made? It will be hard to find them. The law was passed, as I have said, by the old Confederation ; and there never was, in fact, any other party to it. What did they undertake to do? They undertook to establish five articles containing various provisions of more or less importance, affecting the rights and interests of the people then occupying, or who might in all time to come occupy, the region over which the ordinance extended. And they declared that they should never be altered but in the mode pointed out. And will any man seriously contend that is a compact? What other party was there to it? There were some thousands of people then living in that country, not one of whom heard of this contract, which was forever to bind them for years and years after its promulgation. It is an insult to common sense to say, that they and their posterity are bound by such a one-sided instrument as that.

"Besides, if there had not been a single man in those regions, how could a compact be established which was forever to operate on a people thereafter to exist there, when no provision was made for submitting it to their assent, under any circumstances or in any future time? It is idle, sir, to talk of the obligatory nature of a compact thus declared to be such by one party, without the existence of any other party at the time, and without any arrangement for procuring its concurrence when such party should come into existence. This ordinance is destitute of the first essence of mutual obligation.

"But, sir, independent of the fatal objection of the want of parties, there was another equally fatal, and that was the want of power. Nothing was more certain than that the Congress of the Confederation had not the slightest authority to establish territorial governments; and there is no man who will turn to the Articles of Confederation and examine them, who will have the least doubt upon the subject."

"Mr. MADISON said, in speaking upon the subject, 'all this has been done,' that is, governments have been organized, 'without the least color of constitutional authority.' And Mr. ADAMS said 'that the ordinance of 1789 had been passed by the old Congress of the Confederation without authority from the States.'

"These remarks prove that the States of the north-west territory have full power to establish slavery in them if they see fit.

"The Senator from Illinois, Mr. DOUGLAS, told us the other day, proved to us, indeed, that his State recognized the existence of slavery, notwithstanding its eternal interdiction in the ordinance of 1789. And I have never heard, until recently, that the power of the other north-western States to do the same thing was either doubted or denied. If they cannot by their conventions regulate the condition of slavery as they please, they have not a just political equality in the Union."

REMARKS.

1. After the Nebraska bill was passed in the Senate, the " Emigrant Aid Society " was incorporated by the Massachusetts Legislature, on the 4th of May, 1854, which was some weeks before the bill passed the House and became a law. A new charter was received in February, 1855. The object of its formation was to make Kansas a free State, by furnishing aid to emigrants who would go there for that purpose. The general policy of Massachusetts had been to aid men to stay in the Commonwealth, by establishing manufactures, and by other means, rather than to aid them to leave it.

2. The debates in Washington, and the passage of the bill, created a powerful sectional excitement throughout the country, but especially in Kansas, where there was a severe struggle between the pro-slavery and the Free-soil party for the political ascendency. Lecturers went through portions of the Northern States to obtain recruits, and money, and arms, describing the physical advantages of the territory to be such that it could be made a terrestrial paradise. The love of adventure, the love of money, the love of liberty, and hatred or jealousy of the South, were appealed to successfully for obtaining emigrants. Nor were Southern men idle. Border ruffians and free State ruffians met in Kansas as a battle-ground. And elsewhere " shrieking, bleeding Kansas " was successfully employed by demagogues to electioneer for them, as the especial friends of liberty, or of slavery, as the case might be. In Congress, too, those who spoke on this subject became, if possible, more intemperate in their language. Mr. SUMNER's speech entitled " The crime against Kansas," and Mr. BROOKE's assault on him for what he said in that speech concerning South Carolina and Senator BUTLER, were exponents of the feeling which to some extent existed in the two sections of the country to which these gentlemen be-

longed, and proved the means of extending that jealousy and making it more intense.

3. Was the repeal of the Missouri Compromise, which was the great measure of General PIERCE's Administration so far as sectional interests were concerned, a judicious measure? It seemed to be the occasion of aggravating, rather than of diminishing the sectional difficulties and the sectional hatred. But if another course had been taken, it might have proved the occasion of as great or even greater sectional difficulties and sectional hatred. In this latter case, perhaps, there might not have been an opportunity to ring the changes upon the phrases, the " traitor DOUGLAS," the " Kansas swindle." There might not have been so much blackguardism and disgraceful personalities in Congress, or as much ruffianism and bad blood generated in the States, or as much blood shed in the territory, or as many dragon's teeth sown broadcast over the land which have since started up armed men.

But when we undertake to judge of the comparative wisdom of two measures, one of which has been adopted, simply on the ground of results, we are in danger of running into error for the reason that one term of the comparison is wanting. One class of results we never can know, namely, the results of the measure that was not adopted. Human passions are refractory subjects to deal with, especially as exhibited in two great political parties, jealous of each other, each intent on the acquisition of political power, and they will often practically convert the wisest measures into causes of national arrogance and injury. After the passage of the Kansas and Nebraska bill, if things had taken their natural course, and men had emigrated westward according to the more general practice along the same parallels of latitude; if there had not been any unnatural stimulus given to emigration by " Emigrant Aid Societies " on the one hand, and " Friendly Societies " on the other; if means had not been adopted to address the combativeness of young men and to inflame their passions and their conscience, and to appeal to their love of gain, and to put arms into their hands, as if they were to go against enemies to win an empire, the results of the repeal of the slavery restriction north of $36° 30'$ might have been very different from what they were, and the measure might in this case have proved by the results to be a wise one.

In regard to the application of physical force for correcting the evils of the times connected with slavery, Mr. SEWARD, in his speech delivered at Detroit, speaks in the following judicious terms : " You ask, how are these great evils to be corrected, these great dangers to be avoided ? I answer, it is to be done not, as some of you have supposed, by heated debates, sustained by rifles and revolvers at Washington; nor yet by sending armies, and supplies, and Sharp's rifles into Kansas. I condemn no necessary exercise of self-defence in any place where public safety is necessary to practice of the real duties of champions of freedom. But this is a contest in which the race is not to the physically swift, nor the battle to those who have the most muscular strength. Least of all is it to be won by retaliation and revenge."

It was unfortunate that the geographical line of 36° 30', established by the Missouri Compromise, was not made the rule of division afterwards, by being extended to the Pacific Ocean, according to the proposal of Mr. DOUGLAS. It would have prevented the disputes that afterwards arose. This the Northern members repeatedly refused to do. Another mode for settling the difficulty had to be found, namely, the Constitutional mode. If the geographical mode of division adopted in the Compromise of 1820 could not be carried out, then the principles of the Compromise of 1850 had to be applied, namely, the principle of popular sovereignty.

In general, it may be asserted that the Missouri Compromise never ought to have been made; that being made, it ought not to have been repealed ; and having been repealed, it ought never to be restored without some modification.

4. It is not known to the writer that any similar " appeal " by members of Congress, while a question was pending, was ever before made to the people of the United States. Neither is it known to the writer that any similar " protest " was ever addressed to Congress by the clergymen of New England, in their professional character, as distinguished from " private citizens."

CHAPTER XV.

JAMES BUCHANAN'S ADMINISTRATION.

MARCH 4, 1857—MARCH 4, 1861.

MR. BUCHANAN was the candidate of the Democratic party throughout both the Northern and the Southern States. Mr. FILLMORE was the candidate of the Union party, embracing Conservative Whigs and Americans throughout the Northern and the Southern States. JOHN C. FREMONT was the candidate of the Republican party, which was confined mainly to the Northern or non-slaveholding States. This last party grew up out of the troubles and excitements connected with the settlement of Kansas, and was cemented by a common feeling of opposition to slavery and the common hope of gaining political power. It was composed, in part, of the old Liberty party and of the Freesoil party, and in part of the Abolition wing of the Whig party, and in part of others who were disgusted with the repeal of the Missouri Compromise. The origin of the party has been referred to an anti-Nebraska convention held in Auburn, New York, Sept. 27, 1854, which passed the following resolution: "*Resolved* that we recommend that a convention of Delegates from *the Free States*, equal in number to their Representatives in Congress, be held in Syracuse, N. Y., on the 4th of July, 1856, to nominate candidates for the Presidency and the Vice-presidency of the United States for the next presidential election." This resolution was adopted by tremendous cheering. It was also moved to call this the "Republican Organization;" which resolution was also carried. A leading member of that same convention declared it to be an object of that Republican party to "employ all constitutional measures to restrain and cripple slavery where it now exists."

13

The proposed convention was held in Philadelphia, in which only the Free States were represented. Among the Resolutions passed were the two following :

"*Resolved*, That we deny the authority of Congress, of a Territorial Legislature, of any individual or association of individuals, to give legal existence to slavery in any Territory of the United States, while the present Constitution shall be maintained.

"*Resolved*, That the Constitution confers upon Congress sovereign power over the Territories of the United States for their government, and that in the exercise of this power it is both the right and the duty of Congress to prohibit in the Territories those twin relics of barbarism—polygamy and slavery."

I do not quote these resolutions to show their evident inconsistency in admitting the sovereignty of Congress over the Territories, with power to prohibit slavery therein ; and then denying the power to legislate slavery into any Territory, but only to exhibit the sectional relations and bearings, and the spirit of the convention. The ends aimed at were sectional, as were the means used, and the spirit manifested, and the men brought forward as candidates.

IS THE REPUBLICAN PARTY SECTIONAL?

Mr. FILLMORE, in a speech delivered at Albany, in the summer of 1856, not long after his return from abroad, held the following language in relation to the politics of the country, and the approaching election :

"Sir, you have been pleased to say that I have the union of these States at heart. This, sir, is most true ; for if there be one object dearer to me than any other it is the unity, prosperity, and glory of this great Republic. I confess frankly, sir, that I fear it is in danger. I say nothing of any particular section, much less of the several candidates before the people. I presume they are all honorable men. But, sir, what do we see? An exasperated state of feeling between the North and the South on the most exciting of all topics, resulting in bloodshed and organized military array. But this is not all, sir. We see a political party presenting candidates for the Presidency and the Vice-Presidency selected for the first time from the Free States alone, with the avowed purpose of electing these candidates by suffrages from one part of the Union only, to rule over the whole United States.

" Can it be possible that those who are engaged in such a measure can have seriously reflected on the consequences which must inevitably follow in case of success ? Can they have the madness or the folly to believe that our Southern brethren would submit to be governed by such a Chief Magistrate? Would he be required to follow the same rule prescribed by those who elected him, in making his appointments? If a man living south of Mason and Dixon's line be not worthy to be President or Vice-President, would it be proper to select one from the same quarter as one of his cabinet council, or to represent the nation in a foreign country, or, indeed, to collect the revenue, or administer the laws of the United States? If not, what new rule is the President to adopt for selection to office, that the people themselves discard in selecting him?

" These are serious but practical questions, and in order to appreciate them fully, it is only necessary to turn the tables upon ourselves, and suppose that the South, having a majority of the electoral votes, should declare that they would only have slave-holders for President and Vice-President, and should select such by their exclusive suffrages to rule over us at the North, do you think we would submit to it? No, not for one moment. And do you believe your Southern brethren less sensible on this subject than you are, or less jealous of their rights? If you do, let me tell you you are certainly mistaken. And therefore you must see, that if this sectional party succeeds, it leads inevitably to the destruction of this beautiful fabric, reared by our forefathers, cemented by their blood, and bequeathed to us as a priceless inheritance.

" I tell you, my friends, that I speak warmly on this subject, for I feel that we are in danger. I am determined to make a clean breast of it. I will wash my hands of the consequences, whatever they may be; and I tell you that we are treading on the brink of a volcano that is liable at any moment to burst forth and overwhelm the nation."

There were many threats of disunion in case of the election

of Mr. FREMONT. Mr. BURNETT, member of Congress from Kentucky, after speaking of the strong attachment of his State to the Union, goes on to say: "But, sir, if JOHN C. FREMONT should be elected, pledged as he is to make war upon the institutions of the South, composed as his Administration would be of men from one section of the Union, filled as the Federal offices would be with sectional men, all pledged to make a common cause against the South, with a Congress backing up his Administration, such as the present House, who conceive no measure too unconstitutional, too revolutionary, too disgraceful, to meet their sanction, so as it makes war upon the South, the frightful mien of disunion forces itself on them as far the preferable alternative between it and oppression and disgrace in the Union. They would then still be mindful of its past glories, the memories of its great statesmen, the heroic deeds of valor of its noted warriors, and prefer rather to cut short its existence than blacken those brilliant recollections with the record of its future disgrace." This is a type of the feeling that prevailed in the South generally, in opposition to the Republican party.

And in the Republican party there was also a spirit of intolerance and disunion. Mr. HORACE GREELEY declared: "I have no doubt but the Free and the Slave States ought to be separated * * The Union is not worth supporting in connection with the South." Mr. E. P. HURLBURT, a lawyer in Herkimer, New York, made the following declaration: "Rather than admit another slave State into the Confederacy, I would dissolve it. Rather than endure the curse of such another four years' governmental infamy as PIERCE, DOUGLAS, and Co. have inflicted on us, I would dissolve it, so help me Heaven." Mr. G. W. JULIEN, who had been a member of Congress from Indiana, in a speech made the following declaration on behalf of the Republican party: "I tell you we are a sectional party. It is not alone a fight between the North and the South; it is a fight between freedom and slavery; between God and the Devil; between heaven and hell." [Loud applause.] A. P. BURLINGAME, member from Mass., said: "When we shall have elected a President, as we will, who will not be the President of a party, nor of a section, but the tribune of the people, and after we have exterminated a few more miserable doughfaces from the

North, then if the slave Senate will not give way, we will grind it between the upper and nether mill-stone of our power." SIMON BROWN, ex-Lieutenant-Governor of Massachusetts, said : "The object to be accomplished is this, for the Free States to take possession of the Government." TRUMAN SMITH, ex-Senator of Connecticut, declared : " Should Mr. BUCHANAN be elected, it may be written down as certain that, within two years from the fourth of March next, Kansas will be delivered up to the Molochs of slavery. She will be brought in as a Slave State."

These extracts show the state of feeling in both sections of the country. Extensively at the South there was a determination to secede from the Union for the reasons stated by Mr. BURNETT, in case Mr. FREMONT should be elected President.

THE DRED SCOTT DECISION.

Just after President BUCHANAN's inauguration, the Supreme Court of the United States made the famous decision in the case of DRED SCOTT, which seemed to settle certain political questions which had long been pending in the public mind. In the act of Congress, by which Kansas and Nebraska became Territories, the slavery restriction which applied to all territory north of 36° 30' was repealed. The scope and effect of the language of repeal were not left in doubt. It was declared in terms to be " the true intent and meaning of this act, not to legislate slavery into any Territory or State, nor to exclude it therefrom, but to leave the people thereof perfectly free to form and regulate their own institutions in their own way, subject only to the Constitution of the United States."

DRED SCOTT, in the year 1854, was a negro slave belonging to Dr. EMERSON, who was a surgeon in the army of the United States. In that year, Dr. EMERSON took the said Scott to the military post at Rock Island in the State of Illinois. and held him there as a slave until April or May, 1856. At the time last mentioned, said Dr. EMERSON removed to the military post at Fort Snelling, situated on the west bank of the Mississippi River, in the Territory known as Upper Louisiana, acquired by the United States from France, and situated north of the lati-

tude of 36° 30′ north, and north of the State of Missouri. Dr.
EMERSON held the plaintiff, DRED SCOTT, in slavery until the
year 1858. The court decided that said DRED SCOTT did not obtain title to his liberty from the fact that his master took him
first from Missouri to Illinois, where negro slavery does not exist by law, and next to the territory north of 36° 30′, where, by
the Missouri Compromise, slavery was prohibited.

In deciding this case upon certain principles, those principles had to be examined and settled.

1. It was decided that a free negro of the African race,
whose ancestors were brought to this country and sold as slaves,
is not a " citizen " within the meaning of the Constitution of the
United States.

2. It was decided that the clauses in the Constitution which
point to this race, treat them as persons whom it was lawful to
deal in as articles of property, and to hold as slaves.

3. It was decided that since the adoption of the Constitution
of the United States, no State can by any subsequent law make
a foreigner or any other description of persons citizens of the
United States, nor entitle them to the rights and privileges secured to citizens by that instrument.

4. The change in public opinion and feeling in relation to
the African race, which has taken place since the adoption of
the Constitution, cannot change its construction and meaning,
and it must be construed and administered now, according to
its true meaning and intentions, when it was framed and
adopted.

5. The clause in the Constitution authorizing Congress to
make all needful rules and regulations for the government of
the territory and other property of the United States, applies
only to territory within the chartered limits of some one of the
States when they were colonies of Great Britain, and which
was surrendered by the British Government to the old Confed- ·
eration of States, in the Treaty of peace. It does not apply to
territory acquired by the present Federal Government, by treaty
or conquest from a foreign nation.

6. During the time it remains a territory, Congress may legislate over it within the scope of its constitutional powers in relation to citizens of the United States, and may establish a Ter-

ritorial Government, and the form of this local government must be regulated by the discretion of Congress, but with powers not exceeding those which Congress itself, by the Constitution, is authorized to exercise over citizens of the United States, in respect to their rights of persons or rights of property.

7. The territory thus acquired, is acquired by the people of the United States for their common and equal benefit, through their agent or trustee, the Federal Government; Congress can exercise no power over the rights of persons or property of a citizen in the Territory, which is prohibited by the Constitution. The Government and the citizens both enter it with their respective rights defined and limited by the Constitution.

8. Congress has no right to prohibit the citizens of any particular State or States from taking up their home there, while it permits citizens of other States to do so. Nor has it a right to give privileges to one class of citizens which it refuses to do to another. The territory is acquired for their equal and common benefit, and if open to any, it must be open to all upon equal and the same terms.

9. Every citizen has a right to take with him into the territory, any article of property which the Constitution of the United States recognizes as property.

10. The Constitution of the United States recognizes slaves as property, and pledges the General Government to protect it. And Congress cannot exercise any more authority over property of that description, than it may constitutionally exercise over property of any other kind.

11. The act of Congress, therefore, prohibiting a citizen of the United States from taking with him his slaves when he removes to the territory in question to reside, is an exercise of authority over private property which is not warranted by the Constitution; and the removal of the plaintiff by his owner to that territory gave him no title to freedom.

HELPER'S BOOK.

After the nomination for Speaker in the House of Representatives for the 36th Congress, on Dec. 5, 1859, Mr. CLARK, member from Missouri, offered the following resolution:

" Whereas certain members of this House, now in nomination for Speaker, did endorse and recommend the book hereinafter mentioned,

" *Resolved*, That the doctrines and sentiments of a certain book, called ' *The impending crisis of the South—How to meet it*,' purporting to have been written by one Hinton Rowan Helper, are insurrectionary and hostile to the domestic peace and tranquillity of the country, and that no member of this House, who has endorsed and recommended it, or the compend from it, is fit to be Speaker of this House."

The design of the book was to hasten the crisis which it predicts as " impending," by detailing the wretchedness of the Slave States ; " the aim of the revolution " desired ; " the stupid masses in the South," who are described as the " white victims" of slavery ; the results as the " sum of all villanies," as slavery is described to be ; the dependence of the South on the North for the necessary or the convenient articles of life ; with " a revolutionary appeal to Southern non-slaveholders ; " with the declaration that " the North must seize the riches of the South," and " that the revolution must free the slaves ; " and that the North is too scrupulous ; that the revolution must take place, " peaceably if we can, forcibly if we must."

" *The banner to stand or die by.* Inscribed on the banner which we herewith unfurl to the world, with the fixed determination to stand by it or die by it, unless one of more virtuous efficacy shall be presented, are the mottoes which in substance embody the principles, as we conceive, that should govern us in our patriotic warfare against the most subtle and insidious foe that ever menaced the inalienable rights, and liberties, and dearest interests of America."

" 1. Thorough organization and independent political action on the part of the non-slaveholding whites at the South.

" 2. Ineligibility of pro-slavery slaveholders ; never another vote to any one who advocates the retention and perpetuation of human slavery.

" 3. No co-operation with pro-slavery ; no fellowship with them in religion ; no affiliation with them in society.

" 4. No patronage to pro-slavery merchants ; no guestship in pro-slavery hotels ; no fees to pro-slavery lawyers ; no employment of pro-slavery physicians; no audience to pro-slavery parsons.

" 5. No more hiring of slaves by non-slaveholders.

" 6. Abrupt discontinuance of subscription to pro-slavery newspapers.

" 7. The greatest possible encouragement to free white labor."

These are portions of the extracts from HELPER's book, which, at the request of the mover, were read by the clerk of the House. Portions omitted are more outrageously bitter and insulting than the portions quoted.

Mr. CLARK, the mover of the resolution, after the reading of the extracts, proceeded to say : " I have had that document read, in order that the country, as well as this body, might be informed of the position held by certain gentlemen of the Republican party, and especially by those who have been recommended for the Speakership of this House. The extracts which have been read, are, in substance, true extracts from the book itself, which is in the House. Those extracts have been examined and marked. It appears by those extracts that nearly all the Republican members of the last Congress, and certain members of the present, recommended certain things to the non-slaveholders of the South ; and among them, non-fellowship either socially or politically, with slaveholders. If such be the purpose of the gentlemen of this House who signed that paper, let me ask, has it indeed come to this, that gentlemen of the North who live under institutions secured to them by the Constitution of their country, which institutions we have never attempted to invade; that gentlemen living in a bond of union, and under a Constitution that cost so much blood and so much treasure, and under which, by the co-operation of both North and South, our country has grown to its present strength and importance—has it come to this, that they have got their own consent, and expect the country will agree to it, to advise those of the South who do not happen to own slaves, to rise in rebellion and destroy the slave interest, part by non-intercourse in religion, or socially or politically ; and then by advising them not to wait to strike the blow until their arms are powerless, but to exterminate the odious institution, peaceably if they can, forcibly if they must ? Such are the directions recommended by the paper which was signed by at least two members of this House, who have been recommended by the Republicans for the Speakership. * *

"Sir : Do these gentlemen suppose that slaveholders who have won the confidence of their constituents, and who have been sent here to assist in making laws and preserving the Constitution, and keeping the Government intact, feel themselves honored by their association ? If they do, they are greatly deceived. We have been on terms of personal intimacy with them. Every gentleman in this House who knows me, knows that my intercourse with them has been marked with the utmost urbanity. I have met Representatives in this Hall coming from all parts of the country, as my compeers in every relation in life. But can I continue to do so, except gentlemen disclaim having advised my constituents—half of whom are non-slaveholders, to have no intercourse with me ; not to visit the church where I worship ; to strike down and ostracize slaveholding ministers ; to abandon hotels where there are slave waiters ; to discountenance patronage to newspapers that are conducted by slaveholders ? If they expect to play this game, the sooner it is avowed the better. * *

"These gentlemen come in and say that the riches of the South are neglected by the bad management of the South ; that the accursed plague of slavery does it ; and, therefore, that the non-slaveholders of the South should rise in their majesty— peaceably if they can, forcibly if they must—take their arms, drive out the plague of slavery, take possession of the country, and dedicate it to freedom.

"That is the sentiment of the book which those gentlemen recommend to have circulated gratuitously all over the South. Are such men fit to preside over the destinies of our common country ? "

In this book occurs the following paragraph : "This is the outline of our scheme for the obliteration of slavery in the Southern States. Let it be acted upon with due promptitude, and as certain as truth is mightier than error, fifteen years will not elapse before every foot of territory from the mouth of the Delaware to the Rio Grande will glitter with the jewels of freedom."

There was a subscription set on foot in the city of New York for the gratuitous distribution of one hundred thousand copies. To the fund thus raised, it was said that the Governor of New York contributed one hundred dollars.

Besides the sixty-eight members of Congress who recommended HELPER's book, Senator WADE of Ohio said: "I had looked over the book, and saw nothing objectionable." Senator Seward also spoke favorably of it.

A portion of a pamphlet was read, Dec. 20, 1859, at the request of Mr. VALLANDIGHAM, "which was extensively circulated in the Northern, Southern, and Western States of this Union, and which contains the plan of associations to be formed for the purpose of carrying on hostilities against a portion of this Confederacy." After certain annunciation of principles, and after certain preliminaries, it was proposed "to land military forces in the Southern States, who shall raise the standard of freedom, and call the slaves to it, and such free persons as may be willing to join it.

"Our plan is to make war openly or secretly as circumstances may dictate, upon the property of the slaveholders and their abettors, not for its destruction, if that can be easily avoided, but to convert it to the use of the slaves. If it cannot thus be converted, we advise its destruction. *Teach the slaves to burn their masters' buildings,* to kill their cattle and hogs, to *conceal and destroy farming utensils, to abandon labor in seed time* and harvest, and let the *crops perish.* Make slave labor unprofitable in this way if it can be done in no other.

"To make slaveholders objects of derision and contempt by *flogging* them whenever they shall be guilty of flogging their slaves."

This plan JOHN BROWN attempted to carry into practice.

Mr. SHERMAN, the candidate for the Speakership, and against whose election Mr. CLARK's resolution was introduced, as one of the signers of the recommendation of HELPER's book, was defeated.

THE JOHN BROWN INVASION.

JOHN BROWN, in the autumn of 1859, with twenty-three others, obtained forcible possession of the armory at Harper's

Ferry, Virginia. In the Senate of the United States, Mr. MASON, Senator from Virginia, brought forward a resolution to appoint a committee to investigate the facts in the case. This resolution at its introduction had to encounter an amendment offered by Mr. TRUMBULL, of Illinois, designed, it was asserted, to embarrass the action of the Senate in the matter. It also had to encounter the argument and ridicule of Senator HALE, in the same body.

Mr. HALE, of New Hampshire, December 6: "I am free to say, sir, that while I desire now, as I have always desired, this Union may be perpetual, I confess I do see danger to it. I do not see danger from any thing we are doing in the Free States, not the slightest; but I do see danger to this Union from the continued obloquy, reproach, and crimination which is heaped upon the people of the Free States, every time there is any thing calling attention to the subject in the South. * *

"I do not see, for myself, how Southern gentlemen can consent to live in a Union, if they believe that those who are associated with them are the characters which the public press represent us to be; if we are so utterly false not only to the oaths that we have taken to support the Constitution, but to the moral obligations which ought to bind us as patriots and Christians. If the sentiment, that we are so utterly wanting in all those qualities of character, is to be continually and eternally iterated and re-iterated from one of the sections of the country, where these transactions may take place, to the other, there will be a feeling generated which will be fatal to the Union."

Mr. HUNTER, of Virginia, on the same day spoke as follows: "Mr. President, I rise to express my surprise at the manner in which the resolution offered by my colleague has been received —a resolution temperate, proper, and made essentially necessary by circumstances of recent occurrence. I had presumed that no obstacle would be thrown in the way, but that Senators on all sides of the House would agree to go into the inquiry.

"It is known to all that a most atrocious outrage has been committed upon the State which I have the honor in part to represent; that the people of a town reposing in the hours of night, in all the confidence of peace and conscious innocence of all purposes of wrong to mankind, were suddenly invaded, and attacked by a band of armed men from non-slaveholding States; that unarmed men were shot down in the streets; that murders were committed; that an attempt was openly made, not only to subvert the Constitution of the United States, but the Constitution of Virginia; that men were seized and dragged from their habitations at night, and that attempts were made to excite servile insurrection and civil war in its most horrid form. It is known too, sir, that complicity has been charged, not on the part of the South, but by individuals professing to have been in the employment of persons and associations in the non-slaveholding States; and it is also known to those who come from the South, at least, that the public mind has been startled, not so much by the foray of Brown and his twenty-three men, as by the open sympathy and approbation which have been manifested by portions of the North in regard to that attempt, and the apparent indifference with which it has been treated by those who, we had a right to hope, would have been more conservative in their feelings and actions upon such a subject.

" Sir, I had supposed that such indecent exhibitions of sympathy for crime would have been frowned down by an outburst of public opinion on the part of those in the midst of whom such things were perpetrated.   *   *

" And now, sir, when my colleague proposes, in temperate language, merely to inquire into the facts of the case, and to raise a committee to see whether any thing can be done by the authorities of this Government to prevent the repetition of such outrages, how is it met? The Senator from Illinois proposes to stifle such inquiry by making a party issue, and turning the whole subject into a matter of mere partisan warfare and discussion.   *   *

" Still less had we supposed that such a question was to be met with the levity of the Senator from New Hampshire. Why, sir, upon such occasions as these, upon such occasions as this—I will not say as these, for it has no parallel in the history of our Government—to see such a subject treated with the levity in which he is disposed to deal with it, sounds to me, at least, like the laugh of the inebriate or the insensate in the chamber of death itself. I tell him, sir, that much depends upon what is the real state of Northern feeling in regard to these matters. We know that we can defend ourselves against such outrages as this; against the forays of men who may attempt to get up servile war among us; we hope we can defend ourselves against all the hazards to which we may probably be exposed; but it becomes a much graver question to say, how we are to deal with the subject if we become convinced that such attempts find support not only in the sympathy of the great mass of the North, but in contributions that may be actually raised for their assistance."

Mr. Douglas, Jan. 23, 1860: " Without stopping to adduce evidence in detail, I have no hesitation in expressing my firm and deliberate conviction that the Harper's Ferry crime was the matured, logical, inevitable result of the doctrines and teachings of the Republican party, explained and enforced in their platform, their partisan presses, their pamphlets and books, and especially of their leaders in and out of Congress. *

" The great principle that underlies the organization of the Republican party is—*violent, irreconcilable, eternal warfare upon the institution of American slavery*, with a view to its ultimate extinction throughout the land. Sectional war is to be waged until the cotton fields of the South shall be cultivated by free labor, or the rye fields of New York and Massachusetts shall be cultivated by slave labor."

SYMPATHY WITH BROWN.

The admirers of John Brown made a distinction between his acts and his character, the means he employed and the end which he aimed at. The acts and the means they condemned, while his character and the end he aimed to accomplish they seemed to approve and admire. It appears that he spent some years in Kansas, where, being possessed by an evil spirit, he perpetrated acts which were denominated murder, theft, and robbery. " It cannot be disguised that the Northern heart sympathized with Brown and his fate because he died in the cause of what they call liberty." On the day of his death bells were tolled in many places; cannon fired; prayers were offered for him as if he were a martyr; he was placed in the same category with Paul and Silas, for whom prayers were made by the

Church ; churches were draped in mourning ; a motion was made in the Senate of Massachusetts, " that, in view of the fact that this was the day on which JOHN BROWN was sentenced to be hanged, the Senate do now adjourn." The motion was lost ; the vote being 8 to 11. There were *twenty* absentees, who shirked the question. There was also a strong sympathy in the House for BROWN, though that, likewise, by a large majority refused to adjourn. It was moved in the House, " that for the great respect we have for the truthfulness and faith that JOHN BROWN had in man and his religion, and the strong sympathy for the love of liberty (the avowed principle of Massachusetts) for which he is this day to die, this House do now adjourn." Massachusetts elected, as governor, a man who presided at a meeting assembled to express sympathy for BROWN. What was true of the general sentiment in favor of BROWN in portions of Massachusetts, was true of many localities elsewhere in the Free States. This sectional sympathy at the North increased the sectional jealousy at the South.

PERSONAL LIBERTY BILLS.

The effect of " personal liberty bills," was to throw obstructions in the way of carrying out the provisions of the Constitution for the restoration of fugitive slaves to their owners.

States which prohibit their officers and citizens from aiding in the execution of the fugitive slave laws of 1793 and 1850 : Maine, Massachusetts, Pennsylvania, New York, Vermont, Wisconsin, New Hampshire, Connecticut, Michigan, New Jersey, Rhode Island.

States that deny all public edifices in aid of the master: Maine, Massachusetts, Michigan, Vermont, Rhode Island.

States that provide defence for the fugitive : Maine, Massachusetts, Pennsylvania, Wisconsin, Vermont, New York, Michigan.

States which declare the fugitives free, if brought by their masters into the State : Maine, Vermont, New Hampshire.

State that declares him to be free absolutely : New Hampshire. See Report of the Committee of the Legislature of Virginia in 1860.

EXTRACT FROM A PERSONAL LIBERTY BILL OF VERMONT.

" Every person who may have been held as a slave, who
shall come or who may be brought into this State, with the
consent of his or her alleged master or mistress, or who shall
come or be brought, or shall be in this State, shall be free.

" Every person who shall hold, or attempt to hold, in this
State in slavery as a slave, any free person, in any form or for
any time, however short, under the pretence that such person
is or has been a slave, shall, on conviction thereof, be imprisoned in the State prison for a term not less than five years, nor
more than twenty, and be fined not less than $1,000, nor more
than $10,000."

Mr. WEBSTER, in his seventh of March speech, spoke as follows : " I will allude to other grounds of complaint of the South,
and especially to one which, in my opinion, furnishes just foundation of complaint, and that is, that there has been found at
the North among individuals, and among legislatures, a disinclination to perform fully their constitutional duties, in regard
to the return of persons bound to service, who have escaped into
the free States.   In that respect the South, in my judgment,·is
right, and the North wrong.   Every member of every Northern
legislature is bound by oath, like every other officer in the country, to support the Constitution of the United States ; and the
article of the Constitution which says to these States, that they
shall deliver up fugitives from service, is as binding in honor
and conscience as any other article."

Mr. WEBSTER, in his speech at Capon Springs, Virginia, in
1851, said : " I do not hesitate to say and repeat, that if the
Northern States refuse wilfully and deliberately to carry into
effect that part of the Constitution which respects the restoration of fugitive slaves, the South would no longer be bound to
keep the compact.   A bargain broken on one side, is broken on
all sides."

IS SLAVERY A MERE CREATURE OF LOCAL LAW ?

Judge STORY, of the Supreme Court of the United States,
in the decision in the Prigg case, declared that slavery is a mere
creature of local law.   This opinion became fashionable at the

North. But the same eminent judge, in 1827, wrote to Lord STOWEL, that he fully concurred with him in his decision, in which he says that slavery " never was in Antigua the creature of *law*, but of that *custom* which operates with the force of law." Lord STOWEL, in that decision, in effect says, that " the slave who goes to England or to Massachusetts, from a slave State, is still a slave, that he is still his master's property; but that his master has lost control over him, not by reason of the cessation of his *property*, but because those States grant no *remedy* by which he can exercise his control." An invention is in the highest sense the property of the inventor, and a work, of its author, but their rights of property cannot be enforced unless there are patent laws and copyright laws. In barbarous countries, the rights of property exist, though they cannot be enforced by law.

Judge McLEAN, in the Prigg case, said : " But the inquiry is reiterated, Is not the master entitled to his *property ?* I answer that he is. *His right is guaranteed by the Constitution:* and the most summary means are found for its enforcement in the act of Congress." The right of property in slaves exists under the Constitution. In the history of the rights of property, it appears that these rights have existed prior to any written law, and were protected by common law. " The current suggestion that slave property exists but by local law is no more true of this than it is of all other property. In fact, the European socialists, who in wild radicalism (including the Assignation doctrine) are the correspondents of the American abolitionists, maintain the same doctrine as to all property, that the Abolitionists do as to slave property. He who has property, they argue, is the robber of him who has not. And the same precise theory of attack at the North upon the slave property of the South, would, if carried out to their legitimate, necessary, and logical consequences, and will, if successful in this, their first stage of action, superinduce attacks on all property, North and South."—CALEB CUSHING.

" In the treaty with Great Britain formed in 1782, stipulations were entered into that prisoners on both sides shall be set at liberty, and his Britannic Majesty shall, with all convenient speed, and without causing any distinction or carrying away *any negroes* or *other property* of the American inhabitants, &c.,"

14

signed by Richard Oswald, B. Franklin, John Jay, Henry Laurens. Thus the two nations recognized the right of property in negroes.

In the treaty of 1814, there is a similar provision in regard to "slaves and other property." This treaty was signed by Gambier, Henry Coulbourn, William Adams, John Quincy Adams, J. A. Bayard, Henry Clay, Jonathan Russell, Albert Gallatin. If such men could thus recognize the right of property in slaves, why should not others?

"It is historically well known, that the object of this clause in the Constitution relating to persons owing service and labor in one State escaping into another, was to secure to the citizens of the slaveholding States the *complete right and title* of ownership in their slaves, as property in every State of the Union, into which they might escape from the State whence they were held in servitude."—Judge Story, 16 *Peters' Reports*, p. 540.

NORTHERN ABOLITION AND DISUNION SENTIMENTS.

Mr. Lincoln addressed a speech to the Republican State Convention assembled in Illinois in June, 1858, of which the following is an extract:

"In my opinion it (the slavery agitation) will not cease until a crisis shall have reached and passed. A house divided against itself cannot stand. I believe this Government cannot endure permanently half slave and half free. I do not expect the house to fall, but I do expect it will cease to be divided. It will become all one thing, or all the other. Either the opponents of slavery will arrest the further spread of it, and place it where the public mind will rest in the belief that it is in a course of ultimate extinction, or its advocates will push forward until it shall become alike lawful in all the States—old as well as new, North as well as South."

In his Rochester speech in 1858, Senator Seward tells us "that the States must all become free, or all become slave; that the South, in other words, must conquer and subdue the North, or the North must triumph over the South, and drive slavery from its limits."

"It is an irrepressible conflict," he says, "between opposing and ordinary forces ; and it means that the United States must all become either entirely a slaveholding nation, or entirely a free labor nation. Either the cotton and rice fields of South Carolina, and the sugar plantations of Louisiana, will ultimately be tilled by free labor, and Charleston and New Orleans become marts for legitimate merchandise alone, or else the rye fields and wheat fields of Massachusetts and New York must again be surrendered by them to slave culture and to the production of slaves, and Boston and New York become once more markets for trade in the bodies and souls of men."

"Slavery can be limited to its present bounds. It can be ameliorated. It can and must be abolished, and you and I can and must do it."—Mr. SEWARD in Ohio, 1848.

Rev. Mr. WHEELOCK addressed a large congregation in Dover, New Hampshire, in a sermon, of which the following is an extract : "It is a great mistake to term this act (BROWN's) the beginning of bloodshed and war. Never could there be a greater error. We have had bloodshed and war for the last ten years. The campaign began on the 7th of March, 1850. The *dissolution of the Union dates from that day, and we have had no constitution since.* On that day DANIEL WEBSTER was put to death—and such a death ! And from that time to this, there has not been a month that has not seen the soil of freedom invaded and attacked, our citizens kidnapped, imprisoned, and shot, or driven by thousands into Canada."

Gov. CHASE said to W. D. CHADWICK GLOVER, Dec. 27, 1859 : " I do not wish to have the slave emancipated because I love him, but because I hate his master. I hate slavery. I hate a man that will own a slave."

" There is really no union now between the North and the South ; and he believed no two nations on the earth entertain feelings of more bitter rancor towards each other, than these two nations of the Republic. The only salvation, therefore, of the Union is to be found in dividing it entirely from the taint of slavery."—Senator WADE, of Ohio, in Maine.

" I have read the Impending Crisis of the South with great attention. It seems to me a work of great merit ; rich yet accurate in statistical information, and logical in analysis."—WILLIAM H. SEWARD, 1859.

"The time is fast approaching when the cry will become too overpowering to resist. Rather than tolerate national slavery as it now exists, let the Union be demolished at once, and then the sin of slavery will rest where it belongs."—*New York Tribune.*

"I have no doubt but the free and slave States ought to be separated. * * *. The Union is not worth supporting in connection with the South."—*Idem.*

A leading member of the Convention that nominated Mr. FREMONT, namely, JAMES WATSON WEBB, uttered the following as the sentiment of the people: "They (the people) ask us to give them a nomination which, when fairly put before the people, will unite public sentiment, and through the ballot-box will restrain and repel the pro-slavery extension, and this aggression of the slaveocracy. What else are they doing? They tell you that they are willing to abide by the ballot-box, and willing to make that the last appeal. *If we fail there, what then?* We will drive it back sword in hand, so help me, God! *Believing them to be right, I am with them.*" "This sentiment was loudly cheered by the Convention." In July, 1860, he declared: "If a Southern State should attempt to resist, she will be made to submit, and bear herself with deference and respect thereafter to those who are morally and socially her equals, and *politically* and *physically* her superiors, and when provoked to demonstrate it, if need be, her masters."

On page 648 of the Congressional Globe, of the first Session of the thirty-third Congress, Mr. GIDDINGS, Member of Congress from Ohio, is reported to have spoken as follows:

"When the contest shall come; when the thunder shall roll, and the lightning flash; when the slaves shall rise in the South; when, in emulation of the Cuban bondmen, the Southern slaves shall feel that they are men; when they shall feel the stirring emotions of immortality, and shall recognize the stirring truth that they are men, and entitled to the rights that God has bestowed upon them; when the slaves shall feel that, and when masters shall turn pale and tremble, when their dwellings shall smoke, and dismay shall sit on each countenance, then, sir, I do not say, we shall laugh at your calamity and mock when your fear cometh; but I do say, that when that time shall come, the lovers of our race will stand forth and exert the legitimate powers of this Government for freedom. We shall then have constitutional power to act for the good of our country, and do justice to the slave. Then will we strike off the shackles from the limbs of the slave. Then will be a period when this Government will have power to act between slavery and freedom, and when it can make peace by giving freedom to the slaves. And let me tell you, Mr. Speaker, that time hastens. It is rolling forward. The President is exerting a power that will hasten it, though not intended by him. I hail it as I do the dawn of that political and moral millennium, which I am well assured will come on the earth."

" It is written in the Constitution of the United States, that five slaves shall count equal to three freemen, as a basis of representation, and it is written also, in violation of the Divine Law, that we shall surrender the fugitive slave who takes refuge at our fireside from his relentless pursuer."—Senator SEWARD in Ohio, 1848.

In an address delivered in Boston, 1855, Mr. BURLINGAME, Member of Congress, said : " If asked to state particularly what he would do, he would answer, first, repeal the Nebraska bill ; second, repeal the fugitive slave law ; third, abolish slavery in the District of Columbia ; fourth, abolish the internal slave trade ; next, he would declare that slavery should not spread one inch in the Union ; he would then put the Government actually and perpetually on the side of freedom. * * * He would have judges that believed in a higher law ; an anti-slavery Constitution, an anti-slavery Bible, and an anti-slavery God. Having thus denationalized slavery, he would not menace it in the States where it now exists, but would say to the States, It is your local institution ; hug it to your bosom until it destroys you. But he would say, you must let our freedom alone. [Applause.]. If you but touch the hem of her garment we will trample you to the earth. [Loud applause.] This is the only condition of repose, and it must come to this."

On the 9th of June, 1841, JOHN QUINCY ADAMS said " that, in the event of a servile war, his own opinion would be, that if the free portion of people of this Union were called upon to support the institutions of the South by suppressing the slaves,

and a servile war in consequence of it, in that case he would
not say that Congress had no right to interfere with the institutions of the South ; that the very fact, perhaps, that the free portion of the people of this Union were called to sacrifice their blood
and their treasure for the purpose of suppressing a war in a case
in which a most distinguished Southern man, the author of the
Declaration of Independence, had declared that in that event
the Almighty had no attribute that sided with the master, he
would say, that if the free portion of this Union were called
upon to expend their blood and their treasure to support that
cause which had the curse and the displeasure of the Almighty
upon it, he would say, that this same Congress would sanction
an expenditure of blood and treasure, for that cause itself would
come within the constitutional action of Congress, and there
would be no longer any pretension that Congress had not the
right to interfere with the institutions of the South, inasmuch
as the very fact that the people of the free portion of the Union
marching to the support of the masters would be an interference
with those institutions; and that in the event of a war the result of which no man could tell, the treaty-making power came
to be equivalent to universal emancipation."

"Mr. INGERSOLL, Member from Pennsylvania, interrupted
Mr. ADAMS with the expression of the deepest indignation of
his soul at the utterance of such a doctrine."

On the 21st of February, 1843, Mr. DELLET, of Alabama,
asked Mr. ADAMS whether he understood him on another occasion to say, " that in God's good time the abolition of slavery
would come, and let it come."

Mr. DELLET asked Mr. ADAMS if he understood him.

Mr. ADAMS nodded assent, and said with great earnestness,
" Let it come."

Mr. DELLET. Yes, let it come. No matter what the consequences, let it come, said the gentleman. Let it come, though
women and children should be slain, though blood should flow
like water, though the Union itself be destroyed, though Government shall be broken up. No matter though five millions
of the people of the South perish.

Mr. ADAMS, (in his seat.) " Five hundred millions, let it
come." Was this a mental paroxysm, or habitual feeling ?

Senator HENRY WILSON, in Boston, Jan. 21, 1851: "We shall arrest the extension of slavery, and rescue the Government from the grasp of the slave power. We shall blot out slavery in the National Capitol. We shall surround the slave States with a cordon of free States. We shall then appeal to the hearts and consciences of men, and, in a few years, notwithstanding the immense interests of mankind connected with the cause of oppression, we shall give liberty to the millions in bondage. I trust many of us shall live to see the chain stricken from the limbs of the last bondman in the Republic! But, sir, whenever that day shall come, living or dead, no man connected with the anti-slavery movement will be dearer to enfranchised millions, than the name of your guest, WILLIAM LLOYD GARRISON."

CALEB CUSHING IN BOSTON, 1859.

"I showed you how, under the influence of their malign teachings, all party action, North and South, was running in the channel of a desperate and deplorable sectionalism, and that, above all, here in Massachusetts, all the sectional influences dominant in this State were founded upon the single emotion of hate—ay, hate; treacherous, ferocious hate of our fellow-citizens in the Southern States. [Applause, and cries of Good, good.]

"Under the influence of this monomania, they have set up in this Commonwealth a religion of hate—ay, a religion of hate and of blasphemy. O God! that such things are in this our day!

"What more, gentlemen? We have had our ears filled with alleged sympathies for JOHN BROWN; of apologies for his act; of reproaches against the persons whom he was endeavoring to slaughter in cold blood; of sneers at the State of Virginia; of ridicule of the terror of the unarmed women and children of Virginia. I say, sympathy for all this. Gentlemen, it is not sympathy for JOHN BROWN. It is another form of the manifestation of that same intense and ferocious hatred of the people of the South which animates the persons of whom I am speaking. [Applause.] Hatred! Hatred! Now the fact has been told us, that, in all times, hate must have its food of blood. How long are the people of Massachusetts to have their souls

continually perverted with these preachings—ay, pulpit preachings of hatred ? "

RELATIONS OF THE STATES TO THE GENERAL GOVERNMENT.

Senator DAVIS, of Mississippi, Feb. 2, 1860, in the Senate,
submitted six resolutions. In the *first*, he speaks of the action
of the States as independent sovereignties in forming the Constitution of the United States, by delegating a portion of their
power to be exercised by the General Government. In the
second, he speaks of negro slavery's being recognized by the
Constitution. In the *third*, of the equality of the States, in respect to rights in the Territories. The *fourth* is as follows :
" *Resolved*, That neither Congress nor a territorial legislature, whether by direct legislation, or by legislation of an indirect and unfriendly nature, possess the power to annul or impair the constitutional right of any citizen of the United States
to take his slave property into the common territories ; but it
is the duty of the Federal Government there to afford for that,
as for other species of property, the needful protection ; and if
experience should, at any time, prove that the judiciary does
not possess power to insure adequate protection, it will become
the duty of Congress to supply such deficiency."
In the *fifth*, he declares that when a territory forms its constitution, the people can then, for the first time, have power to
say whether slavery, as a domestic institution, shall be maintained or prohibited in its jurisdiction ; and if Congress shall
admit them as a State, they shall be received into the Union
either with or without slavery, as their constitution may pre-
scribe, at the time of admission.
In the *sixth*, he speaks of the opposition made by the States
to the return of fugitive slaves, as hostile in its character, and
subversive of the Constitution, and revolutionary in its effect.
The South insists that what is recognized as property in the
States, and what is treated as property in the Constitution, and
in treaties with other nations, and in congressional legislation,
and in judicial decisions, shall be recognized as property in the
territories, and protected as property.
In opposition to this view, the Republican party, in their

platform, Chicago, 1860, has the following declaration : "That the new dogma that the Constitution, of its own force, carries slavery into any or all of the territories of the United States, is a dangerous political heresy, at variance with the explicit provisions of that instrument itself, with cotemporaneous exposition, and with legislative and judicial precedents, is revolutionary in its tendency, and subversive of the peace and harmony of the country."

POWER OF CONGRESS OVER TERRITORIES.

As heretofore stated, Northern men have claimed for Congress the power to prohibit slavery in the Territories, on the strength of that clause in the Constitution which declares that " Congress shall have power to dispose of and make all needful rules and regulations respecting the territory and other property belonging to the United States ; " and for other reasons.

Does "territory" here mean *land* or *inhabitants?* If "public lands" be substituted for "territory," it will then in the Constitution stand, "public lands" and other property ; but if you substitute "colony," that is, inhabitants, it will stand, "Congress shall have power to make all needful rules concerning the ' colony ' and other property." Where now is the power to dispose of the public lands ? See Senator GEYER's speech, in 1856.

It is evident, then, that this clause conferred upon Congress no *political* power over the "territory" then owned by the United States, but only power to dispose of it, and make rules and regulations about it as " property."   .

TERRITORY OF LOUISIANA.

" The inhabitants of the ceded territory *shall be* incorporated in the Union of the United States, and admitted *as soon* as possible, according to the principles of the Federal Constitution, to the enjoyment of all the rights, and advantages, and immunities of the citizens of the United States, and in the mean time shall be maintained and *protected* in the enjoyment of their liberty, *property*, and the religion they profess."—*Treaty with France*. 1803.

"At this time slaves were held by the people of Louisiana, through the whole length of the Mississippi valley. These people had an unrestricted right of settlement with their slaves under legal protection throughout the entire ceded province. Here is a treaty promise to protect that *property*, that *slave* property in that Territory before it should become a State. This promise was violated at the time of the Missouri Compromise, by Northern votes." Here by treaty the General Government engage to protect slave property.

In 1820, Mr. MADISON wrote: "The questions to be decided seem to be, first, whether a territorial restriction be an assumption of illegitimate power; or, second, a misuse of legitimate power; and if the latter only, whether the injury threatened to the nation from an acquiescence in the misuse, or from the frustration of it, be greater. On the first point, there is certainly room for a difference of opinion; though, for myself, I must own that I have always leaned to the belief that *the restriction was not within the true scope of the Constitution*. This opinion of Mr. MADISON, the "Father of the Constitution," is in harmony with the DRED SCOTT decision.

In the Republican platform, (1860,) there is the following declaration: "That the normal condition of the territory of the United States is that of freedom; that as our republican fathers, when they had abolished slavery in our national territory, ordained that no person should be deprived of life, liberty, or property, without due process of law, it becomes our duty, by congressional legislation, whenever such legislation shall become necessary, to maintain this provision of the Constitution against all attempts to violate it; and we deny the authority of Congress, of a territorial legislature, of any individual or association of individuals, to give legal existence to slavery in the United States."

On this declaration, Senator TOOMBS, of Georgia, remarks: "Then you declare that the treaties made by Mr. JEFFERSON, in 1803, are null and void, and no law; then you declare that the acts by which property in slaves was protected and allowed, both by territorial and congressional acts, in Florida, in Louisiana, in Missouri, in Mississippi and Alabama, are all null, void, and no law; you declare that the decision of the Supreme Court is

null, void, and no law; that there is no Constitution but the
Chicago platform; yet you propose to come here and take possession of this, and swear to maintain the Constitution with this
reading, and you are quite astonished at our having any objections to the peaceable proceedings.   *   *   But no matter what
may be our grievances, the honorable Senator from Kentucky
says we cannot secede.   Well, what can we do?   Submit?
They say they are the strongest, and they will hang us.   Well,
I suppose we must be thankful for that boon.   We will take
that risk.   We will stand by the right.   We will take the Constitution.   We will defend it by the sword, with halter around
our neck."

WHO WERE PARTIES TO THE CONSTITUTIONAL COMPACT.

March 8, 1860, in the Senate, Mr. COLLAMAR, of Vermont:
" I deny, in the first place, that the States, as States, entered into
this compact.   That is repeated so often, I do not know but
it is believed.   When a State acts, it acts in its organized capacity, by its organs, by its Legislature, or by its Executive.
There never was one of the States that acted in this way in the
adoption of the present Constitution.   The people of the United
States, meeting in the Conventions in the several States, adopted
the United States Constitution.   The States never acted on it
as States.   It would be a paradox that they should have done
so.   How could the Legislature of North Carolina, for instance,
invested as it was, at that time, by the people with the power
to levy and collect duties upon imports,—how could the State
in its organized capacity, through that organ, delegate that
power to another body?   It could not be done.   It never was
done.   It never was attempted to be done.   The people of the
United States had to meet in their several States in their original condition, as a people in convention, for these reasons : first,
it was more convenient ; next, if the people of North Carolina
had invested their Legislature with the power to levy and collect duties, the people of North Carolina alone would have the
power to invest that in another body, to wit, Congress.   If you
called the whole people of the United States, it would be a different people—it would be a different set of people to take that

power away from the one that gave it. No, sir, it is not true that this is in that sense a Confederacy. It is a National Government. This is a clear statement of the theory that the States were not parties to the constitutional compact. But it is not supported by facts or comparative weight of authority.

MR. WEBSTER'S RESOLUTIONS IN THE SENATE, 1832.

1. "That the Constitution of the United States is not a league, confederacy, or compact, between the people of the several States in their sovereign capacities; but a Government proper, founded on the adoption of the people, and creating direct relations between itself and individuals.

2. "That no State authority has power to dissolve these relations; that nothing can dissolve them but revolution; and that, consequently, there can be no such thing as secession without revolution.

3. "That there is a supreme law, consisting of the Constitution of the United States, acts of Congress passed in pursuance of it, and treaties; and that, in cases not capable of assuming the character of a suit at law or equity, Congress must judge of, and finally interpret, this supreme law, so often as it has occasion to pass acts of legislation; and in cases assuming the character of a suit, the Supreme Court of the United States is the final interpreter.

4. "That an attempt by a State to abrogate, annul, or nullify an act of Congress, or to arrest its operation within her limits, on the ground that, in her opinion, such law is unconstitutional, is a direct usurpation on the just powers of the General Government, and on the equal rights of other States, a plain violation of the Constitution, and a proceeding essentially revolutionary in its character and tendency."

These resolutions touching nullification, which was under consideration, rather than secession, were not adopted by the Senate.

Mr. MADISON, on the other hand, takes a different view of the parties to the compact of the Constitution.

"On examining the first relation, it appears, on one hand,

that the Constitution is to be founded on the assent and ratification of the people of America, given by deputies elected for
the special purpose; but on the other, that this assent and ratification is given by the people, not as individuals composing
one entire nation, *but as composing the distinct and independent
States to which they respectively belong.*

" This assent and ratification is to be given by the people,
not as individuals composing one entire nation, but as composing the distinct and independent States to which they respectively belong. It is to be the assent and ratification of the several States, derived from the supreme authority in each State—
the authority of the people themselves. The act, therefore,
establishing the Constitution, will not be a *national*, but a *Federal* act.

" That it will be a *Federal* and not a national act, as these
terms are understood by the objectors, the act of the people, as
forming so many independent States, not as forming an aggregate nation, is obvious from this single consideration, that it is
to result neither from the decision of a *majority* of the people,
nor from a majority of the States. It must result from the
unanimous assent of the several States that are parties to it,
differing no otherwise from their ordinary consent than in its
being expressed, not by the legislative authority, but by that
of the people themselves."

Mr. MADISON also said : An observation fell from a gentleman on the same side as myself, which deserves to be attended
to. " If we be dissatisfied with the National Government, if
we should choose to renounce it, this is an additional safeguard
to our defence." Here Mr. MADISON expresses his concurrence
with the gentleman mentioned, in the declaration, that if the
State of Virginia is dissatisfied with the General Government
in its practical workings, she can renounce it.

In reference to the Federal Government and its powers and
purposes, in the forty-fifth number of the Federalist, this language is used :

" The powers delegated to the Federal Government are few
and defined. Those which are to remain to the State Government are numerous and indefinite."

This, then, is the distinction between the two Governments.

The powers granted to the Federal Government are "few and defined," those reserved to the States are "numerous and indefinite."

"The former [the Federal Government] will be exercised principally on external objects, as war, peace, negotiation, and foreign commerce; with which last the power of taxation will for the most part be connected. The powers reserved to the several States will extend to all the objects which, in the ordinary course of affairs, concern the lives, the liberties, and the properties of the people, and the internal order, improvement, and prosperity of the State."

"I have never believed that a State could nullify, and remain in the Union; but I have always believed that a State might secede when it pleased, provided she would pay her proportion of the public debt; and this right I have considered the best guard to public liberty and to public justice that could be devised, and it ought to have prevented what is now felt in the South—oppression."—NATHANIEL MACON, of North Carolina, Feb. 9, 1833.

Mr. MACON was regarded as an eminently wise man in the Senate of the United States, of which, for a long time, he was regarded as the father.

ORDINANCE OF SECESSION PASSED BY THE PEOPLE OF THE STATE OF GEORGIA, JANUARY 19, 1861.

"We, the people of the State of Georgia, in convention assembled, do declare and ordain, and it is hereby declared and ordained, that the ordinance adopted by the people of Georgia in convention, in the year 1788, whereby the Constitution of the United States was assented to, ratified and adopted, and also acts and parts of acts of the General Assembly ratifying and adopting amendments to the said Constitution, are hereby repealed, rescinded, and abrogated; and we do further declare and ordain, that the Union now subsisting between the State of Georgia and the other States, under the name of the United States of America, is hereby dissolved, and that this State is in the full possession of those rights of sovereignty which belong and appertain to a free and independent State."

The people of South Carolina passed the ordinance secession Dec. 20, 1860, thus leading the way in .that great sectional movement.

MR. MADISON ON SECESSION.

In a letter written in 1833, Mr. MADISON uses the following language : " It surely does not follow from the fact that the States, or rather the people embodied in them, having, as parties to the constitutional compact, no tribunal above them, that in controverted meanings of the compact a minority of the parties can rightfully decide against the majority, still less that a single party can at will withdraw itself altogether from its compact with the rest."

In 1787 he used the following language : " It has been alleged that the confederation, having been formed by unanimous consent, could be dissolved by unanimous consent only. Does this doctrine result from the nature of compacts ?   Does it arise from any particular stipulation on the articles of confederation ?   If we consider the Federal Union as analogous to the fundamental compact by which individuals compose our society, and which must, in its theoretic origin at least, have been the unanimous act of the component members, it cannot be said that no dissolution of the compact can be effected without unanimous consent.   *A breach of the fundamental principles of the compact by a part of the society would certainly absolve the other part from their obligations to it.*"

" Whether a State can or cannot secede, and what others may do towards her, or she towards them—these are questions behind the Constitution of the United States, and, if I may say so without inconvenience, far above it.   These are questions of political science and not of constitutional construction ;   questions upon which empires are often dismembered and dynasties overthrown."—Mr. Pugh, in the Senate, Dec. 20, 1860.

" The whole theory of our Government is built upon the expectation that the States will not secede, but that all will continue to be integral parts of the confederacy.   If you ask, where is authority under the Constitution for a State to secede ? I would ask, where is there any thing in the Constitution to prevent its secession ? "—Senator Pugh, Dec. 20, 1860.

"It depends on the State itself whether to retain or to abolish the principle of representation, because it depends on itself whether it will remain a member of the Union. To deny this right, would be inconsistent with the principle on which all our political systems are founded; which is, that the people have in all cases a right to determine how they will be governed.

"The secession of a State from the Union depends on the will of the people of such State. The people alone, as we have already seen, have the power to alter the Constitution."—WILLIAM RAWLE, of Pennsylvania, 1825.

This very able man was offered the office of Attorney-General, by WASHINGTON.

President BUCHANAN, in his annual Message, 1860 :

"In order to justify secession as a constitutional remedy, it must be on the principle that the Federal Government is a mere voluntary association of States, to be dissolved at pleasure by any one of the contracting parties. If this be so, the confederacy is a rope of sand, to be penetrated and dissolved by the first adverse wave of public opinion in any of the States. In this manner our thirty-three States may resolve themselves into as many petty jarring and hostile republics, each one retiring from the Union without responsibility, whenever any sudden excitement might impel them to such a course. By this course a Union might be entirely broken up into fragments in a few weeks, which cost our fathers many years of toil, privation, and blood to establish.

"It is not pretended that any clause in the Constitution gives countenance to such a theory. It is altogether founded on inference, not from any language contained in the instrument itself, but from the sovereign character of the several States by which it was ratified. But is it beyond the power of a State, like an individual, to yield a portion of its sovereign rights to secure the remainder? In the language of Madison, who has been called the father of the Constitution, it was formed by the States—that is, by the people in each of the States acting in their highest sovereign capacity; and formed, consequently, by the authority which formed the State Constitutions.

"Nor is the Government of the United States created by the

Constitution less a Government in the strict sense of the term within the sphere of its powers, than the governments created by the Constitutions of the States are within their several spheres." The whole argument of President Buchanan in his annual Message of 1860, is one of the ablest against secession.

"I believe that it contravenes no provision of the Constitution, for one or more of the States to secede from the Union; not by virtue of any power conferred upon them by that instrument, but in consequence of the States never having surrendered it to the General Government: the Constitution declares that 'the powers not delegated to the United States by the Constitution are reserved to the States respectively, or the people.' I apprehend that it will be admitted that the States may exercise any or all of their reserved powers without a violation of the Constitution. If, then, they have never parted with their right to resume their original sovereignty, when, in their opinion, the Government becomes destructive of the ends for which it was instituted, it is no violation of the Constitution for them to secede. If there is any clause in the Constitution by which they deprived themselves of this right, it has escaped my observation."—Senator Hunter, of Virginia, Jan. 15, 1861.

This expresses the Southern view, as President Buchanan in his message does the Northern.

THE COERCION OF A STATE BY PHYSICAL FORCE.

On the subject of coercion, Alexander Hamilton said: "It has been observed, to coerce the States is one of the saddest projects that was ever devised. A failure of compliance will never be confined to a single State; this being the case, can we suppose it wise to hazard a civil war? Suppose Massachusetts, or any larger State should refuse, and Congress should attempt to compel them, would they not have influence to procure assistance, especially from those States that are in the same situation as themselves? What a picture does this idea present to our view? A complying State at war with a non-complying State: Congress marching the troops of one State into the bosom of another; the State collecting auxiliaries, and forming, perhaps, a majority against its Federal head. Here is a nation at war
15

with itself. *Can any reasonable man be well disposed towards a Government which makes war and carnage the only means of supporting itself?*—a Government that can exist only by the sword? Every such war must involve the innocent with the guilty. This single consideration should be sufficient to dispose every peaceable citizen against such a Government."

On the same subject, GEORGE MASON, of Virginia, said: "The most jarring elements of nature, sin and malice, are not more incompatible than such a mixture of civil liberty and military execution. Will the militia march from one State into another, in order to collect the arrears of taxes from the delinquent members of the Republic? Will they maintain an army for this purpose? Will not the citizens of the invaded States assist one another till they rise and shake off the Union altogether? * * * To punish the non-payment of taxes with death, is a severity not yet adopted by despotism itself; yet this unexampled cruelty would be mercy, compared to a military collection of revenue, in which the bayonet could make no distinction between the innocent and the guilty."—See Mr. MADISON's views on this subject, page 49.

JOHN QUINCY ADAMS, in his special Message, Feb. 5, 1827, in respect to the resistance of Georgia to Federal requisitions, said: "In abstaining at this stage of the proceedings from the application of any military force, I have been governed by considerations which will, I trust, meet the concurrence of the Legislature. Among these, one of prominent importance has been, that these surveys have been attempted and partly effected under color of legal authority from the State of Georgia; that *the surveyors are, therefore, not to be viewed in the light of individual and solitary transgressors, but as the agents of a sovereign State acting in obedience to authority which they believed to be binding upon them.*"

Mr. MADISON, on the 8th of June, 1787, said in convention: "Any Government for the United States formed on the supposed practicability of using force against the unconstitutional proceedings of the States, would prove as visionary and fallacious as the Government of Congress," evidently meaning the then existing Congress of the Confederation.

Mr. BUCHANAN in his annual address, 1860, discusses the

question, "Has the Constitution delegated to Congress the power to coerce a State into submission which is attempting to withdraw, and has actually withdrawn from the confederacy? If answered in the affirmative it must be on the principle that power has been conferred upon Congress to declare and to make war against a State. After much serious reflection, I have arrived at the conclusion that no such power has been delegated to Congress, or to any other department of the Federal Government. It is manifest upon an inspection of the Constitution, that this is not among the enumerated powers granted to Congress; and it is equally apparent that its exercise is not 'necessary and proper for carrying into execution' any one of these powers. So far from this power having been delegated to Congress, it was expressly refused by the convention which formed the Constitution." See MADISON papers, p. 761.

"Without descending to particulars, it may be safely asserted that the power to make war against a State is at variance with the whole spirit and intent of the Constitution.

"But if we possessed this power would it be wise to exercise it under existing circumstances? The object doubtless would be to preserve the Union. War would not only present the most effectual means of destroying it; but would banish all hope of its peaceable re-construction." * * *

"The fact is that our Union rests upon public opinion, and can never be cemented by the blood of its citizens shed in civil war. If it cannot live in the affections of the people, it must one day perish. Congress possesses many means of preserving it by conciliation, but the sword was not placed in its hands to destroy it by force." These views he repeats in a special Message on the subject.

President BUCHANAN, in his special Message, Jan. 8, 1861, after denying the right of secession, on the part of the States, and the right of coercion on the part of the General Government against seceding States, says: "But the right and duty to use military force defensively against those who resist the Federal officers in the execution of their legal functions, and against those who spoil the power of the Federal Government, is clear and undeniable."

To this Senator DAVIS, of Mississippi, Jan. 10, 1861, replies:

" Is it so ? Where does he get it ? Our fathers were so jealous of a standing army that they would scarcely permit the organization and maintenance of any army. Where does he get the 'clear and undeniable' power to use the force of the United States in the manner he then proposes ? To execute a process, troops may be summoned as a *posse comitatus ;* and here in the history of our Government, it is not to be forgotten that in the earlier, better days of the Republic—and painfully do we feel that they were better indeed—a President of the United States did not recur to the army ; he went to the people of the United States. Vaguely and confusedly, indeed, did the Senator from Tennessee (ANDREW JOHNSON) bring forward the case of the great man, Washington, as one, in which he had used a power which was equivalent to the coercion of a State, for he said that Washington used the military power against a portion of the people of a State ; and why might he not have used it against the whole State ?

" Let me tell that Senator that the case of General Washington has no application as he supposes. It was a case of insurrection within the State of Pennsylvania ; and the very message from which he read communicated the fact that Governor MIFFLIN thought it necessary to call the militia of adjoining States to co-operate with those of Pennsylvania. He used the militia not as a standing army. It was by the consent of the Governor ; it was by his advice. It was not the invasion of the State. It was not the coercion of the State ; but it was aiding the State to put down insurrection, and in the very manner provided in the Constitution itself.

" But, I ask again, what power has the President to use the army and navy except to execute process ? Are we to have drumhead courts substituted for those which the Constitution and the laws provide ? Are we to have sergeants sent over the land instead of civil magistrates ? Not so thought the elder Adams. * * * I say then, when we trace our history to its early foundation under the first two Presidents of the United States, we find that this idea of using the army and the navy to execute the laws at the discretion of the President, was not even entertained, still less acted upon, in any case."

DECLARATION BY THE CONVENTION OF SOUTH CAROLINA OF CAUSES
WHICH LED TO THE SECESSION OF THAT STATE.

Dec. 24, 1860.

The people of the State of South Carolina, in Convention assembled, on the 2d day of April, A. D. 1852, declared that the frequent violations of the Constitution of the United States by the Federal Government, and its encroachments upon the reserved rights of the States, fully justified this State in their withdrawal from the Federal Union ; but in deference to the opinions and wishes of the other slaveholding States, she forbore at that time to exercise this right. Since that time these encroachments have continued to increase, and further forbearance ceases to be a virtue.

And now the State of South Carolina, having resumed her separate and equal place among nations, deems it due to herself, to the remaining United States of America, and to the nations of the world, that she should declare the immediate causes which have led to this act.

In the year 1765, that portion of the British Empire embracing Great Britain, undertook to make laws for the Government of that portion composed of the thirteen American Colonies. A struggle for the right of self-government ensued, which resulted, on the 4th of July, 1776, in a Declaration, by the Colonies, " that they are, and of right ought to be, FREE AND INDEPENDENT STATES ; and that, as free and independent States, they have full power to levy war, conclude peace, contract alliances, establish commerce, and to do all other acts and things which independent States may of right do."

They further solemnly declared, that whenever any " form of Government becomes destructive of the ends for which it was established, it is the right of the people to alter or abolish it, and to institute a new Government." Deeming the Government of Great Britain to have become destructive of these ends, they declared that the Colonies " are absolved from all allegiance to the British Crown, and that all political connection between them and the State of Great Britain is, and ought to be, totally dissolved."

In pursuance of this Declaration of Independence, each of

the thirteen States proceeded to exercise its separate sovereignty ; adopted for itself a Constitution, and appointed officers for the administration of Government in all its departments— Legislative, Executive, and Judicial. For purposes of defence they united their arms and their counsels ; and, in 1778, they entered into a League, known as the Articles of Confederation, whereby they agreed to intrust the administration of their external relations to a common agent, known as the Congress of the United States, expressly declaring, in the first article, "that each State retains its sovereignty, freedom, and independence, and every power, jurisdiction, and right, which is not, by this Confederation, expressly delegated to the United States in Congress assembled."

Under this Confederation the War of the Revolution was carried on ; and on the 3d of September, 1783, the contest ended, and a definite Treaty was signed by Great Britain, in which she acknowledged the Independence of the Colonies in the following terms :

" ARTICLE 1. His Britannic Majesty acknowledges the said United States, viz. : New Hampshire, Massachusetts Bay, Rhode Island and Providence Plantations, Connecticut, New York, New Jersey, Pennsylvania, Delaware, Maryland, Virginia, North Carolina, South Carolina, and Georgia, to be FREE, SOVEREIGN, AND INDEPENDENT STATES ; that he treats with them as such ; and, for himself, his heirs and successors, relinquishes all claims to the Government, propriety, and territorial rights of the same and every part thereof."

Thus were established the two great principles asserted by the Colonies, namely, the right of a State to govern itself ; and the right of a people to abolish a Government when it becomes destructive of the ends for which it was instituted. And concurrent with the establishment of these principles, was the fact, that each Colony became and was recognized by the mother country as a FREE, SOVEREIGN, AND INDEPENDENT STATE.

In 1787, Deputies were appointed by the States to revise the articles of Confederation ; and on 17th September, 1787, these Deputies recommended, for the adoption of the States, the Articles of Union, known as the Constitution of the United States.

The parties to whom this Constitution was submitted, were the several sovereign States; they were to agree or disagree, and when nine of them agreed, the compact was to take effect among those concurring; and the General Government, as the common agent, was then to be invested with their authority.

If only nine of the thirteen States had concurred, the other four would have remained as they then were—separate, sovereign States, independent of any of the provisions of the Constitution. In fact, two of the States did not accede to the Constitution until long after it had gone into operation among the other eleven; and during that interval, they each exercised the functions of an independent nation.

By this Constitution, certain duties were imposed upon the several States, and the exercise of certain of their powers was restrained, which necessarily impelled their continued existence as sovereign States. But, to remove all doubt, an amendment was added, which declared that the powers not delegated to the United States by the Constitution, nor prohibited by it to the States, are reserved to the States respectively, or to the people. On the 23d May, 1788, South Carolina, by a Convention of her people, passed an ordinance assenting to this Constitution, and afterwards altered her own Constitution to conform herself to the obligations she had undertaken.

Thus was established, by compact between the States, a Government with defined objects and powers, limited to the express words of the grant. This limitation left the whole remaining mass of power subject to the clause reserving it to the States or the people, and rendered unnecessary any specification of reserved rights. We hold that the Government thus established is subject to the two great principles asserted in the Declaration of Independence; and we hold further, that the mode of its formation subjects it to a third fundamental principle, namely, the law of compact. We maintain that in every compact between two or more parties, the obligation is mutual; that the failure of one of the contracting parties to perform a material part of the agreement, entirely releases the obligation of the other; and that, where no arbiter is provided, each party is remitted to his own judgment to determine the fact of failure, with all its consequences.

In the present case, that fact is established with certainty. We assert that fourteen of the States have deliberately refused for years past to fulfil their Constitutional obligations, and we refer to their own statutes for the proof.

The Constitution of the United States, in its fourth Article, provides as follows :

" No person held to service or labor in one State under the laws thereof, escaping into another, shall, in consequence of any law or regulation therein, be discharged from such service or labor, but shall be delivered up, on claim of the party to whom such service or labor may be due."

This stipulation was so material to the compact that without it that compact would not have been made. The greater number of the contracting parties held slaves, and they had previously evinced their estimate of the value of such a stipulation by making it a condition in the Ordinance for the Government of the territory ceded by Virginia, which obligations, and the laws of the General Government, have ceased to effect the objects of the Constitution. The States of Maine, New Hampshire, Vermont, Massachusetts, Connecticut, Rhode Island, New York, Pennsylvania, Illinois, Indiana, Michigan, Wisconsin, and Iowa, have enacted laws which either nullify the acts of Congress, or render useless any attempt to execute them. In many of these States the fugitive is discharged from the service of labor claimed, and in none of them has the State Government complied with the stipulation made in the Constitution. The State of New Jersey, at an early day, passed a law in conformity with her constitutional obligation ; but the current of Anti-Slavery feeling has led her more recently to enact laws which render inoperative the remedies provided by her own laws and by the laws of Congress. In the State of New York even the right of transit for a slave has been denied by her tribunals ; and the States of Ohio and Iowa have refused to surrender to justice fugitives charged with murder, and with inciting servile insurrection in the State of Virginia. Thus the constitutional compact has been deliberately broken and disregarded by the non-slaveholding States ; and the consequence follows that South Carolina is released from her obligation.

The ends for which this Constitution was framed are declared by itself to be "to form a more perfect Union, to establish justice, insure domestic tranquillity, provide for the common defence, promote the general welfare, and secure the blessings of liberty to ourselves and our posterity."

These ends it endeavored to accomplish by a Federal Government, in which each State was recognized as an equal, and had separate control over its own institutions. The right of property in slaves was recognized by giving to free persons distinct political rights; by giving them the right to represent, and burdening them with direct taxes for three-fifths of their slaves; by authorizing the importation of slaves for twenty years; and by stipulating for the rendition of fugitives from labor.

We affirm that these ends for which this Government was instituted have been defeated, and the Government itself has been destructive of them by the action of the non-slaveholding States. Those States have assumed the right of deciding upon the propriety of our domestic institutions; and have denied the rights of property established in fifteen of the States and recognized by the Constitution; they have denounced as sinful the institution of slavery; they have permitted the open establishment among them of societies, whose avowed object is to disturb the peace of and eloin the property of the citizens of other States. They have encouraged and assisted thousands of our slaves to leave their homes; and those who remain have been incited by emissaries, books, and pictures, to servile insurrection.

For twenty-five years this agitation has been steadily increasing, until it has now secured to its aid the power of the common Government. Observing the *forms* of the Constitution, a sectional party has found within that article establishing the Executive Department, the means of subverting the Constitution itself. A geographical line has been drawn across the Union, and all the States north of that line have united in the election of a man to the high office of President of the United States, whose opinions and purposes are hostile to slavery. He is to be intrusted with the administration of the common Government, because he has declared that that "Government cannot endure permanently half slave, half free," and that the public mind must rest in the belief that slavery is in the course of ultimate extinction.

This sectional combination for the subversion of the Constitution has been aided, in some of the States, by elevating to citizenship persons who, by the supreme law of the land, are incapable of becoming citizens ; and their votes have been used to inaugurate a new policy, hostile to the South, and destructive of its peace and safety.

On the 4th of March next, this party will take possession of the Government. It has announced that the South shall be excluded from the common territory, that the Judicial tribunal shall be made sectional, and that a war must be waged against slavery until it shall cease throughout the United States.

The guarantees of the Constitution will then no longer exist ; the equal rights of the States will be lost. The slaveholding States will no longer have the power of self-government, or self-protection, and the Federal Government will have become their enemy.

Sectional interest and animosity will deepen the irritation ; and all hope of remedy is rendered vain, by the fact that the public opinion at the North has invested a great political error with the sanctions of a more erroneous religious belief.

We, therefore, the people of South Carolina, by our delegates in Convention assembled, appealing to the Supreme Judge of the world for the rectitude of our intentions, have solemnly declared that the Union heretofore existing between this State and the other States of North America is dissolved, and that the State of South Carolina has resumed her position among the nations of the world, as a separate and independent State, with full power to levy war, conclude peace, contract alliances, establish commerce, and to do all other acts and things which independent States may of right do."

After making the above declaration, the Convention of South Carolina appointed R. W. BARNWELL, J. H. ADAMS, and JAS. L. ORR, commissioners to proceed to Washington, as commissioners to treat with the Government of the United States, on various subjects connected with the secession of the State. This they ineffectually attempted, Dec. 29, 1860, President BUCHANAN declining to receive them in their official character.

THE PEACE CONGRESS.

On January 19, 1861, the General Assembly of Virginia passed a preamble and resolutions inviting the States to send commissioners to Washington to adjust the sectional difficulties which threatened the integrity of the Union. These resolutions recommended the CRITTENDEN resolutions as the basis of settlement.

THE CRITTENDEN RESOLUTIONS.

In order to settle the sectional disputes, Senator CRITTENDEN brought forward a resolution embracing several articles with the following preamble: " Whereas serious and alarming dissensions have arisen between the Northern and Southern States, concerning the rights of the slaveholding States, and especially their rights in the common territory of the United States, and whereas it is eminently desirable and proper that these dissensions, which now threaten the very existence of the Union, should be permanently quieted and settled by constitutional provisions which shall do equal justice to all sections, and thereby restore to the people that peace and good will which ought to prevail between all the citizens of the United States; therefore,

" *Resolved, by the Senate and House of Representatives of the United States, in Congress assembled,* (two-thirds of both Houses concurring,) that the following articles be and hereby are proposed and submitted as amendments to the Constitution of the United States, which shall be valid to all intents and purposes, as part of said Constitution, when ratified by conventions of three-fourths of the several States."

Article 1—Provided for prohibiting slavery north of 36° 30' in all the territory now held or which may hereafter be held, and recognizing it as existing in all the territory south of that line, and for allowing any territory to come into the Union, when it has a sufficient population for a member of Congress, according to the then ratio of representation of the people of the United States, on an equal footing with the other States either with or without slavery, as the Constitution of such new State shall provide.

Article 2—Declares that Congress shall have no power to abolish slavery in places under the exclusive jurisdiction of Congress and within the limits of States that permit the holding of slaves.

Article 3—Declares that Congress shall not have power to abolish slavery in the District of Columbia except on certain conditions.

Article 4—Declares that Congress shall not interdict the transportation of slaves from one State to another where the laws permit slavery.

Article 5—Declares that the fugitive slave law shall be modified in such a manner, that in case the owner meets with forcible obstruction from people to the recovery of his slave, the United States shall pay for such fugitive slave; it being provided that the county where this force, or intimidation, or rescue takes place, shall be liable for the amount paid, with authority to remunerate itself by a suit against the rescuers or wrong-doers.

Article 6—Provides that these and some other articles already in the Constitution shall not be altered hereafter.

It also contained certain recommendations in respect to the personal liberty bills, and the fugitive slave law, and the slave trade.

LETTERS OF SENATORS BINGHAM AND CHANDLER.

WASHINGTON, *Feb.* 15, 1861.

DEAR SIR,

When Virginia proposed a convention in Washington, in reference to the disturbed condition of the country, I regarded it as another step to debauch the public mind, and a step towards obtaining that concession which the imperious slave power so insolently demands. I have no doubt, at present, that this was the design; I was, therefore, pleased that the Legislature of Michigan was not disposed to put herself in a position to be controlled by such influences.

The convention has met here, and within a few days the aspect of things is materially changed. Every free State except Michigan and Wisconsin is represented, and we have been assured by friends upon whom we can rely, that if those two

States should send delegations of true unflinching men, there would probably be a majority in favor of the Constitution as it is, who would frown down rebellion by the enforcement of the laws. These friends have recommended the appointment of delegates from our State, and in compliance with their request Mr. CHANDLER and myself telegraphed to you last night. It cannot be doubted that the recommendations of this convention will have considerable influence upon the public mind and upon the action of Congress. * * *

I have the honor with much respect, to be truly yours,

K. S. BINGHAM.

His Excellency, Governor BLAIR.

WASHINGTON, *Feb.* 11, 1861.

MY DEAR GOVERNOR,

Governor BINGHAM and myself telegraphed to you on Saturday at the request of Massachusetts and New York, to send delegates to the peace or compromise congress. They admit that we were right and they were wrong; that no Republican State should have sent delegates; but they are here and cannot get away. Ohio, Indiana, and Rhode Island are caving in, and there is danger of Illinois; and now they beg us, for God's sake, to come to their rescue, and save the republican party from rupture. I hope you will send *stiff-backed* men or none. The whole thing was got up against my judgment, and will end in thin smoke. Still I hope as a matter of courtesy to some of our erring brethren, that you will send the delegates.

Truly your friend,

Z. CHANDLER.

His Excellency AUSTIN BLAIR.

P. S.—Some of the manufacturing States think that a fight would be awful. Without a little blood-letting, this Union will not, in my estimation, be worth a rush.

The peace Congress was a failure. The South, goaded on by wrongs real, and wrongs imaginary, was rushing into secession. The North called for " blood-letting." Blood was forthcoming.

REMARKS.

1. Causes were in operation when Mr. BUCHANAN entered upon his administration, and during its continuance, which raised the sectional feeling, both North and South, to such a degree of antagonism, that the Union of the States was ruptured by the secession of South Carolina, Georgia, Alabama, Mississippi, Louisiana, and Florida. What those causes were, both proximate and remote, may be seen or inferred from the facts stated in the preceding pages. The sectional character attributed to the Republican party; the opposition to the DRED SCOTT decision; the recommendation by sixty-eight Northern members of Congress of Helper's incendiary abolition book; the JOHN BROWN invasion, and the sympathy expressed for him by Northern communities; the personal liberty bills passed by the Legislatures of at least twelve Northern States; the declaration of the Northern dominant party, that there should be no more slave territory; the spirit with which that party was coming into power, the exclamation of the victorious Gauls, addressed to the conquered Romans, *væ victis*, being in their hearts, if not on their lips;—these were some of the proximate causes of the secession. The sceptre was departing from Judah, and the lawgiver from between his feet. For fourteen presidential terms the candidate, favored by the South, had been elected; while the favorite candidates of the North had been elected for only four presidential terms. And with respect to these four, who were the favorite candidates of the North, namely, JOHN ADAMS, JOHN QUINCY ADAMS, General HARRISON, and General TAYLOR, there was no great dissatisfaction at the South. The two latter were by birth Southern men, and in favor of protecting Southern institutions. But now, for the first time, an anti-slavery man, Mr. LINCOLN, was elected president upon an anti-slavery platform, with the expectation on the part of the electors that anti-slavery men would "take possession of the Government," and would control the councils of the nation. Moreover, the Northern triumphant party, as belonging to the most numerous section, expected to hold the Government in perpetuity, so that all that was left to the South

was to exclaim with the fallen statesman Wolsey, "Farewell, a long farewell to all my greatness!"

But the North might justly, in turn, complain against the South, on account of grievances which, to some extent, furnish an apology for the injuries just mentioned. It might justly complain that it had been, for a long time, practically excluded from its appropriate share of influence, and office, and emolument, in the administration of the Federal Government. It might say, You of the South have had possession of the Federal Government, with all its attendant advantages, for fifty-six years out of seventy-two; and when you have refused to admit us to an equal participation in these advantages, and when you have foiled us again and again, in our attempts to gain the presidential election, you must not think it strange that we should, in our desperate efforts to obtain our rights, have used means that would be unpardonable in other circumstances. You must not think it strange, if you deprive us of our appropriate share of political power, that we, in retaliation, should deprive you of your appropriate share in the territories. You must not think it strange that, if the slave States go in a solid column against our presidential candidates, we should oppose the admission of new slave States. You must not think it strange that, if you attempt to nullify Tariff laws, which protect our manufacturing property, we should, by our personal liberty bills, nullify your fugitive slave law, which protects your slave property. You must not think it strange that, if you attack our commercial interests, as you did during the administration of Mr. JEFFERSON and of Mr. MADISON; and our manufacturing interests, as you did during the administration of General JACKSON and of Mr. POLK; we should attack your interests in slaves. You must not think it strange, if you magnify the reserved rights of the States and threaten secession, that we should magnify the powers granted to the Federal Government, and threaten military coercion.

2. In the progress of years, a thorough alienation of feeling had grown up between large masses at the North, and large masses at the South. Men hate those whom they injure as well as those who injure them. In the North there was the feeling of contempt mingled with the hatred, namely contempt

for the supposed imbecility and poverty of the South, and its dependence on the North for conveniences and necessaries of life manufactured at the North. There was also a deep moral abhorrence of Southern men as slaveholders, inasmuch as slavery was supposed to include in it " the sum of all villanies." The supposed " barbarism of the South " furnished the staple for speeches, and newspaper articles, and local conversation. There were those, and not a few, who felt that those Southern barbarians were not any better entitled to equal rights in the territories, according to the guarantees of the Constitution, than were the children of Ishmael to the promises made exclusively to the seed of Isaac, or than were the descendants of Esau to a share with the children of Israel in the territories of the Promised Land. In short, they felt that, as " Saints," Northern men should " inherit the North "; that they should take possession of the common territories by a direct grant from Congress, overriding the Constitution ; and that, in due time, under a patent from the Almighty, they should take possession of the Southern States, as fast as they could expel the Canaanites from the land.

And, on the other hand, Southern men repaid, if possible, this Northern hatred with interest ; for their hatred was intensified by the fear of those who politically had power to injure them. They distrusted men who claimed to have large powers from the Constitution to injure the South, while in cases in which the Constitution expressly protects the interests of the South, they would place themselves under the subterfuge of a " higher law," in order to violate their constitutional obligations. They feared and distrusted men who would thus act under the Constitution with their own construction of it, or the higher law with their own construction of it, according as the one or the other would help to enlarge the rights of the North, and lessen the rights of the South. They distrusted, and feared, and hated men, who, under a pretence of the right of petition, and of the freedom of the press, and liberty of speech, would deluge the floor of Congress with insults and slanders, and fill the mail bags with incendiary publications ; and send insurrectionary apostles of abolitionism, to kindle the flames of rebellion in the South. They distrusted, and feared, and hated men, sixty-eight of whose representatives had recommended a book, written to injure Southern institutions protected by the Constitution—men who sympathized with a convict, and crowned him with sepulchral honors, because he hated slavery; who, thirty years ago, would have been "hung like a felon, and buried like a dog." They distrusted, and feared, and hated men, who ostracized and excluded from office some of the ablest and best men in the Northern States, and put abolitionists in their place, simply upon the suspicion that the former were national and not sectional in their politics; who had let loose their war dogs to pursue their great man, DANIEL WEBSTER, even into his grave; and who, for a season, instead of allowing ministers of the Gospel to preach Christ and him crucified, demanded that they "should preach DOUGLAS and him damned"; all because they suspected these two men of favoring the South. They distrusted, and feared, and hated men, who could aid in passing personal liberty bills, which violate and nullify the Constitution in one of its clauses, and who can vilify and set at nought the decision of the Supreme Court of the United States, which many of them had never even read.

Senator IVERSON of Georgia, Dec. 6, 1860, in the Senate, made the following remarks: "Sir, disguise the fact as you will, there is an enmity between the Northern and the Southern people that is deep, and you can never eradicate it—never. Look at the spectacle exhibited on this floor. How is it? There are the Republican Northern Senators on that side. Here are the Southern Senators on this side. How much social intercourse between us? You sit on that side, sullen and gloomy; we sit on ours with portentous scowls. Yesterday I observed there was not a solitary man on that side of the chamber came over here, even to extend the civilities and courtesies of life; nor did any of us go over there. Here are two hostile bodies, on this floor, and it is but a type of the feeling that exists in the two sections. We are enemies as much as if we were hostile States. I believe the Northern people hate the South worse than ever the English people hated France; and I can tell my brethren over there, that there is no love lost on the part of the South.

16

"In this state of feeling, divided as we are by interest, by geographical position, by every thing that makes two people separate and distinct—I ask, why should we remain in the same Union together? We have not lived in peace; we are not now living in peace. It is not to be expected, or hoped, that we ever shall live in peace. My doctrine is, that whenever man and wife find that they must quarrel and cannot live in peace, they ought to separate; and these two sections, the North and the South, manifesting, as they have done and.do now, and probably ever will manifest, feelings of hostility, separated as they are in interests and objects—my own opinion is, that they can never live in peace; and the sooner they separate the better."

3. Does the Northern dominant party desire the extinction of slavery in the Southern States, and does it propose to adopt only political means to promote that extinction? Senator Seward, in his speech in Ohio, said: "Slavery can be limited to its present bounds. It can be ameliorated. It can and must be abolished, and you and I can and must do it." Mr. Douglas said of this: "Every appeal they make to Northern prejudice is against the institution of slavery everywhere, and they would not be able to retain their abolition allies, the rank out-and-out abolitionists, unless they held out the hope that it was the mission of the Republican party, if successful, to abolish slavery in the States as well as territories of the Union." They, the people of Ohio, and he, a New Yorker, must abolish slavery in Virginia.

Mr. Joshua R. Giddings said of the Helper book: "Every sentence of the book finds a response in the hearts of all true Republicans."

Senator Sumner said, that "slaveholders are base, false, and heedless of justice. It is vain to expect that men, who had screwed themselves up to become the propagandists of this enormity, will be restrained by any compromise, compact, bargain, or plighted faith. As the less is contained in the greater, so there is no vileness of dishonesty, no denial of human rights, that is not plainly involved in the support of an institution, which begins by changing men, created in the image of God, into a chattel, and sweeps little children away to the auction block." How strangely is this in contrast to the language of another Massachusetts Senator!

In 1835, at a meeting in Faneuil Hall, HARRISON GRAY OTIS, in reference to anti-slavery associations, said " that almost all the epithets of vituperation which the language affords, have been applied to slaveholders and their principles—to the principles of WASHINGTON, and JEFFERSON, and MADISON, and the RUTLEDGES, and the PINCKNEYS; and the thousands of other great and estimable persons who have held, or who yet hold slaves." He pointed to the portraits of HANCOCK and WASHINGTON, which hung in the Hall, and said :

" Let us imagine an interview between them, in the company of friends, just after one had signed the commission of the other; and, in ruminating on the lights and shadows of futurity, HANCOCK should have said : I congratulate my country on the choice she has made, and I foresee, that the laurels you gained in the field of Braddock's defeat, will be twined with those which will be earned by you in the war of Independence ; yet, such are the prejudices in my part of the Union against slavery, that although your name and services may secure you from apprehension during your life, yet your countrymen, when the willows weep over your tomb, will be branded by mine as man-stealers and murderers ; and the stain consequently annexed to your memory! Would not such a prophecy have been imputed to a brain disturbed, and its accomplishment regarded as a chimera? "

And yet such a prophecy has been verified to a wide extent, not only in Massachusetts, but in the North generally. Much that is uttered in conversation, in political speeches, in sermons, and in public prayers, *can be accounted for only on the supposition* that there are large classes of men who desire the abolition of slavery in the States, as well as its exclusion from the territories, and that, if they had the political power, they would not scruple to use it for the attainment of both of those objects, whatever should be the consequences to the South.

4. *Southern prejudices.*—As early as 1671, these prejudices existed. At that time, Sir WILLIAM BERKLEY, Governor of Virginia, stated " that the Navigation Act cutting off all trade with foreign countries was very injurious to them, (the Vir-

ginians,) as they were obedient to the laws. And this is the cause why no great or small vessels are built here, for we are obedient to the laws, while the New England men trade to every place that their interests lead them."

Mr. J. Taylor, in the Convention assembled to ratify the Constitution in North Carolina, said : " We plainly see that men that come from New England are different from us ; they are ignorant of our situation ; they do not know the state of our country. They cannot legislate for us."   •

Many Southern statesmen have been under the impression, that the Northern States have very little reverence for the Constitution, and that they would be very ready to enlarge or diminish its powers, if, by so doing, they could advance their own material interests, and their own political power; that under the pretence of advancing the " general welfare," they would sacrifice the vested rights of the South ; that under the pretence of promoting " the greatest good of the greatest number," they would violate sacred compacts ; that from their greed of money and their greed of political power, they are ready to sacrifice honor and duty to self-interest, and that they love negroes only because they hate their masters.

5. Was the new Confederacy or Union expected to be permanent? The Union of the Old England Colonies established in 1643, though solemnly declared in the Constitution to be " perpetual," was dissolved. The Union, under the British Constitution, of the Colonies with the mother country, which was supposed to be organic, and claimed to be perpetual, was dissolved. The Union formed by the Federal Constitution, or " Articles of Confederation and Perpetual Union," and which was in that instrument solemnly declared to be perpetual, was dissolved.

Was the new Union, like those three Unions, expected to be dissolved and pass away?

The States were familiar with the idea, that " Governments derive their just powers from the consent of the governed," and that " when any form of Government becomes destructive of the ends for which it was established, it is the right of the people to alter or to abolish it, and institute a new Government." By an article in the new Constitution, " the ratification of the

Convention of nine States shall be sufficient for the establishment of this Constitution *between the States* ratifying the
same;" thus justifying the doctrine, that nine States might
secede from the remaining four, notwithstanding the article in
the old Constitution, namely, "And the Articles of this Confederation shall be inviolably observed by every State, and the
Union shall be perpetual; nor shall any alteration at any time
hereafter be made in any of them, unless such alteration be
agreed to in a Congress of the United States, and be afterwards
confirmed by the Legislatures of every State."

In the new Constitution there is no declaration that the
Union shall be perpetual, no promise on the part of the States
to abide in it, and no power delegated to the Federal Government to retain them in it by force. Will they stay in it?

Many of the fathers had their fears and misgivings. Even
WASHINGTON hardly dared to look into the future. "Let experience," said he, "solve the question. To look to speculation
in such a case were criminal." He evidently feared to reason
on the subject, lest he should be carried to the conclusion,
that the Union could not be preserved, however much he
loved it.

JOHN ADAMS expected the dissolution of the Union. "The
Rev. Mr. COFFIN of New England, who is now here soliciting
donations for a College in Greene County, Tennessee, tells me
that when he first determined to engage in this enterprise, he
wrote a letter recommendatory of the enterprise, which he
meant to get signed by clergymen, and a similar one for persons of a civil character, at the head of which he wished to
have Mr. ADAMS to put his name, he being the President of
the United States, and the application going only for his name,
and not for a donation. Mr. ADAMS, after reading the paper,
and considering, said he saw no possibility of continuing the
Union of the States; that their dissolution must necessarily
take place; that he therefore saw no propriety in recommending to New England men to promote an institution in the
South; that it was, in fact, giving strength to those who were
to be their enemies, and therefore he would have nothing to do
with it."—JEFFERSON's WORKS, Dec. 13, 1803.

In the following letter to Mr. HOLMES, of Maine, April 22,

1820, Mr. JEFFERSON makes known his own views : "I thank you, dear sir, for the copy you were so kind as to send me of the letter to your constituents, on the Missouri question. It is a perfect justification to them. I had, for a long time, ceased to read the newspapers, or pay any attention to public affairs, confident that they were in good hands, and content to be a passenger in our boat to the shore from which I am not far distant. But this momentous question, like a fire-bell in the night, awakened and filled me with terror. I considered it at once as the knell of the Union. It is hushed, indeed, for the moment, but this is a reprieve only, not a final sentence. *A geographical line coinciding with a marked principle, moral and political, and conceived and held up by the angry passions of men, will never be obliterated, and every new irritation will make it deeper and deeper.* * * I regret, now, to die in the belief that the useless sacrifice of themselves by the generation of 1776, to acquire self-government and happiness to their country, is to be thrown away by the unwise passions of their sons, and that my only consolation is to be, that I do not live to weep over it."

Many patriotic statesmen, like WASHINGTON, and ADAMS, and JEFFERSON, have looked with fear and trembling into the future condition of these States. They were apprehensive that the original thirteen States were too extensive for one Government. What would they have said of the magnitude of the thirty-four States united in one Confederacy ? *Suis et ipsa Roma viribus ruit.*

But there are other considerations on this subject that have attracted the attention of another class of men. COLERIDGE, in his *Table Talk*, 1833, p. 201, says : "Can there be any thorough national fusion of the Northern and the Southern States ? I think not. The fact is, the Union will be shaken almost to dislocation, whenever a very serious question between the States arises. The American Union has no centre, and it is impossible to make one. The more they extend their borders into the Indian land, the weaker will the national cohesion be. I look upon the States as splendid masses to be used by-and-by in the composition of two or three Governments."

A Russian writer, IVAN GOLOVIN, remarked in 1856 : " A

visit to the United States has the strange property of cooling democrats. Again, I tell you, the manifest destiny of the States is disunion. I do not give the Union eight years to last."

ALEXANDER HAMILTON speaks of the new Constitution, when it was before the country for adoption, in the following terms :

"If the Government be adopted, it is probable General WASHINGTON will be the President of the United States. This will insure a wise choice of men to administer the Government, and a good administration. A good administration will conciliate the confidence and affections of the people, and perhaps enable the Government to acquire more consistency than the proposed Constitution seems to promise for so great a country. *It may thus triumph altogether over the State Governments, and reduce them to an entire subordination, dividing the larger States into smaller districts.* The *organs* of the General Government may also acquire additional strength.

"If this should not be the case, in the course of a few years, it is probable that the contests about the boundaries of power between the particular Governments and the General Government and the *momentum* of the larger States, *will produce a dissolution of the Union. This, after all, seems to be the most likely result.*"

BENJAMIN HARRISON, father of President HARRISON, in a letter to Gen. WASHINGTON, 1787, says : "I cannot divest myself of the opinion, that the seeds of civil discord are plentifully sown in very many of the powers, given both to the President and the Congress ; and if the Constitution is carried into effect, the States south of the Potomac will be little more than appendages to those northward."

In the progress of time the seeds of civil discord germinated. Causes became apparent that threatened the dissolution of the Union.

WASHINGTON, in his letter to ALEXANDER HAMILTON, July 27, 1792, says : "On my way home, and since my arrival here, I have endeavored to learn from sensible, moderate men, known friends of the Government, the sentiments that are entertained of public measures. These all agree that the country is prosperous and happy, but they seem to be alarmed at that system

of policy, and those interpretations of the Constitution, which
have taken place in Congress." These interpretations tended
to enlarge the powers of the General Government, as was supposed, at the expense of State rights.

There were men all along, from the days of WASHINGTON to
the present time, who understood the danger of disunion, and
endeavored to avoid the causes that would produce it. They
were prescient of the future, and saw events in their causes.

In 1849, ROBERT E. SCHENCK, member from Dayton, Ohio,
said : " If we of the Northern States will not vote for a Southern man, merely because he is a Southern man, and men of the
South will not vote for a Northern man, merely because he is
a Northern man, and if that principle is to be carried out in all
our national politics and elections, what must be the result?
Disunion. THAT ITSELF IS DISUNION. You may disguise and
cover it up as you please, but that it will be. It may be regarded as but the first step in disunion, but its consequences
follow as inevitably as fate. One section—the North or the
South—must always have the majority. Disfranchise all upon
the other side, and the Union could not hold together a day ; *it
ought not to hold together upon such conditions a day.*"

On the other hand, from the first, there were those who
never indulged any fears of secession and disunion. They were,
indeed, inclined to ridicule the fears of others as entirely groundless, in words like these: "The Southern States cannot be
kicked out of the Union, and if they were inclined to go out,
the North would not let them go. All the threats and all the
fears of disunion are as wild as the visions of Southern fanatics
and the dreams of Northern Union-savers. They are all got up
for political effect, and to carry on elections by frightening
weak-minded Union-savers."

6. *Meaning of certain Terms.*—STATES. The word State,
says Mr. MADISON, sometimes means *territory* occupied by a
political society ; sometimes the *Government* established by
that society ; sometimes the *people* composing that society in
their highest sovereign capacity. It is used in this last sense
when it is said that the State, or States, ratified the Constitution or acceded to the Constitution. The people ratified the

Constitution as the act of the State. Thus each State, acting by itself, and for itself, in Convention, became a party to the constitutional compact. It should be added, that the term State replaced the term colony, which was in use before the Declaration of Independence.

The States made the Declaration of Independence, each State acting for itself, and each State becoming " free and independent." The States formed the articles of Confederation, each State still retaining its sovereignty as to all that was not delegated. The States formed the present Constitution. " The Convention which formed it, was called by a portion of the States; its members were all appointed by the States; received their authority from the separate States; voted by States in forming the Constitution, transmitted it to Congress to be submitted to the States for their ratification; it was ratified by the people of each State in Convention, each ratifying by itself and for itself, and bound exclusively by its own ratification; and by express provision it was not to go into operation unless nine out of twelve States should ratify, and then binding only between the States ratifying. Any four States, great or small, could have defeated its adoption."

ROGER SHERMAN and OLIVER ELLSWORTH, in their letter to Governor HUNTINGTON, say : " We wish it, the Constitution, may meet with the approbation of the several States, and be a means of securing their rights, and lengthening out their tranquillity."

The States retained their sovereignty for the reason that it was not delegated to the Constitution. In the case of the Bank of Augusta *vs.* Earle, 13 Peters' Reports, p. 590, it was decided by the Supreme Court that the " rules of international law apply to the States *inter se*, and the Chief Justice declared that they are sovereign States. The Constitution was a Federal compact, done in Convention, by the unanimous consent of the States present."

Judge CHASE, of the Superior Court of the United States, in Dallas' Reports, p. 199, says : " I consider the Declaration of Independence as a declaration, not that the United Colonies jointly, in a collective capacity, were independent States, but that *each of them was an independent State.*" It asserts the separate and individual independence, freedom, and sovereignty of each of the thirteen States. The treaty with Great Britain recognizes the sovereignty of each State by name.

UNITED STATES.—This term replaced the term "United Colonies," on the Declaration of Independence. The use of the term United Colonies did not annul the separate distinctive rights of the Colonies. The use of the term United States does not annul the separate distinctive rights of the States, whether before the adoption of the Articles of Confederation, or after the adoption of the Articles of Confederation, or after the adoption of the Federal Constitution. The word "United," used in these four different sets of circumstances, does not imply that the Colonies or the States were one people, in the sense in which a colony or a State is one, but only that the several Colonies before the Declaration of Independence, and the several States before the adoption of the Articles of Confederation, and after their adoption, and after the adoption of the Constitution, *united for certain purposes and in certain respects.*

In the minds of the framers and friends of the Constitution, the plural idea was the ruling idea in the use of the term "United States." The term was equivalent to the "States of the Union." Thus General WASHINGTON, in his reply to CORNPLANTER: "The United States desire to be the *friends* of the Indians." "The United States will be true and faithful to *their* engagements."

But in the minds of foreigners, and those ignorant of the structure of our Government, the singular idea is attached to the term. They sometimes say, "the United States *is* able to take care of itself."

In the Convention of Virginia, which ratified the Constitution, PATRICK HENRY objected to the words, " We, the people of the United States," lest it might be supposed that it meant the inhabitants of all the States as one homogeneous mass or aggregate. But Mr. MADISON replied, "The parties to it are to be the people, but *not the people as composing one great society, but the people as composing thirteen sovereignties.*" The accession or adoption was the separate act of the people of each State, quite independent of the people of any other State. And the articles at the end are declared to be " done in Convention by the unanimous consent of the States present."

PEOPLE.—This term was used in application to the individuals who composed a separate Colony or a separate State. " The good people of these Colonies," meant the good people in the *several* Colonies. It meant those for whom the delegates severally acted, and it did not mean those people in the aggregate. The several peoples represented in the Convention acted by their respective delegates. Thus, the people of Connecticut acted for themselves by their delegates ROGER SHERMAN, SAMUEL HUNTINGTON, WILLIAM WILLIAMS, OLIVER WOLCOTT. In the Articles of Confederation, the following phrases are employed : " among the people of the different States "; " and the people of each State "; " their own people," that is, the people of the respective States. In the Constitution the word " people " is used only for reference to the inhabitants of the *several States*, or portions of the same, and in no case for the collective inhabitants of all the States in the aggregate. It is applied to those who were accustomed to act together under State authority, at a particular time or place, or to portions of them. Thus, " The powers not delegated to the United States by the Constitution, nor prohibited by it to the States, are reserved to the States or to the people," (that is, to the people of the States.) In the phrase, " We, the people of the United States," there is an equivalent for we, the people of New Hampshire, and the people of Massachusetts, &c. The articles of the Constitution was a compact " *between* the States ratifying the same." The " style " of the Federal Union in the new Constitution was borrowed from the old, namely, the Articles of Confederation, and has the same meaning.

The reason why the Constitution was submitted to the *people* of each State, and not to the several Legislatures, was because it was apprehended that the latter would oppose it. Said WILSON : " I know that they, the Legislatures and the State officers, will oppose it ; I am for carrying it to the people of each State." The ratification was the act of each State, and not of the Federal Government, which then had no existence, or of the aggregate people under that Government.

Massachusetts, in Convention, in ratifying the " new Constitution," speaks of the " rights of the people," that is, the people of the several States ; and also uses the language, " in the name and by the authority of the people of this Commonwealth." " The freedom of the people," was understood to mean the freedom or the rights of the States, or of the people of the States, in distinction from the granted rights or powers of the Federal Government.

CONSTITUTION.—The people in the Colonies were under the BRITISH CONSTITUTION.

A CONSTITUTION was framed in 1643 by the colonies of Massachusetts, Plymouth, Connecticut, and New Haven. It was composed of twelve articles. The first fixes the name, " The United Colonies of New England." Second : " The said United Colonies, for themselves and their posterity, do jointly and severally enter into a firm and *perpetual league of friendship* and amity, for offence and defence, mutual advice and succor upon all just occasions, for their mutual safety and general welfare."

Besides State Constitutions, the people of the Colonies, when they became " free and independent States," through their Legislatures formed a Constitution under which they could act for specific purposes set forth in that instrument. This was familiarly known as " the Articles of Confederation," though it was also denominated the " FEDERAL CONSTITUTION," in popular language, in the acts of the States, and in the Convention assembled to revise it. Thus, Massachusetts, in the appointment of delegates to the Convention which formed the " new Constitution," uses the term " Federal Constitution" as equivalent to " the Articles of Confederation."

It was solemnly ratified by all the Legislatures, and declared to be of perpetual obligation. " And the Articles of this Confederation shall be inviolably observed by every State, and the *Union shall be perpetual.* Nor shall any alteration, at any time hereafter, be made in any of them, unless such alteration be agreed to in a Congress of the United States, and be afterwards confirmed by the Legislature of every State."

It is not strange that LUTHER MARTIN should express the following reprobation of the violation of federal obligation by forming a new Constitution in 1787 : " Will you tell us that we ought to trust you because you now enter into a solemn compact with us ? This you have done *before*, and *now* treat with the utmost contempt. Will you now make an appeal to the Supreme Being, and call on Him to guarantee your observance of this compact? The same you have formerly done for your observance of the Articles of Confederation, which you are now violating in the most wanton manner. The same reason which you now urge for destroying our present Federal Government, may be urged for abolishing the system, which you now propose to adopt."

It should be kept in mind, that sectional views of the Constitution had an influence in producing a sectional policy in the administration of the Government. The South, from the start, favored a strict construction of the Constitution. The leading statesmen of that section, from THOMAS JEFFERSON to JEFFERSON DAVIS, generally inquired for the " enumerated powers," and the " delegated powers " contained in the Constitution, and insisted that federal action must be carefully limited by these powers. And if, in any case, the action of the Federal Government, in any of its branches, should go outside of these " granted powers," to usurp the powers reserved to the States, it is then null and void, because unconstitutional.

On the other hand, the North has been inclined to a broad construction of the Constitution. The leading statesmen of that section, from ALEXANDER HAMILTON to DANIEL WEBSTER, generally were disposed to magnify the " granted powers," though at the expense of the powers reserved to the States. /

To these general statements there are many exceptions, both in the North and the South.

Is a national bank constitutional ? The Southern statesman examines the Constitution, and finding no grant of power to Congress to establish such a bank, therefore pronounces the establishment of a bank unconstitutional. A Northern statesman, on the other hand, while he acknowledges that the Constitution contains no express grant of power to Congress to establish a bank or any corporation, says that, inasmuch as a bank would be convenient or appropriate for carrying into operation other grants of power, it is therefore constitutional.

Are internal improvements constitutional? On the same grounds as in the other case, the Southern statesman says no, the Northern yes.

Are high tariffs for protection constitutional? On the same ground as before the Southern statesmen say no, inasmuch as the Constitution empowers Congress to lay duties for revenue, but not for protection or prohibition. The Northern statesmen say yes; because, as they judge, they are "necessary" in order to promote the "general welfare," or at least the welfare of their section of the country.

[Mr. Jefferson to Mr. Giles,]

"Monticello, Dec. 25, 1825.

"I see as you do, and with the deepest affliction, the rapid strides with which the federal branch of our Government is advancing towards the usurpation of all the rights reserved to the States, and the consolidation in itself of all power, foreign and domestic; and that, too, by constructions which, if legitimate, leave no limits to their power. Take together the decisions of the Federal Courts, the doctrines of the President, (J. Q. Adams,) and the misconstructions of the constitutional compact acted on by the legislation of the federal branch, and it is but too evident that the three ruling branches of this department, are in combination to strip their colleagues, the State authorities, of the powers reserved to them; and to exercise themselves all functions, foreign and domestic. * * And what is our resource for the preservation of the Constitution? Reason and argument? You might as well reason and argue with the marble columns encircling them. The representatives chosen by ourselves? They are found in the combination, some from incorrect views of government, some from corrupt ones, sufficient, voting together, to outnumber the sound party, and with majorities only of one, two, or three, bold enough to go forward in defiance.

Mr. Madison declared "that the divergence between us (Colonel Hamilton and myself) took place from his wishing to *administration*, or rather to administer the Government (these

were Mr. MADISON's very words) into what he thought it ought
to be ; while, on my part, I endeavored to make it conform to
the Constitution, as understood by the Convention that produced and recommended it, and particularly by the State Conventions that *adopted* it."

FEDERAL GOVERNMENT.—The word Federal is derived from
the Latin word *fœdus*, a league or compact. Ours is a
Federal Government, as appears from the recommendation of
Congress, 1787 : "Resolved, that in the opinion of Congress,
it is expedient that, on the second Monday of May next, a Convention of delegates, who shall have been appointed by the
several States, be held at Philadelphia, for the sole and express
purpose of revising the Articles of Confederation, and reporting
to Congress and the several Legislatures, such alterations and
provisions therein as shall, when agreed to in Congress and
confirmed by the States, render the *Federal Constitution* adequate to the exigencies of the Government and the preservation
of the Union. With this the commissions from the States to
the delegates corresponded. So intent were the Conventions
upon making a Federal and not a consolidated Government,
that, at the motion of Mr. ELLSWORTH, the term "national Government" was by an unanimous vote struck out from the Constitution, and instead of it the "Government of the United
States" was substituted.' It is in its origin and nature Federal,
having been framed by the States as parties, and depending for
its existence on the action of the States.

The letter addressed to Congress by General WASHINGTON,
President of the Convention, and agreed to by that body, by
paragraphs, speaks of the "Federal Government of *these States*,"
and not of a national Government. The word Federal indicates
that the Constitution is a compact between the States. The
term "national Government" is used in a popular sense.

ACCEDE.—Mr. WEBSTER, in his speech, Feb. 16, 1833, said.
in regard to the first resolution of Mr. CALHOUN, which declares
that the several States "acceded" to the Constitution or constitutional compact, "that the word *accede* is not found in the
Constitution itself, or in the ratification of it by any of the

States. The natural converse of *accession* is *secession*, and therefore, when it is stated that the people of the States *acceded* to the Union, it may more plausibly be argued that they may *secede* from it. If, in adopting the Constitution, nothing was done but *acceding* to a compact, nothing would seem to be necessary in order to break it up, but to *secede* from the same compact. *But the term is wholly out of place.*"

The first resolution of Mr. CALHOUN is in the following words : " *Resolved*, that the people of the several States, composing these United States, are united as parties to a constitutional compact, to which the people of each State acceded as a separate and sovereign community, each binding itself by its own particular ratification; and that the Union, of which the said compact is the bond, is a Union *between the States* ratifying the same.*"

Is Mr. WEBSTER right in this declaration, that this term is wholly out of place? Was Mr. CALHOUN wrong in the use of the term?

FRANKLIN says, vol. x., 351, " An eighth State has since *acceded.*"

" The influence of each *accession* to the Constitution on the remaining States might be considerable." G. T. CURTIS, His. Con., vol. ii., p. 529.

The Governor of Rhode Island, 1789, says: " Our not having *acceded* to or adopted the new system of Government formed and adopted by our sister States, we doubt not, has given uneasiness to them."

General WASHINGTON, in his letter to BUSHROD WASHINGTON, Nov. 10, 1787, says: " Let the opponents of the proposed Constitution in this State (Virginia) be asked, and it is a question they ought certainly to have asked themselves, What line of conduct they would advise it to adopt, if nine other States, of which I think there is no doubt, should *accede* to the Constitution. Would they recommend that it should stand single? Will they connect it with Rhode Island?"

In a letter to JAMES MADISON, Dec. 7, 1787, he says: " If these, (South Carolina and Georgia,) with the States eastward and northward, should *accede* to the Federal Government, I think the citizens of this State will have no cause to bless the opposers of it here if they should carry their point."

.In a letter to James Madison, Jan. 10, 1788, he says : " But of all the arguments that may be used at the Convention which is to be held, the most prevailing one will be that nine States, at least, have *acceded* to it, that is, to the Constitution.

In his letter to Count Luzerne, Feb. 7, 1780 : " It is also said that Georgia has *acceded*."

Thus the language " accede to the Constitution," " accede to the Union," was current and correct long ago, as applied to the States. The phrase " members of the Union," as applied to States that had acceded to the Constitution, or ratified the Constitution, was also in use. The States are members of the Union.

Secede, secession, are the opposite of *accede, accession*. The use of the two latter words, in relation to the Federal Constitution, and their supposed correlation to the two former, have already been noticed.

(" The Union was formed by the voluntary agreement of the States, and in uniting together they have not forfeited their nationality, nor have they been reduced to the condition of one and the same people. If one of the States chose to withdraw its name from the contract, it would be difficult to disprove its right of doing so.") This opinion De Tocqueville expresses in his work entitled " *Democracy in America*," p. 419. He was as well qualified as any other foreigner to judge correctly concerning the nature of our institutions.

(" Any State may, at any time, constitutionally withdraw from the Union, and thus virtually dissolve it. It was not certainly created with the idea that the States, or several of them, would desire a separation. But whenever they chose to do it, they have no obstacle in the way.") Thomas Colley Grattan's *Civilized America*, vol. i., p. 287. Mr. Macon, and Mr. Rawle, and Gouverneur Morris's opinions have been already quoted as agreeing with that of these distinguished foreigners. *See* pp. 68, 216, 218.

The Northern members of Congress, on one occasion in the early part of General Washington's administration, " threatened secession and dissolution." *See* p. 37. Massachusetts and Connecticut seemed at one time to believe in the right of secession, under certain circumstances. We have the declaration of

17

John Quincy Adams, "that the continuance of the embargo, in 1809, much longer would certainly be met by forcible resistance supported by the Legislature, and probably by the judiciary of the State," (Massachusetts.) "That their object (the leaders of the party) was and had been for several years, a dissolution of the Union," as he knew from "unequivocal evidence," that this design had been formed in the winter of 1803 and 1804, immediately after and as a consequence of the acquisition of Louisiana." ' See p. 70. Massachusetts interposed her authority, pronounced the embargo unconstitutional. Mr. Jefferson wisely yielded, and the embargo was repealed. In thus avoiding a collision with the State of Massachusetts, and showing his respect for State rights, he set an example which General Jackson intentionally or unintentionally followed, in advising the modification of the tariff laws in 1833, by which he wisely avoided a collision with South Carolina.

The *Boston Centinel* of Nov. 9, 1814, in noticing the appointment of delegates from Connecticut and Rhode Island, to the Hartford Convention, says: " they are the second and third pillars of the new Federal edifice."

John Quincy Adams, in his oration delivered in 1839, on the jubilee of the Constitution, seems to countenance the right of secession under certain limitations: " To the people alone is thus reserved, as well the dissolving as the constituent power, and that power can be exercised by them only under the tie of conscience binding them to the retributive justice of heaven.' With these qualifications we may admit the same rights vested in the *people of every State in the Union* with reference to the General Government." The following from his *Memoir*, by Josiah Quincy, p. 98, has a bearing on the same point : " There is now every appearance that the slave question will be carried by the superior ability of the slavery party. For this much is certain, that if institutions are to be judged by their results, in the composition of the councils of the Union, the slaveholders are much more ably represented than the simple freemen. With the exception of Rufus King, there is not one in either House of Congress, a member of the free States, able to cope in powers of the mind with William Pinkney and James Barbour. In the House of Representatives they have no one

to contend on equal terms with JOHN RANDOLPH or CLAY. Another misfortune to the free party is, that some of their ablest
men are either on this question with their adversaries, or luke-
warm in the cause. The slave men have indeed a deeper immediate stake in the issue than the partisans of freedom. Their
passions and interests are more profoundly agitated, and they
have stronger impulses to active energy than their antagonists,
whose only individual interest in the case exists from its bearing on the balance of political power between the North and
the South."

"The impression produced on my mind by the progress of
this discussion (the Missouri) is, that the bargain between freedom and slavery, contained in the Constitution of the United
States, is morally and politically vicious; inconsistent with the
principles on which alone our revolution can be justified, cruel
and oppressive, by riveting the chains of slavery, by pledging
the faith of freedom to maintain and perpetuate the tyranny of
the master; and grossly unequal and impolitic, by admitting
that slaves are at once enemies to be kept in subjection, property to be secured and returned to their owners, and persons
not be represented themselves, but for whom their masters
are privileged with many a double share of representation.

"I have favored this Missouri Compromise, believing it to be
all that could be effected under the present Constitution, and
from extreme unwillingness to put the Union at hazard. But
perhaps it would have been a wiser and a bolder cause to have
persisted in the restriction on Missouri, until it should have
terminated in a Convention of the States to revise and amend
the Constitution. This would have *produced a new Union of
thirteen or fourteen States, unpolluted with slavery, with a
great and* glorious object, that of rallying to their standard the
other States, by the universal emancipation of their slaves. If
the Union must be dissolved, slavery is precisely the question
upon which it ought to break."

COERCION.—The founders of the Federal Government did
not rely for its preservation, mainly upon physical force, as if
it were a military despotism, but upon mutual confidence and
" conciliated interests." We have no evidence that it was the

intention of the Convention that formed the Constitution, or of the States that were parties to the compact, to clothe the Government with power to use military coercion against a State that had placed itself on its reserved rights. If there was such an intention, where is it recorded? What they did rely upon was *legal coercion*, acting through the forms of law upon individuals. Mr. CURTIS, in his excellent history of the Constitution, vol. ii., pp. 62, 63, says: " One of the leading objects in forming the Constitution, was to obtain for the United States the means of coercion, without a resort to force against the people of the States collectively." " The introduction, therefore, of the judicial department into the new plan of Government, of itself evinces an intention to clothe that Government with powers that could be *executed peacefully*, and without the necessity of putting down the organized opposition of subordinate communities."

WASHINGTON, in a letter addressed to ALEXANDER HAMILTON, Aug. 26, 1792, having spoken of " mutual forbearance and yielding on all sides," adds, " without these, I do not see how the reins of Government are to be managed, or how the *Union of the States* can much longer be preserved."

With respect to the coercion of a State, I have found no evidence that WASHINGTON differed from MADISON and BUCHANAN, with respect to the constitutional power to coerce a State. In the case of the whiskey insurrection, he acted in harmony with the executive authority of the State then represented by Governor MIFFLIN, and also in harmony with the views of Judge WILLSON, of Pennsylvania, an associate Justice of the Supreme Court of the United States. He was careful to keep the military in subordination to the civil authority.

In the farewell address of General JACKSON, March 3, 1837, is the following: " But the Constitution cannot be maintained, nor the Union preserved in opposition to public feeling by the mere *exertion of coercive powers of the Government*. The foundations must be laid in the *affections of the people*, in the security it gives to life, liberty, and property in every quarter of the country; and in the fraternal attachments which the citizens of the several States bear to one another, as members of one political family, materially contributing to promote the happiness of each other."

It appears evident from the debates in the United States Senate, Feb. 8, 1831, and from other facts, that General Jackson endorsed the opinions of Mr. Hayne, on the subject of State rights, and not those of Mr. Webster. The tone and language of Mr. Webster's speeches, on that well-known occasion, were extremely well adapted to popular effect, and were greatly and deservedly admired even by many who felt that he leaned towards a construction of the Constitution which would make the General Government consolidated rather than Federal.

What the opinions of General Jackson were, in respect to nullification, in the case of South Carolina are well known from his proclamation, written by Edward Livingston, then Secretary of State. On that occasion he was in favor of carrying the olive branch in one hand and the sword in the other. South Carolina was in the Union, and, of course, subject to the laws of the Union. These laws General Jackson was determined to execute, but he and other wise men on that occasion, pursued a conciliatory course that rendered the forcible execution of the laws unnecessary.

"If it be supposed that, among the States which are united by the Federal tie, there are some which exclusively enjoy the principal advantages of Union, or whose prosperity depends on the duration of that Union, it is unquestionable that they will always be ready to support the Central Government in enforcing the obedience of others. But the Government would then be exciting a force not derived from itself, but from a principle contrary to its nature. States form confederations in order to derive equal advantages from their union ; and in the case just alluded to, the Federal Government · would derive its power from the unequal distribution of those benefits among the States.

"If one (or more) of the Confederate States have acquired a preponderance sufficiently great to enable it to take exclusive possession of the central authority, it will consider the other States as subject provinces, and it will cause its own supremacy to be respected under the borrowed name of the Sovereignty of the Union. Great things may then be done in the name of the Federal Government, but in reality that Government will have ceased to exist. In both of these cases, the power which acts in the name of the Confederation becomes stronger, the more it abandons the natural state and the acknowledged principles of Confederation."—DE TOCQUEVILLE, p. 419.

"I understand the Senator from New Hampshire, Mr. HALE, to proclaim not the gospel of peace between brethren, but a circumspect waiting to ascertain whether Mr. BUCHANAN would or would not send a Federal army to coerce South Carolina. I trust, sir, if Mr. BUCHANAN should do so high-handed and fatal an act of violence as that, his term is not too brief, as President of the United States, for him to be arraigned at our bar by an impeachment. What would South Carolina be worth to herself or to us if she were dragged captive in chains? I wish no State of this Union subjugated by her sisters. If she cannot be retained by the bonds of affection, by acts of kindness, why then, in God's name, horrible as I esteem such an alternative—let her depart in sorrowful silence."—Senator PUGH, Dec. 10, 1860.

Mr. CLAY, in deprecating a civil war, used the following language: "But if they were to conquer, whom would they conquer? A foreign foe, one who had insulted our flag, invaded our shores, and laid our country waste? No, sir, no. It would be a conquest *without laurels, without glory*, a self-*suicidal conquest*, a conquest of brothers over brothers, obtained by one over another portion of the descendants of common ancestors, who, nobly pledging 'their lives, their fortunes, and their sacred honor,' had fought and bled side by side in many a hard battle on land and ocean, severed our country from the British crown, and established our national independence."

It was provided in the Constitution that *legal coercion* should be exerted against *individuals* who violate the laws made in pursuance of the Constitution. This, it was supposed, would supersede the necessity of making any provision for the coercion of a State by military force.

The Constitution recognizes *treason against a State as a crime*, and requires a traitor who has fled into another State to be delivered up. It thus acknowledges the Sovereignty of the States: *Treason is a crime against sovereignty.* "The Constitution does not," in the language of Chief-Justice ELLSWORTH, "attempt to coerce sovereign bodies." Such an attempt is equivalent to an act of war of a government of *delegated sovereignty*, against a government of *original and inherent sovereignty*.

CONCILIATION AND COMPROMISE.—In 1794, when combinations were formed in Pennsylvania to defeat the execution of the laws laying duties upon spirits distilled within the United States, commissioners were appointed by the Federal Government to *persuade* the actors to return to their duty. Thus WASHINGTON pursued a conciliatory course, even in case of an insurrection which received no encouragement from a State, in its organized capacity.

"Now, for one, I am not ready yet to take the responsibility of absolutely closing the door of reconciliation. I cannot persuade myself to forget the warnings that have descended to us from many of the wisest and best statesmen of all time against this rigid and haughty mode of treating great discontents. I cannot overlook the fact that, in the days of our fathers, the imperious spirit of CHATHAM did not feel itself as sacrificing any of his proud dignity by proposing to listen to their grievances, and even to concede every reasonable demand, long after they had placed themselves in armed resistance to all the power of Great Britain. Had George the Third listened to his words of wisdom, he might have saved the brightest jewel of his crown. He took the opposite course. He denied the existence of grievances. He rejected the olive branch. History records its verdict in favor of CHATHAM and against the king."—C. F. ADAMS, of Massachusetts, in the House of Representatives, Jan. 31, 1861.

This language of conciliation was in harmony with the feelings of a great portion of the people in the States both North and South, at that time.

On the other hand, Mr. EGERTON, of Ohio, Jan. 31, 1861, said :

1. "I will not compromise, because I have no faith that any compromise we can make would stand any longer than it ministered to slavery.

2. "I will not compromise, because I would not further strengthen slavery.

3. " I will not compromise, finally, because slavery is a sin, an outrage against humanity, and an insult to God."

This language was probably in harmony with the feelings of a large portion of people in some of the Northern States.

" This is a mighty empire. Its existence spreads its influence through the civilized world. Its overthrow will be the greatest shock that civilization and free governments have ever received; more extensive in its consequences, more fatal to mankind, than the French Revolution, with all its blood, and with all its war and violence. And for what ? Upon questions concerning this line of division between slavery and freedom ? Why, Mr. President, suppose this day all the Southern States being refused their right, being refused this partition, being denied this privilege, were to separate from the Northern States, were to do it peaceably, and then were to come to you and say : ' Let there be no war between us ; let us divide fairly this territory of the United States ; ' could the Northern section of the country refuse so just a demand ? what would you then give them ? what would be the fair proportion ? If you allowed them their fair relative proportion, would you not give them as much as is now proposed to be assigned on the Southern side of that line, and would they not be at liberty to carry their slaves there if they pleased ? "—Mr. CRITTENDEN, Dec. 28, 1860.

Mr. EVERETT, May 29, 1860, made the following declaration : " Our political controversies have substantially assumed an almost purely sectional character—that of a fearful struggle between the North and the South. It would not be difficult to show at length the perilous nature and tendency of this struggle, but I can only say, on this occasion, that, in my opinion, it cannot much longer be kept up without rending the Union. * * * A spirit of *patriotic moderation* must be called into activity throughout the Union, or it will assuredly be broken up."

Senator BROWN, of Mississippi, Dec. 12, 1860, said : " If the same spirit could prevail which now actuated the Senator who has just spoken, (Mr. DIXON, of Connecticut,) a different state of things might prevail in twenty days."

President BUCHANAN used the following language on this subject : " The proposition to compromise by letting the North have the exclusive control of the territory above a certain line, and giving Southern institutions protection below that line, ought to receive universal approbation. In itself, it may not be entirely satisfactory, but when the alternative is between a reasonable concession on both sides, and the destruction of the Union, it is an imputation on the patriotism of Congress to assert that its members will hesitate for a moment."

Listen, also, to the following patriotic sentiments from Senator SEWARD : " Beyond a doubt, Union is vitally important to the Republican citizens of the United States; but it is just as important to the whole people. Republicanism and Union are not convertible terms. Republicanism is subordinate to Union as every thing else is; Republicanism, Democracy, every other political name and thing—all are subordinate, and they ought to disappear in the presence of the great question of Union. So far as I am concerned, it shall be so."

The plan of compromise proposed by Mr. CRITTENDEN, Jan. 12, 1861—and which was regarded with favor by a large portion of the Peace Congress assembled at Washington, and which was acceptable generally to the Border States—was not satisfactory to the extremists either North or South. The majority of the Senate was not in favor of it. Whether the greater share of the blame of the failure of this attempt at compromise was due to the North or to the South, it is not necessary here to inquire. The terrible consequences of the failure soon became alarmingly evident. " Blood-letting " was substituted for the counsels of peace and conciliation.

CONSTRUCTION OF THE CONSTITUTION.—" It is evident that a Confederation so vast and so varied, both in numbers and in territorial extent, in habits and interests, could only be kept in national cohesion by the strictest fidelity to the principles of the Constitution, as understood by those who have adhered to the most restricted constructions of the powers given by the people and the States. Interpreted and applied according to those principles, the great compact adapts itself with healthy ease and freedom to an unlimited extension of that benign system of federative self-government, of which it is our glorious, and, I trust, immortal charter. Let us then, with redoubled vigilance, be on our guard against yielding to the temptation to the exercise of doubtful powers, even under the pressure of the motives of conceded temporary advantage and apparent temporary expediency.

"The minimum of Federal Government, compatible with the maintenance of national unity and efficient action in our relation with the rest of the world, should afford the rule and measure of construction of our powers under the general clauses of the Constitution. A spirit of strict deference to the sovereign rights and dignity of every State, rather than a disposition to subordinate the States into a provincial relation to the central authority, should characterize all our exercise of the respective powers temporarily vested in us as a sacred trust from the generous confidence of our constituents."—FRANKLIN PIERCE. First Annual Message.

Mr. MADISON, in his letter to Mr. WEBSTER, March 15, 1833, says: "The Constitution of the United States being established by a competent authority, by that of the sovereign people of the several States who were parties to it, it remains only to inquire what that Constitution is."

The evidence in this inquiry is largely philological. The common rules for interpreting language must be applied to the Constitution in order to learn what it is. The meaning attributed to the several clauses by the Convention that formed it, and the several State Conventions which adopted it, may be safely considered as the true meaning.

Practically, the true course to be pursued by the Federal Government in the construction of the Constitution, is NEVER TO ATTEMPT TO EXERCISE ANY DOUBTFUL POWERS. The benefit of a doubt should always accrue to the residuary powers reserved to the States, and never to the delegated powers intrusted by the Constitution to the Federal Government.

The burden of proof rests on the Federal Government. In the last resort the parties to the constitutional compact must be the judges. See p. 268.

GOUVERNEUR MORRIS TO TIMOTHY PICKERING, DEC. 22, 1814. —"But, after all, what does it signify that men should have a written Constitution, containing unequivocal provisions and limitations. The legislative lion will not be entangled in the meshes of a logical net. The Legislature will always make the power which it wishes to exercise, unless it be so organized as to contain, in itself, the sufficient check. Attempts to restrain it from outrage by other means will only render it the more outrageous. The idea of binding Legislatures by oaths is puerile. Having sworn to exercise the powers granted according to their true intent and meaning, they will, when they desire, go further and avoid the shame, if not the guilt of perjury, by showing the true intent to be, according to their comprehension, that which suits their purpose."

"There is no difference between a Government having all power and a Government having the right to take what power it pleases."—J. C. CALHOUN.

In 1802, ALEXANDER HAMILTON called the Constitution the "frail and worthless fabric," and spoke of it as "a temporary bond." He had endeavored to infuse energy and strength into it by a broad or loose construction of its powers, but the States had decided against such a construction; hence the epithets which he applied to it.

Mr. MADISON says of General WASHINGTON, "that he signed Jay's treaty, but he did not at all like it. He also signed the bank, but he was very *near* not doing so; if he had refused, it would, in my opinion, have produced a crisis."

"I am satisfied that had it been his veto, there would have been an effort to nullify it; they would have arrayed themselves in a hostile attitude."—Mr. TRIST, 1827.

A dominant party in the Government is often tempted to enlarge the Federal powers at the expense of State rights; and when the opposing party becomes dominant, it, in turn, is tempted to follow bad precedents, and thus sanction what it had asserted to be a violation of the Constitution. Thus Mr. MADISON, with his party, opposed, with great ability, the charter of the first bank of the United States. But when his own party came into power, and passed a vote to charter the second bank of the United States, he, in opposition to his own declared constitutional views on the subject, gave his signature to the bill.

An unconstitutional act in a given case " will be recorded as a precedent, and many an error, by the same example, will rush into the State."

REVOLUTION.—A revolution does not necessarily imply war or the shedding of blood, as it is supposed by many to do. What is the cause of this erroneous supposition? Why, in the case of the American Revolution there was war and the shedding of blood. In the case of the French Revolution there was war and the shedding of blood, and so the conclusion is drawn that revolution necessarily implies war and the shedding of blood.

"I acknowledge, to the fullest extent, the right of revolution, if you call it a right, and of the destruction of the Government under which we live, if we are discontented with it, and on its ruins to erect another more in accordance with our wishes; but they that undertake it, undertake it with this hazard: if they are successful, then all is right, and they are heroes; if they are defeated, they are rebels."—Senator WADE, of Ohio, Dec. 17, 1850.

"We are confusing language very much. Men speak of revolution, and when they speak of revolution they mean blood. Our fathers meant nothing of the sort. When they spoke of revolution, they spoke of an inalienable right." If our fathers had the "inalienable right" to change their "systems of Government," where was the right of Great Britain in the premises to wage war against the States?

In Mr. FORCE's published volumes is a pamphlet, the title page of which is as follows: "An account of the late REVOLUTION in New England, together with the declaration of the gentlemen, merchants, and inhabitants of Boston and the country adjacent, April, 18, 1689; written by Nathaniel Byefield, a merchant of Boston, in New England, to his friends in London." Concerning this revolution, it is said "through the goodness of God there has been no blood shed." In this revolution from the Government of JAMES to that of WILLIAM, Sir EDMOND ANDROSS, Kt., was ordered to "surrender and deliver up the Government and fortifications," and he consented without resistance. The great English revolution of 1689, when JAMES II. was dethroned, and WILLIAM and MARY reigned in his stead, was not attended by war or much violence; and yet, how beneficent it proved! Revolution is not necessarily connected with war and bloodshed.

SOVEREIGNTY OR SUPREME POWER.—In a despotism, the monarch is sovereign. In Great Britain, the sovereignty, or supreme power, is lodged with the Kings, Lords, and Commons. In the United States, it rests with the people of the several States.

In the Continental Congress, 1774, PATRICK HENRY, speaking for Virginia, thought it would be unjust " for a little colony to weigh as much in the councils of America as a great one." Mr. SULLIVAN, of New Hampshire, responded that " a little colony had its all at stake as much as a great one," thus announcing in the outset the great doctrine of the equality of States, as sovereign and independent communities. Accordingly, it was resolved that " each colony shall have one vote."

· In June 27, 1776, the Continental Congress declared " that all persons owing allegiance to any of the United Colonies, who shall bring war against any of the citizens, are guilty of treason " against the colony to which they owe allegiance, thus recognizing the sovereignty of each colony.

In the Constitution, of Massachusetts, formed 1780, is the following form : " I, A B, do truly and sincerely acknowledge, profess, testify, and declare, that the Commonwealth of Massachusetts is, and of right ought to be, a free, *sovereign*, and independent State ; and I do swear that I will bear true allegiance to the Commonwealth, and that I will defend the same against traitorous conspiracies."

The States are sovereign in all that relates to the powers reserved to themselves, and which they did not delegate to the Federal Government in creating it. In creating the Federal Government, the States delegated a portion of their individual sovereignty to it, to be employed for the common benefit. The Federal Government was endowed, by the States acting in conventions, with the powers of exercising sovereignty in respect to war, taxation, and treaties with foreign nations, and other enumerated subjects. In the language of Mr. MADISON, the enumerated powers vested in the Government of the United States are of as high and sovereign a character as any of the powers reserved to the State Governments.

" Nor is the Government of the United States created by the Constitution, less a Government, in the strict sense of the term, within the scope of its powers, than the Governments created by the Constitutions of the States are within their several spheres."

" My own general idea was that the States should severally preserve their *sovereignty*, and that the exercise of the *Federal sovereignty* should be divided among these several bodies, legislative, executive, and judiciary, as the *State sovereignties* are, and that some peaceable means should be contrived for the Federal head to force compliance on the part of the States." This refers to legal coercion, to the exclusion of war.

The people of each State, at the time they adopted the Federal Constitution, delegated to the Federal Government a portion of the sovereignty which was inherent in the State, but they reserved to it all that was not delegated. They delegated to the Federal Government the power to act on individuals, but not to act against the State by military coercion. To act against a State in this way, would be to make war against a sovereign power, to which the people of the State, as individuals, owe allegiance as well as obedience, and against which they may commit treason by withholding allegiance and obedience.

Whenever a question arises in regard to the line of division between the delegated sovereignty of the Federal Government and the original sovereignty of the States, it was intended that the Federal Court shall, by its decision, settle that question in all those cases which can be brought before it for adjudication, and that the Executive shall carry out those decisions in their applications to individuals.

" This Constitution, and the laws of the United States which shall be made in pursuance thereof, and all treaties made, or which shall be made, under the authority of the United States, shall be the superior law of the land ; and the Judges in every State shall be bound thereby, any thing in the Constitution or laws of any State to the contrary notwithstanding." This applies only to distinct and not to doubtful powers.

But if a State should place itself on its reserved powers, and should deny the constitutionality of a Federal act, whether of the legislative, or executive, or the judicial branch of the

Government, then the true mode of settling the same question is to summon a Convention of the States to declare that act constitutional or otherwise, and thus prevent a dangerous collision between the delegated sovereignty of the Federal Government and the residuary sovereignty of the States. *War is a contest between sovereignties.*

" The Gordian knot of the Constitution seems to be in the problem of collision between the Federal and State powers, especially as eventually to be exercised by their respective tribunals. If the knot cannot be untied by the text of the Constitution, it ought not certainly to be cut by any political Alexander."—Mr. Madison, Jan. 29, 1821.

Allegiance.—On the 2d of July, 1776, the Continental Congress passed the following resolution :

Resolved, That the United Colonies are, and of right ought to be, free and independent States ; that they are absolved from all *allegiance* to the British crown, and that all political connection between them and the State of Great Britain is, and ought to be, totally dissolved."

On the passage of this resolution, a special committee was appointed to prepare a preamble declaring the causes which led to its adoption, to accompany its promulgation to the world. On the Fourth of July, this Declaration of Independence received the unanimous sanction of the delegates from each State, by the signature of their names.

In 1777, the following oath of " abjuration and allegiance" was adopted by the State of South Carolina: " I, A B, do acknowledge that the State of South Carolina is, and of right ought to be, a free, and independent, and sovereign State, and that the people thereof owe no *allegiance* or obedience to George the Third, King of Great Britain ; * * * and I do further swear that I will bear faith and true *allegiance* to the said State, and to the utmost of my power will support, maintain, and defend the freedom and independence thereof."

The present Constitution of South Carolina contains the following : " I solemnly swear (or affirm) that I will be faithful, and true allegiance bear to the State of South Carolina, so long as I continue a citizen thereof."

In the Constitution of Massachusetts, formed in 1780, is the following form : " I, A B, do testify and sincerely acknowledge, profess, testify, and declare, that the Commonwealth of Massachusetts is, and of right ought to be, a free, *sovereign*, and independent State, and I do swear I will bear true *allegiance* to the Commonwealth, and that I will defend the same against all traitorous conspiracies."

Is allegiance due both to the State sovereignty and to the Federal sovereignty, also, in the scope of its delegated powers ? Can sovereignty, or at least its exercise, be divided between the State Government and the General Government ? May not a corresponding division be made of allegiance ? Why not ?

There are those who say that allegiance cannot be divided. They say that, under the Constitution of the United States, every citizen owes allegiance to the State, and obedience to the Federal Government.

4. *Northern Views of Slave Property.*—In March, 1798, when the bill for the erection of a Government in Mississippi Territory was before Congress, it was moved that the same should be in all respects similar to that established in the Northwestern Territory, except that " slavery should not be forbidden." Mr. THATCHER, of Massachusetts, moved to strike out the excepting clause, thus excluding slavery from the Territory.

Mr. OTIS, of Massachusetts, " hoped his colleague would not withdraw his motion ; and the reason why he wished this was, that an opportunity might be given *to gentlemen who came from the same part of the Union* with him to manifest that it is not their disposition to interfere with the Southern States as to *that species of property in question.* He thought it was not the business of those who had nothing to do with that kind of property *to interfere with that right.* If the amendment prevailed, it would declare that no slavery should exist in the Natchez country. This would not only be a sentence of banishment, but of war."

The amendment did not prevail, and slavery was permitted in the Territory.

Chief-Justice SHAW, of Massachusetts, 1836, in a legal decision, said : " Slavery, to a certain extent, seems to have crept into the colonial government, not probably by force of law, for none such is found to exist; but either, it is presumed, from that universal custom pervading through the colonies, in the West Indies, and on the continent of America, and which was fostered and encouraged by the commercial policy of the times. That it was so established is shown by this: that by several provincial acts, passed at various times in the early part of the last century, *slavery was recognized as an existing fact*, and various regulations were prescribed in reference to it."

Judge BISSEL, of Conn., has said, 1837, " that the principle was recognized and acted upon that one man might have property in another, might command his services for life without compensation, and dispose of him as he would of any other chattel."

Judge BALDWIN, of the United States Court, in the case of Johnson *versus* Tompkins, declares that " the foundations of this (the Federal) Government are laid, and rest on the rights of *property* in slaves, *and the whole fabric must fall by disturbing the corner-stone.*"

ALEXANDER HAMILTON remarks that " it is the unfortunate situation of the Southern States to have a great part of their population, as well as property, in blacks." He, like other leading statesmen contemporaneous with him, had no difficulty in considering slaves as property.

7. PERSONAL LIBERTY BILLS.—" If the property of an American citizen is taken by a foreign nation, and, upon a demand for redress, it is not given up, or paid for, war follows; and if instead the foreign Government legislates to protect the wrongdoer, war is inevitable." " It would be the case if the same thing took place between any foreign States. But we (the Southern States) are in a vastly worse condition than would be the people of any foreign State, because those States of the Union that legislate to prevent the recapture of our property are doing it with perfect safety. The proceedings of the old Barbary powers, when they used to send out cruisers and capture property on the high seas, were brave and honorable enterprises compared with these proceedings, because they run the risk of having their cities bombarded."—Senator CLINGMAN, Dec. 4, 1860.

18

This statement of the case, evidently a fair one, places in a strong light the injustice of certain personal liberty bills, violating, as they do, the principles of the Constitution, and having the effect to defeat one of its provisions. Any State which has passed a personal liberty bill designed to defeat a plain provision of the Constitution for the return of fugitive slaves, cannot consistently complain of the States injured by those bills, if they refuse to act with them in the Confederacy. Without the introduction of the article for the return of fugitive slaves, we know that the Constitution would not have been adopted, and if States, by their legislation, make that article null and void, they release the other States which hold slaves from their obligation to continue in the Confederacy. "A compact broken on one side is broken on all sides."

8. Who are to judge, in the last resort, in respect to the constitutionality of the acts of the Federal Government? Evidently the same organized bodies that *originally adopted the Constitution*, and *that now have power to amend the Constitution.* "Nine," or three-quarters of the States that sent delegates to the Convention, had power to adopt the Constitution and make it binding *between* the States; and three-quarters of the States now acting by their Legislatures or their Conventions, have power to amend the Constitution. They can declare what the meaning of the Constitution is in doubtful cases.

In common cases, which are capable of assuming, and actually assuming, the character of a suit, the Supreme Court of the United States is the interpreter.

In cases not capable of assuming the character of a suit at law or in equity, Congress, when called to act, must interpret the Constitution in such a way as *never to exercise any doubtful powers.*

When the Supreme Court or Congress, or, more comprehensively, when the General Government exercises doubtful power or powers that any of the States claim to be not delegated, but reserved, then the States, acting in Convention or by their Legislatures, can determine whether the power in question is delegated or reserved. The States are to judge in the last resort of the constitutionality of the acts of the Federal Government. The Constitution gives to them this authority, in giving them power to amend the Federal Constitution. If three-fourths of the States refuse to act by their Legislatures or by Convention, in the manner prescribed by the Constitution, then the aggrieved States have to choose between bearing the evil complained of, or vindicating the right of revolution ; just as the colonies did when they made the Declaration of Independence, and sustained it by a seven years' war against the unreasonable demands of the mother country. And as the aggrieved States have in such a case the right to determine what it is their duty to do; so in like manner the other States, acting through the forms of the Federal Government, have also the right to determine what it is their duty to do in their relations to the aggrieved States.

www.ingramcontent.com/pod-product-compliance
Lightning Source LLC
Chambersburg PA
CBHW060612030726
47498CB00005B/1643